D0438670

The Fate of Gender

BY THE SAME AUTHOR

The Vanishing Land

The American Way of Crime: From Salem to Watergate, a Stunning New Perspective on American History (with John Gerassi)

The Culture of Desire: Paradox and Perversity in Gay Lives Today

A Queer Geography: Journeys Toward a Sexual Self

Apples: The Story of the Fruit of Temptation

An Apple Harvest: Recipes and Orchard Lore (with Sharon Silva)

The Monk and the Skeptic: Dialogues on Sex, Faith, and Religion

The Fate of Gender

Nature, Nurture, and the Human Future

FRANK BROWNING

B L O O M S B U R Y
NEW YORK • LONDON • OXFORD • NEW DELHI • SYDNEY

Bloomsbury USA
An imprint of Bloomsbury Publishing Plc

1385 Broadway	50 Bedford Square
New York	London
NY 10018	WC1B 3DP
USA	UK

www.bloomsbury.com

First published 2016

ISBN: HB 978-1-62040-619-9
ePub: 978-1-62040-621-2

Library of Congress Cataloging-in-Publication Data has been applied for.

2 4 6 8 10 9 7 5 3 1

Typeset by RefineCatch Limited, Bungay, Suffolk
Printed and bound in the U.S.A. by Berryville Graphics Inc., Berryville, Virginia

For Neil Chudgar, without whom this book
could not have happened

Contents

Part IV: Fluidities

Part V: Gender and Being

Introduction

To a New World of Genders

Next to cutting and hanging tobacco, tomato canning (my current activity as I write these introductory notes) was about the most unpleasant summer work I remember from my childhood in Kentucky. Late August and the outdoor temperature always burned past ninety matched by a humidity even higher. Indoors the kettles of boiling water pushed it over one hundred. Sweat dripped from every pore. Canned the same day they were picked from muddy, prickly vines, the fresh tomatoes were first washed, then skinned by plunging them briefly into the boiling water, then packed into quart jars before being lowered in a rack into the pressure canner, a sealed stovetop container that if not properly closed could explode, permanently scarring anyone who happened to be nearby. Tempers in the kitchen were seldom lower than the temperature.

Canning in my childhood was women's work, like mopping and laundering and bathing the baby. Today, canning is a nearly forgotten art. Of the few people who do still can, most I know these days are men. Very few women have either the time or the inclination to undergo this annual punitive exercise no matter how much better the end result may taste when compared to tins of flavorless red stuff sold on supermarket shelves. Men, however, seem to find it a fascinating test of their culinary skills and a demonstration of how flexibly fluid they can show themselves to be in today's gender-diffuse times, when the lead breadwinners in half the households in America are women and baby bathing and diaper changing are about equally divided. None of which was really imaginable during my early adolescence at the peak of Beatles and Rolling Stones fame a generation ago. Males in rural Georgia or Kansas or Virginia or Ohio would in those days have been banned from the poker club or shunned at the pickup basketball court had their fingernails betrayed the traces of peach and tomato flesh.

I was lucky, I suppose, to have grown up in Kentucky, officially a border state, a locution that derives from the Civil War when slaveholding sons bayonetted their Yankee cousins on the battlefields. But Kentucky's border mentality extended much farther into the psyches of men and women, boys and girls I grew up with. To be passionately both and neither and ready to talk about it across the table over a shot of bourbon was, if not a norm, an ideal—just as the Baptist preachers would hedge their Sabbath rules by coming to buy our apples on Sundays promising to return on Monday to pay the IOU they had left. Race remains a ragged and volatile piece of the border fabric, but in odd ways, gender borders were always more porous—even if the men kept far away from the house during canning time. Older men—men in the 1960s when I was fifteen—regularly called young guys "honey." Any family with six or more children most always had one who was "well he's just Uncle Jack (or Aunt Frances)," meaning everyone early on understood that "that one" wouldn't marry or carry on the line (which, we will see later, is a natural statistical distribution in large families); out of a dozen cousins one normally would be the florist or take up nursing, or among the girls one would handle the tractor and the hay baler more expertly than any of her brothers. So long as they declared nothing about their "privacies" and embarrassed no one at Thanksgiving dinner, they were welcome and even encouraged to shred some conventional gender borderlines. The perennial bachelors could even bake cakes—at least sturdy chocolate if never fluffy angel cakes.

Today all of these roles and behaviors that once defined what and how men and women could be and do seem terribly antiquated, detritus on the cultural battlefield of what has for the last half century been labeled the gender revolution. The term itself—*gender*—would have baffled most everyone in the first years after World War II when legions of women known collectively as Rosie the Riveter returned to the kitchen after running tobacco farms and serving in wartime factories building tanks and B-52 bombers. While the boys had shipped away to Dunquerque and Yokohama, expediency transferred women onto the shop floor to replace them, even as they kept canning beans and tomatoes by night. No one then saw it as a "gender revolution." It wouldn't be until the late 1950s that the term itself began to seep into academic discourse, not least concerning many of those women who had discovered that they liked working for their own out-of-house independence. Even early frontline feminists like Betty Friedan or the French philosopher Simone de Beauvoir made sparse distinction between "sex" and "gender." Beauvoir's most famous book, remember, was entitled *Le deuxième sexe* (and in English translation *The Second Sex*). Only with the arrival of the Baby Boom generation did activists, sociologists, and philosophers, most notably the Berkeley theoretician Judith Butler and her followers, begin to separate the two terms. *Sex* referred to biology and, to a larger degree, to nature. *Gender* came to be seen as learned social behavior distinguishing male and female roles—or nurture. Women canned. Men harvested. (At least in America, though those roles were always much muddier in Asia, Africa, and Latin America.)

When I was a twelve-year-old visiting one of my spinster aunts in the city, she took it upon herself to educate me in proper male comportment: I was always to stand up and offer my seat on a public bus when a lady entered, always to hold the door for a lady, always to pass the plate at Thanksgiving dinner first to the ladies at the table. Generally I still do those actions though frequently young women on crowded subways stand up to make room for me when I enter. These are gestures of politeness, of course, but as many angry feminists argued at the height of the women's movement in the early 1970s, they are also *enacted* statements about power and who holds it. A much younger woman who cedes her place to me now both pleases me and reminds me that I have become less vigorous, less forceful, or simply *less* than those people who are thirty years younger than I. To offer your arm to a girlfriend similarly indicated protection as well as a public demonstration of affection, but at the same time the gesture served—and still serves—as a statement of ownership: She is mine; don't touch. Now when in major American and European cities young men similarly link their arms, that too is a performance—an act intended to declare both affection between the two and pride in their affection—whereas two women linking arms indicates nothing more than friendship. Physical gestures far more subtle than these fill volumes of anthropological history—from Romans who quietly signaled their availability to one another by lightly scratching their heads with a middle finger to portions of New Guinea where pointed lips are still more often used than pointed fingers to signal directions. Smart phones and near universal Internet access, even in the remote forests of New Guinea, may have mixed and blended these steadily evolving forms of bodily gesture, but gestures do remain. Likely they will always remain with us as powerful signals of power, attachment, and personhood, regardless of how we accept or challenge gender conventions. Moreover, these essential gender expressions, whether they signal forms of personal relations or indicate structures of authority and submission in a symphony orchestra, call us to reconsider still further what we believe is "natural" in the greater realm of Nature.

As late as the postwar era, only the most radical of feminists (among them Planned Parenthood founder Margaret Sanger) dared dissent from the assumption that men *by nature* are better suited to run universities or direct orchestras, just as most Americans and Europeans accepted that women *by nature* were better equipped to nurture and raise children. In France, the schools that Americans and Nordic peoples call *kindergarten* are still called *école maternelle*, plainly if not consciously indicating that women are naturally the best keepers of the young. Fundamentalist religious leaders, whether they are French Catholics or Kentucky evangelicals, insist more loudly than ever that these gender roles are simply natural enactments established by the deity and *his* prophets on earth. So it is that the march of the gender revolution has reached far more deeply and far more broadly into nearly every element of human behavior and society.

Liberal-minded citizens of the West express shock at the renewed declarations by Salafist and other Islamist scholars who do not merely defend the subordination of women to men but also justify the flogging or outright enslavement of any woman whom they judge to be an infidel. As much as mainstream Muslim doctrine rejects the Salafist arguments, and as much as mainstream Christians now denounce them, it is wise to remember that little more than a century ago much more conventional Christianity continued to defend enslavement. If Southern Baptists were the most notorious apologists for slavery before and even after the Civil War, the Catholic Church, the world's largest Christian sect, continued to defend enslavement until nearly the dawn of the twentieth century, and even afterward it enforced a sort of near slavery on unmarried pregnant young women in its infamous Magdalene laundries. Easily forgotten as well, women in America did not win the right to vote until 1920 while in France, that other supposed bastion of liberty, women only won the franchise in 1944 at the end of the Nazi occupation—a mere twenty years before I entered university.

Wartime's reliance on Rosie the Riveters and the subsequent social upheavals of the 1960s had certainly loosened the reins of masculine control that had long blocked gender equity and had regimented individual expressions about how men and women could comport themselves in public—the clothes they could wear, the songs they could sing, the jobs they could hold, the mates with whom they could bed, even down to how they could raise their children or even decide whether and how to bring a child into the world. Both the Civil Rights and the anti–Vietnam War demonstrations of the 1960s were critical and often contradictory antecedents to what became the feminist movement of the 1970s and the slightly later gender-bending campaigns for gay and lesbian rights.

Yet all these public social movements and the raucous, joyous effervescence that surrounded them drew not only on two centuries of post-Enlightenment movements for personal freedom. They also drew deeply on broad public education about science and health, which contributed to sturdier bodies for men and women, greater longevity, deeper understanding of how our bodies function—and most importantly on a radical social vision aimed on ensuring individual, personal autonomy over our own bodies. Toward that latter end nothing counted more than the long campaign first articulated by Margaret Sanger for women to control their own fertility—and their own freedom from forced procreation. The very first oral birth control pill, Enovid, won FDA approval in 1960, following on a decade of research initially funded by Sanger—who had been sentenced to jail a half century earlier for promoting contraception. The pill represented a light-year leap not only in freeing sexually active women from the risk of becoming pregnant: It broke the nature-nurture wall that for millennia had united erotic pleasure with reproduction. Sex, all the global monotheisms had taught (and official Vatican liturgy still teaches), serves only one function: procreation, creating babies. All non-erotic pleasure equals a form of sin. Once erotic pleasure was safely isolated—or mostly isolated—from reproduction, all kinds of barriers began to break down, exactly as all the popes, imams, and orthodox rabbis had warned. Women became *biologically* free to act on the political and philosophical feminist arguments that Beauvoir and Friedan had advanced. Work agendas need not be blocked by babies. And indeed the age of when women experienced their initial pregnancies began steadily moving upward. Ownership of one's own body became a real possibility, as the authors of the real bible of sexual liberty, *Our Bodies, Ourselves*, argued in passionate detail when the book first appeared in 1971. It has sold more than four million copies in twenty-nine languages and has been continually updated and revised to reflect changing medical knowledge and social perspectives.

But as much as the pill and *Our Bodies, Ourselves* originally aimed to free women from what its authors saw as the tyranny of male-enforced pregnancy, the reverberations echoed across the entire erotic and behavioral landscape, altering almost overnight how college boys and girls behaved between the sheets. As behavior changed, so too changed the language of sex and sexuality, the openness with which sex could be discussed and portrayed in everything from comic books to rock concerts. Hippie encampments that were hardly more than starlight bordellos spread from California to Iowa to Vermont. "Saving it for marriage" became an ongoing joke once pregnancy disappeared as a risk. Indeed the fissures in the institution of marriage itself grew into cracks and crevasses until by the mid-1970s a minority of brides took to the bridal sheets as virgins.

Little surprise: Once the sanctions and persecutions for heterosexual sex began to collapse, so exploded as well the liberation campaigns for a steadily expanding array of other erotic expression. The older, quiet suit-and-tie Mattachine advocates who had fought to decriminalize homosexual acts flowered into fierce on- and off-campus demonstraters for gay liberation, for bisexuality, for transsexuality. Once the idea that each individual *owned* his or her own body and the risk of burning in Hell for committing sodomy went away, the human body in all its tortures and treasures became an open turf for discovery and debate. Why should women who didn't hunger for the erotic caress of male hands and genitals not find their pleasures elsewhere: alone, with other women, with toys or cucumbers or not at all? And why should men who desired other men's bodies and longed for the taste of other men's fluids not pursue them? Or for those whose erotic motors revered equally clitoris and penis not kiss both with equal passion carrying no thought of procreation?

Soon enough came that not insignificant slash of humanity who saw and felt themselves lodged in bodies that did not match their spirits, as people who were not exactly male, not exactly female. If pretty women off the ranch could wear Wranglers and Levis, why shouldn't square-shouldered males who loved silk not wear skirts? And indeed more and more did and do, responding to their hormonal impulses, to their neo-Freudian conscious and unconscious impulses, and to an irrepressible fashion industry that has paid brilliant attention to both, leading us to the ever more fluid sense of sex and gender that has become the hallmark of our current era, in which molecular neuroscientists identify intersexuality and transsexuality not as aberrance or perversion but simply as merely further evidence of nature's diversity.

The cultural right wing was quickly proved correct in its analysis of all the risks that came with the liberation of the erotic from the reproductive, even if their program was bankrupt in its morality. As we felt free to couple and behave as we wished, the traditional bonds of reproductive law quickly unraveled. Gay bars and cafés, lesbian "sewing circles," and raucous Pride marches not only swept across the urban landscape; within less than a generation, gay men had mostly shed their fearful, limp-wristed stereotypes to become CEOs and founders of global corporations, notable among them Apple CEO Tim Cook and PayPal founder Peter Thiel, while the bull dyke profile gave way to Google's Megan Smith (named chief technology officer of the United States in 2014) or Genentech's Nancy Vitale. The ever-expanding LGBTQ alphabet tag had by the 1980s become nearly as common as, sometimes more so than, earlier hyphenated ethnic heritage and pride. By the time a dozen states had enacted same-sex marriage laws in the first decade of the millennium, all of them finally certified by a majority Supreme Court in 2015, gender battles had steadily displaced the simplistic notion of a male-female binary with an ever-expanding perception that all individuals exist on a shifting spectrum of gender, sexuality, and personal identity. David Bowie, Boy George, Michael Jackson, Brittany Howard, Grace Jones, even the legendary Nina Simone. By voice and profile they all questioned the gender tag they had been popularly assigned and awakened parallel senses of fluidity in their fans and listeners. The ultra-glam star Lady Gaga, who came on the scene in 2005, once explained, "I love Grace Jones and David Bowie because they both played with gender and what sexy means." Or as a married Brooklyn carpenter friend who performs occasionally at the Imperial Court of New York as Kay Sera—the Boy as Cute as the Girl Next Door—once put it to me, "My line is simple: Straight in the sheets, Queer in the streets."

While the politicized feminist movement focused its energy on gender equity, the cultural movements that grew from sexual liberation—from Freud to Lady Gaga—unleashed a still more disturbing (to both conservatives and leftists) campaign for gender fluidity, and both would find their legal foundation in what came to be known as Title IX, a portion of the Education Amendments of 1972 that expanded the 1964 Civil Rights Act to prohibit discrimination against women.

Title IX was directed at ensuring that women have equal rights to federally funded education. Its most immediate effects were on expanding college enrollment and on opening athletic programs to female students who had long been ignored or outright excluded. But Title IX reached much farther, declaring that "no person in the United States shall, on the basis of gender, be excluded from participation in, be denied the benefits of, or be subjected to discrimination under any education program or activity receiving federal financial assistance." Indiana senator Birch Bayh, the author of Title IX, defended the act against an alliance of Southern Dixiecrats and northern Republicans who, like today's opponents of gay marriage, viewed it as a war against God and Nature. "We are all familiar with the stereotype of women as pretty things who go to college to find a husband," Bayh said on the Senate floor, "[who] go on to graduate school because they want a more interesting husband, and finally marry, have children, and never work again. The desire of many schools not to waste a 'man's place' on a woman stems from such stereotyped notions. But the facts absolutely contradict these myths about the 'weaker sex' and it is time to change our operating assumptions."

Title IX did in fact change many of the most common stereotypes about women's place in modern American society. Suddenly school and university admission policies had to change. At the end of World War II barely 38 percent of college students were women. By 1988 54 percent were women, and by 2010 women made up 56 percent of public university students—and now women are 33 percent more likely than men to graduate college. Across the developed world men now trail women in university enrollment 48 percent to 52 percent. The roots of Title IX, of course, were long and tangled. The law in effect resurrected the gender equity reforms that had been championed by the first women's rights movement born at Seneca Falls, New York, in 1848; later the abolitionist Susan B. Anthony led the first serious movement for women's voting rights, after which the suffrage movement expanded with Margaret Sanger, who was sentenced to a New York workhouse in 1917 for advocating birth control and distributing contraceptive materials. If Sanger and her allies won the right to vote, another half century would pass before women's physical autonomy would win any serious attention.

The failure of the states to ratify the Equal Rights Amendment to the Constitution further blunted the political movement for gender equity. Women's pay in the professions still remains a third behind men's pay in equivalent job categories, even as women like Sheryl Sandberg at Facebook, Ginni Rometty at IBM, and Marilyn Hewson at Lockheed Martin have famously risen to run some of the world's most powerful corporations.

As much as the struggle for women's equality has characterized the outward form of the gender story, our understanding of acceptable male behavior has also changed profoundly, not merely moving toward gender equity but opening the way toward gender fluidity. Women have clearly inched forward to dismantle the barriers to full human participation in the world, but so too have the rules regulating masculinity unwound. Much to the shock of my father's generation, men have gradually moved toward behaviors and methods of expression that have been classically defined as feminine, from diaper changing to baking cookies to shifting more and more fluidly between standardized sexual roles. Prior to the twentieth century men were strictly constrained by acceptable work roles, by dress, by speech mannerisms, by which topics they could safely discuss in public or even among themselves, and, not least, by their physical comportment. Perhaps even more than the strictures imposed on respectable women, the constraints governing masculinity up until World War II were defined by public expectations of sobriety, rigor, and emotional restraint. Northern European and American intellectuals saw themselves as the Aryan descendants of classical Greek ideals. They and their fellow eugenicists argued from pulpit and podium that a well-formed physique reveals the interior character of civilized men and the notion of a "civilized" character was directly linked to national identity and race. Frailty, weakness, and deformation evidenced both genetic and moral inferiority—the basis upon which the "science" of eugenics sought to purify the future world of the "lesser, weaker, more feminine races"—including most notably Jews, "Mohammedans," Africans, and Asians. Too close an association with any of these "lesser species" (or with the voluptuous form of the female—hence the near total exclusion of women from parliaments and the corridors of state) could only lead to masculine enfeeblement and national degeneration. Among the titans of the eugenics movement were no less than Teddy Roosevelt, Woodrow Wilson, George Bernard Shaw, and even Helen Keller. That linkage of manhood and nationalism, historian George Mosse argued in *The Image of Man*, met its apogee in the imagery, statuary, and politics of German nationalism, after which it found a new home in the triumphalism of mid-century America where science and technological innovation created supersized automobiles, intergalactic missiles, and the thermonuclear bomb that (for a time) seemed to guarantee America's role as the world's singular source of civilized power, now perhaps challenged by the bare-chested horseman, Vladimir Putin.

All of those masculine conceits were placed under threat, conscious or not, by the gender equity movement that provoked Betty Friedan to lead her collective children away from the ironing board and into the boardroom. In their wake came Britain's Iron Lady, Margaret Thatcher, disciplining the wayward Falkland Islands, followed a generation later by the world's most powerful pantsuit-clad woman, Angela Merkel. In America the iconic *Father Knows Best* would be bested by the ultimate in gender fluidity shows, *Transparent.* At the same time it fell to a former mayor of hippie-homo San Francisco, Senator Diane Feinstein, to expose the systematic torture techniques that the men of the CIA had invented and refined along the shores of the Potomac. None of these outgrowths of the empowerment of women was spelled out directly by the feminist activists of the sixties and seventies, nor were those decades the sole progenitors of the chaotic gender world in which we now all live. There were, and remain, bitter conflicts between the original Civil Rights leaders, including Martin Luther King Jr., and the Women's Rights movement, just as deep divisions opened between some sectors of the women's movement and many gay and lesbian activists. Many gay activists still cringe at linking arms with transsexual people. Yet the feminist movement undeniably helped remake a world where all these gender transformations became possible. Equal employment access, counseling for pregnant undergraduates, reshaping classroom and lab environments, striking back at sexual harassment (however feebly in macho fraternity houses), and acting forcefully to open engineering and high-tech training to women: All these were framed initially as issues of simple equality between the sexes. To the traditional pinstriped executive in his smoking room or to the laid-off line workers at U.S. Steel, or to the evangelical ministers in Alabama, Kentucky, and Arkansas, these arguments for "equity" constituted nothing less than a full-fledged assault on the natural order of the universe as designed by a singular and unmistakably male god leading to the current unwinding of strict masculine and feminine roles.

Upending the routines, rituals, and rules of gender has, as the cultural conservatives rightly predicted, led to radical transformations in how we as moderns lead our lives all around the world. The mission of this book is to track, explore, and interrogate those ongoing transformations: from rough-and-tumble kindergarten classes in Oslo to masturbation seminars in Shanghai, from same-sex rent-a-womb agencies in Los Angeles to transsexual parenting clubs in Salt Lake City, from high-tech women engineering teams in Silicon Valley to geriatric rebellions in Tokyo. Thanks to the endless and rarely censored explosion of smartphone talk and imagery, hardly anyone outside North Korea or Yemen is isolated from these cultural convulsions—including those who find the changes utterly blasphemous. Gay farm boys raise organic beef down the road from Holy Roller churches and men push baby strollers through Walmart aisles a few miles from my childhood farm in Kentucky—and no one notices, an all but unthinkable tableau in 1965.

In the world we now inhabit, apart from dangerous fundamentalist sectarianism, nothing seems to stimulate or threaten conventional stability so deeply as the shifting terrain of gender—and indeed it may well be that the steady erosion of gender roles motivates fundamentalist rage even more than the historic abuses of race, poverty, and imperial presumption. Without question, the savage fundamentalist attacks in France that shocked the world in 2014 and 2015 were inseparable from both fear and hatred of the occidental upheaval in how men and women treat each other in every domain—from sexual submission to child-rearing to state governance. All that may seem like a very long leap from canning garden produce, but it is the argument of this book that the most ordinary activities and assumptions we express in daily life concerning masculinity and femininity are at the foundation of today's headlines over the gender conundrum. Gender, as philosopher Judith Butler has explained throughout her career, is not merely a labeled identity: Gender is a performance that we all collectively enact in our mostly unconscious daily routines. What fearful conservatives denounce as pending chaos, other so-called gender radicals celebrate as "the death of gender." Both are profoundly confused. Gender distinctions are hardly disappearing. Rather, this book argues, traditional gender categories are undergoing profound fracture and reformulation in nearly every family and town in America. Where religion and patriarchy once defined men as the people who naturally run business, lead governments, and make war, we have been forced to examine what it means to be a man and to be a woman—and for a growing slice of humanity to refuse to be either. Kindergartens in Norway, China, and Chicago teach toddlers not to accept all the old categories of what it means to be a girl—on the playground, in the laboratory, or in bed. Sex acts and behaviors that brought criminal prosecution a generation ago are now protected as a matter of personal right just as marriage is now open to any gender and any sexuality regardless of protests from religious extremists. And in the last fifteen years geneticists and brain scientists have shown us that no matter what XX and XY chromosomes may suggest to the outward eye, masculinity and femininity as well as sexual attraction are far more complex biologically than anyone had previously imagined. The categories that distinguished Nature (our supposed biological identity) from Nurture (how we were raised and cared for) are false categories always in flux. We all exist on what is called a gender spectrum carrying both "masculine" and "feminine" traits whether we lust for the opposite sex, our own sex—or no sex. Moreover the way in which our hormones and neurology express themselves fluctuates across our lifetimes in response to where we live, how we live, and the joys and stresses we experience.

Gender, unlike what some radicals of both the right and the left claim, is not dead nor is it being betrayed. From the moment we pop out of the womb until we're dumped into our final box, the way we express the multitude of genders we contain is in continual flux whether we acknowledge it or not. All that is truly new is that we in the West can hardly turn on our radios or TVs without hearing some new discovery or battle concerning gender. The fears and anxieties seem to beset the left as much as the right.

Feminist radicals of a generation ago, once clad in chenille work shirts and marching in sturdy Birkenstocks, seem baffled by their militant granddaughters who stride through the courthouses in three-inch heels as they direct corporate prosecution teams. Fashions that once signaled conventionality or rebellion have proved as unstable as the gender roles beneath the fashions. Work-shirt feminism disappeared in less than a decade and along with it the notion that free and independent women should resemble their male bosses and cohorts. Long hair on men passed from being sexually suspect to marking super studs, just as ear pins spread from gay to gangbanger zones and tattoo-free shoulders became hard to find on anyone under thirty-five. In the mid-1970s the Sears catalog marketed toys for boys and girls in a rainbow fan of colors and displayed science kits with no gender reference. A quarter century later

Lego construction kits targeted boys almost exclusively while warrior toys were aimed at both—except that bow-and-arrow kits for girls were mostly pink while boys' bows stuck to blue and black. Princess dresses for little girls' first birthday parties sold like never before at the beginning of this century, only to be replaced by running shoes once the girls passed age ten and joined soccer teams. By midway through Barack Obama's second presidential term, the Department of Education ruled that the still embattled Title IX regulations would thenceforth apply to discrimination by students or by teachers against any transgender child or any student who displayed "non-conforming" masculine or feminine traits and behaviors. The end of the twentieth century and beginning of the twenty-first, in short, saw the steady fracturing and erosion of any fixed gender conventions or counter-conventions.

Challenge and reaction to the fracturing of traditional gender notions, however, has hardly proved to end the story any more than Martin Luther resolved the conflicts within the Catholic Church when he nailed his ninety-five theses to the church door in Wittenberg in 1517. At the core of all the liberation movements of the '60s and '70s ran one fundamental phrase: *the personal is political.* Or in its earlier counterculture formulation: *the right to be you and me.* The collective liberation movements that had once aimed at cracking a feminine mystique defined by universal, white, heterosexual male dominance shifted steadily toward the terminology of identity politics. Especially in America, a resurgence of flamboyant individualism was perhaps best personified in Lady Gaga's 2011 hit "Born This Way." If conservative traditionalists had appealed to Nature as the basis on which males and females should behave—males the warriors and breadwinners, females the cooks and caregivers—a new sort of appeal to Nature emerged by the end of the last millennium. Unlike the social constructionists who followed Judith Butler's original argument that most gender roles are formed to reinforce male dominance over daily life—in short, nurture—these new militants quickly scanned biological texts to argue that natural diversity in almost all plants and animals has produced myriad *natural* identities, all of which are biologically if not genetically determined.

By 2014 Facebook formally acknowledged the use of some fifty-six distinct gender identities ranging from agender to pangender. Girls who once had been teased as tomboys, these new Nature advocates insisted, had been *born* to drive trains and trucks. Boys who gathered flowers and taught themselves to sew, once ridiculed as sissies, were *born* to love daffodils and silk. Their tastes and manners were encoded in their genes, they insisted; hence their identities should be protected by new customs and new laws. Replacing the earlier language of fluidity in human behavior and perception there surfaced a fracture of ethics in which each nature-based identity stood only for itself and was justified in asserting its exclusion of other identities. Rather than celebrate the search for shifting, fluid gender sensibilities in all of us across our lives, a counter self-protective expression sought labeling and self-definition and sometimes outright separatism.

For actual biologists and neuroscientists, these shifting tides of gender ideology seem especially strange. One of the world's leading evolutionary biologists, Richard Bribiescas at Yale, has simply and clearly explained just how fluid and variable are the early stages of human development. During their first weeks, male and female fetuses cannot be distinguished in the womb. Later, as identifying genitalia begin to develop, external social influences—stress, fear, excitement, catastrophe—can intensify an array of hormones in the mother's body that in turn can affect the child's eventual character, comportment, and erotic identity. Or in a word, as Bribiescas told one interviewer, it is simply absurd to see nurture and nature as distinct, opposing forces.

For actual gender radicals who had grown up in the heyday of the civil rights, antiwar, gay liberation, and various feminist waves, the new appeal to Nature as destiny has also proved more than mildly worrisome. A movement that once sought solidarity based on tolerance and equality risked feeding division and generalized resentment with the very real possibility of resurrecting a refurbished variety of nineteenth-century eugenics based not on race but on "innate" gender distinctions—distinctions that have already won support among ultratraditional Catholics in France, Poland, and Slovakia, not to mention within the growing antiscience, evangelical homeschooling movement in the United States. As the signs and signals of outward personal freedom have gone viral, access to anonymous tweets and Instagrams has also revealed just how deep and persistent are the undercurrents of uncertainty and confusion. While Facebook managers may recognize more than fifty "genders," Facebook and Twitter pages abound with misogynist, hateful blasts at women in power. Male students, even in elite universities, spew out vile invective about the "rotten cunts" who have been their professors while hotbeds of male supremacy from deep Appalachia to the heart of Texas to the Canadian border rant on with young followers about the emasculation of America at the hands of "dykes and perverts." A powerful sector of black evangelical churches has taken a parallel view, joining with right-wing white evangelicals to denounce at once the so-called "murderer abortionists" in Planned Parenthood and feminist-led acceptance of androgyny. At a more sophisticated level the former minister Jefferis Kent Peterson has built something of an evangelical career based on his founding 1996 essay "Androgyny in Pop Culture" in which he discussed the popularity of performers like Cindy Lauper, Michael Jackson, and Boy George: "The ideal of androgyny in contemporary culture," he wrote, "represents the breakdown of a healthy social structure ... it is a reflection of the inhumanity of contemporary culture and a sign of its possible demise." Rather than opening modern life to a broader, more creative array of sexual and gender roles, Peterson and his followers warn continuously of a moral and cultural breakdown that has seduced men and women to abandon their God-given sexual and gender roles.

Nor is the backlash limited to America. The esteemed Cambridge classical scholar Mary Beard has recounted repeated misogynist attacks against her from all across Britain both for her sex and her age, while the freshly appointed French minister of education, Najat Vallaud-Belkacem, the first woman to hold the post, suffered vitriolic denunciations from the first day she took office in 2014. Antiwoman, antigay, and antitrans movements are plainly not restricted to the hard-line Islamist zones of the earth. Neither on the other hand does it appear that fractionalized fear and resentment are likely to drive those who have tasted freedom and independence backward into the caves of invisibility. What the Internet and its uncountable authors and their critics have let loose in a global atmosphere of curiosity and exploration seems, at least today, beyond the capacity of repression as the once simplified and even crude radical notion of creating a "new man" edges ever closer.

The most militant of gender revolutionaries may still insist that gender is a purely social construction, but for most who study the issue the picture is getting more and not less complex. How are we to understand for instance the fundamental physiological and hormonal differences between males and females of all species, differences expressed in the size and shape of skeletons and their calcium content—not to mention distinct organs of reproduction and the ability to lactate or fabricate sperm? If Sigmund Freud's now discredited diagnosis of hysteria has at last been put to rest, the effect of hormones on our emotions remains very real—be they the sometimes calming effects of estrogen during pregnancy or the exaggerated levels of testosterone that seem to accompany men in aggressive sports and warfare. Males are biologically different from most females. But are those differences essential elements of Nature?

Nature, Helga Nowotny argues in *Naked Genes: Reinventing the Human in the Molecular Age*, is more than ever a problematic notion, a territory where progressive ecologists and ultraconservative evangelicals are sometimes startled to find themselves dancing to the same tune if in a different key. For the evangelicals, Nature is the outward, visible expression of the presence of the deity. For the strict ecologists, deceived and disappointed by the official deities, nature has replaced the divine, which for centuries, Nowotny writes, provided us "a naturally given order (created by God or the gods) whose laws stood above human law and the political order and was therefore absolutely valid." The trouble with that notion of nature is that the more molecular science tells us about the genetics of the natural world, the more we have come to realize just how ephemeral the natural world is and always has been. Nothing in nature is fixed, stable, or durable. "For millennia, whole civilizations imposed on human behavior and communal order an imperative, accompanied by the symbols and rituals of the various religions. All this has collapsed in the last few decades in the face of scientific-technological achievements. Nature has ceased being a moral order in the double sense of the term: It is no longer regarded as a world in which eternal, unchangeable principles rule, and it is therefore less and less in a position to impose these principles on humans."

Startling as Nowotny's statement may seem to the citizens of today's global megalopolises, farmers since the ancient Egyptians and even fruit-gatherers roaming wild forests have always understood how variable and fickle nature is. Nothing is a better illustration than the common apple, *Malus domesticus*, which almost certainly found its origins in the wild apple forests of the Tian Shan Mountains on the border between western China and Kazakhstan. Nearly all the knotty red, green, and yellow fruits growing there on frequently thorny saplings from the Rosaceae family are far too bitter to bite (though many are excellent for making cider), but from time to time over the millennia, pollen from the flowers of one drifted to the blossoms of another; the sun appeared at just the right moment; a normal seeming fruit was born and nourished some decidedly abnormal seeds; the following autumn those seeds were gobbled up by a roaming bear or a migrating bird that then dropped one of them in a new soil where it in turn germinated and grew into a new tree that had never before existed, heavily laden with crisp, sweet, juicy apples whose descendants, thanks to the ancient camel caravans, followed by Roman legions and eventually supersonic jets, found their way into today's hypermarket stands.

Any high school biology student has read some version of the apple saga. Not until the last decades, however, has molecular genetics enabled us to look more closely at our own kindred cousins whose bodies, attractions, and sentiments have fallen far from the mother trees. Moral traditionalists, be they the recruits of Boko Haram in Nigeria or the cross-carrying followers of Pope Benedict XVI, still refuse to see just how essentially diverse are the gender profiles of *Homo sapiens*. Moreover, there is little new in that diversity. Only recently a traveler who works with the indigenous peoples of northeastern Australia told me about the very, very ancient traditions of the Torres Strait Islanders. "In any family that has had three boys," he told me, "if the fourth child is born a boy, he will be raised as a girl, he'll be dressed in girl's clothes, and he'll be taught to cook and behave as a girl. He'll be called a 'sister girl.'" Sometimes, he elaborated, later-born boys will naturally gravitate toward femininity. Traditional Western social critics may blame these "aberrant" gender behaviors on media marketing, but until very recently the Torres Strait Islanders were almost totally isolated. Parallel gender variations have existed nearly everywhere from the Zapotec muxes in Oaxaca to the Chippewas around Lake Superior to the Albanian burnneshas, the South Asian hijras, or even the ancient Scythian "Amazon" fighters. Gender variation, when we dare to look closely, is as natural as any modern apple is unnatural.

But what makes it so? In the case of the sister girls and brother boys on the Torres Strait Islands, the apparent answer is . . . diverse. Sometimes a biological predisposition leads a girl to perform as a male, or a boy as a female, while in other situations where a community appears to have a "shortage" of one sex, the gender roles are assigned by the parents and a boy with fully male genital equipment is raised as a sister girl all the way to adulthood, at which point she may choose to marry a woman and make children with her. For many Western gay and lesbian militants, these socially imposed roles are as offensive as forcing lesbians to marry straight men. The social constructionist militants of the 1970s and '80s sought fiercely to show that we are, all of us, creatures of social influence and formation and that biology—or nature—is nothing more than an excuse for enforced conformity. Little by little, however, a newer and more complex understanding of sexuality, gender, and nature has begun to emerge.

Canadian researchers, for example, have found that late-born boys in large North American families (see Chapter 3) seem much less likely to be heterosexual than their older brothers. Social scientists offer no biological explanation; they merely observe the reality. Yet whatever the biological source may be, the greater issue concerns how our genetic inheritance can be affected by exogenous or external societal and environmental stimulus, thereby altering our internal natures. A key recent case from the world of sport is illustrative. In 2007 the organizers of the New York City Marathon issued a startling new rule that placed music in the same category as anabolic steroids and other performance-enhancing drugs, or PEDs. Athletes plugged into their iPods, it turns out, can experience an emotional—and thereby hormonal—effect on the body's oxygenation system, which in turn can provide one runner an advantage over another. Coaches, for example, have long known that runners training at higher altitudes temporarily develop more red blood cells than identical twin runners training at sea level. Changing altitude is accepted as personal choice and natural, but music that can affect metabolic activity and brain waves and thereby enhance physical stamina and coordination is judged to be, like steroids, an unnatural alteration of our genetically coded and constructed bodies. These are realities that have long been understood by basketball coaches and chanting cheerleaders, not to mention the ancient drummers who usually accompanied African warrior bands. From the moment of conception forward, our genetic codes, our DNA, may be essentially fixed, but how our genetic codes express themselves in relation to external stimulation by stress, excitement, reassurance, stability, and calm can also produce dramatic differences in who we become and how we behave.

Or, to come back to the ever more complex universe of gender display, how we walk, how we sing, how we dance, how we copulate, how we fight, even how we develop bone and muscle form, and indeed how we comprehend what it means to be male or female, or both or neither, appear more and more to be infinitely fluid. That, as Helga Nowotny and a growing legion of researchers tell us, is the real gift of nature: to be always in transition. It is in that sense that gender as a distinction understood by our grandparents seems very quickly to be disappearing. Some who are given to panic and quick judgment, like Reverend Peterson, have declared that we are witnessing the death of gender; a more prudent view, as this work aims to illustrate, is that gender is rather experiencing an unprecedented proliferation of meanings, forms, and expression.

Perhaps even the sons or grandsons of Reverend Peterson and all those other boys who would do anything to escape the kitchen during tomato canning season are now ready to reexplore the steamy kitchens of their ancestors and embrace the magical sweat of culinary invention.

PART I

Gender Visions

CHAPTER 1

Simple Justice or Gender Chaos?

The signs are everywhere. Not only do little girls excel in preschools more quickly than little boys, but reams of data show that women's mental agility persists seriously longer than men's as everyone's life expectancy grows longer. Those of us who carry XX chromosomes are more durable, more flexible, and, say geriatric specialists, more resilient than XY companions. The resilience of what used to be called the weaker sex, however, reveals only one small if important window on today's radical reformulation of the gender dialogue. The roles, the perceptions, and the performances that signal the meanings of masculine and feminine are everywhere in flux. A quick survey of Midwestern high school athletic programs, a visit to the ever more ubiquitous home cooking schools, or even a scan of Presbyterian marriage registers should turn anybody weaned on *The Adventures of Ozzie & Harriet* or *Father Knows Best* topsy-turvy. Nothing in the raucous circus of gender revision, however, nearly matches the hyperbolic battles sweeping today's college campuses (and many high schools). The upheavals prove distressing not simply to stuffy members of the Lions Club; aging feminists of Gloria Steinem's generation frequently seem equally baffled by the gender battles among contemporary twenty-somethings. Where Steinem sought to replace salutations of Miss or Mrs. by Ms. as a liberation for unmarried women, now Ms. as well is crumbling before fearful school administrations intimidated by younger people who refuse any gender labels.

The question of how teachers should address students in the classroom first surfaced, not surprisingly, in a handful of elite private colleges. It was in autumn 2013 that I received a note from my friend Neil, a young gay professor of literature at Macalester College in St. Paul, Minnesota; he had just received a circular from his administration that left him temporarily dumbfounded. Henceforth, the memorandum instructed, professors were to refrain from using terms like Mr., Miss, or Ms. Instead, they were advised to ask each student to declare "their" PPC, otherwise known as Preferred Pronoun Choice (sometimes known as PPP, Preferred Personal Pronoun). The directive had come in response to a small but vocal number of undergraduates who felt that their preferred gender identity was not being respected in the classroom. More than a few Brendas had become Brads even though they appeared not to have Adam's apples, while more than a few students who had registered as Brads were plainly developing upper-body curves and abandoning Brad for Brenda within their friendship circles.

At about the same time, Calliope Wong, a person born with both X and Y chromosomes but who had been living for several years as a female, applied to Smith College in Northampton, Massachusetts. She was quickly rejected. "Smith is a women's college, which means that undergraduate applicants to Smith must be female at the time of admission," the rejection letter read. "Your FAFSA [Free Application for Federal Student Aid] indicates your gender as male. Therefore Smith cannot process your application." Calliope Wong's high school grades were excellent, and all the other documents she submitted to Smith indicated she was female, but because she had not yet gone through the lengthy bureaucratic process of registering her federal ID as female, and because she had applied for federal aid, that single document identified her by her birth gender: male. To make the point still clearer Smith's vice president in charge of admissions sent an e-mail to Calliope pointing out that the college was founded for the specific purpose of educating women. "We don't define what constitutes a woman—we leave that to other entities or agencies to affirm [but] we do require that it BE affirmed, at the point of admission."

Sex and gender have long been particularly sensitive terrains for Smith, once known as the sister school to Yale when Old Blue was all male. But by the last decades of the last century Smith was rumored to be a hotbed of lesbianism—so much so that Smith's then-president Mary Maples Dunn felt compelled to issue a statement about the college and lesbianism in which she articulated "a doctrine of tolerance of all lifestyles," aimed not least at more conservative alumnae upon whose bequests Smith, like other women's colleges, highly depends. More succinctly, Dunn wanted to assure alumnae that they need not fear that the large but still minority lesbian student body would be intimidating to innocent heterosexual applicants. "When asked about the lesbian problem, the alums will deny it up, down and backward," Sophie Godley, the political chair of Smith's Lesbian-Bisexual Alliance, told a reporter for the *Los Angeles Times* in 1991. "It's the image that they're worried about, the packaging," Godley, who went on to become a public health advisor and teacher in Boston, said. "They don't want Smith to be known as a lesbian school."

Other elite women's colleges have taken dramatically different approaches. At Mount Holyoke, a new production of *The Vagina Monologues* was canceled after some students protested that "not all women have vaginas." Further complicating the issue for these colleges founded in the nineteenth century to help women who were generally excluded from private male universities is that the federal Department of Education has ruled that all the protections granted under Title IX of the Education Amendments of 1972 are now extended to transgender individuals. Or in short, when is a woman really a woman and how is she to prove her womanliness?

What first surfaced in the hothouse atmosphere of a handful of elite liberal arts colleges has spread like the morning dew to public universities everywhere—even in Mormon Utah where Campus Pride, the intercollegiate gay association, has ranked the University of Utah among America's twenty-five friendliest LGBTQ campuses. The Preferred Pronoun Choice battles have permeated campuses nationwide (though it's been slower to surface in Europe, where pronouns—such as he, she, they, it—more frequently agree with an object than a speaker). Once the City University of New York Graduate Center in New York, with 1,700 faculty and 4,600 students, joined the fray, the pronoun war had reached its apogee. "Allowing students to use their preferred name and eliminating the use of pronouns in official correspondence is a necessary step toward protecting the rights, privacy, and safety of students," said Dominique Nisperos, cochair of the Doctoral Students' Council at CUNY, which had been at the forefront of defending "gender nonconforming" students. Money was next on their gender liberation agenda, calling on the budget-strapped administration to construct gender-neutral bathrooms and dormitories. Now, more than one hundred campuses have established gender-inclusive residence halls. That was a tough and expensive issue at the University of Maryland outside Washington, D.C., said Amy Martin, a director in the school's residence program: "Students told us that they felt they would be targeted [in gender neutral bathrooms]. We also have a number of Living and Learning programs where you live in residence halls based on which program you are a part of, so if we had only one location for gender neutral housing, students wouldn't be able to be with their Living and Learning programs."

Genny Beemyn, who directs the Stonewall Center at the University of Massachusetts at Amherst, also says she's seen a steady progression in sensitivity to transsexual students' needs since her school became the first to offer gender-neutral housing in 1992. "Trans students and allies have been working now for a number of years at many schools to create gender-inclusive bathrooms and gender-inclusive housing options, because those are pretty basic—to have a place to sleep and a place to pee," she said. More than seventy campuses now include hormonal and some transsexual surgical procedures in their college health plans. And even major schools like the University of Michigan, the University of Maryland, Duke, and most of the University of California campuses now offer what they call gender-neutral or gender-inclusive student housing. Administrators at the University of North Carolina and the University of Texas prepared similar housing services only to have them rejected by their politically appointed boards of governors. But the trend toward making American campuses more trans friendly continues to advance—even in Texas, where hard-right politicians regularly denounce any policy that appears to promote the safety and equality of gay, lesbian, trans, or otherwise gender-independent identities—as they did in a nationally financed campaign to reverse a Houston ordinance that would have outlawed discrimination against LGBT people. Support for gender-inclusive policies and programs, not surprisingly, comes as much from faculty and student counseling services as from student activists themselves. "I am a firm believer in battering down the binary model of gender however we need to do it, despite the anxiety of people who prefer a black-and-white world," said Nancy Daley, an adjunct assistant professor at the University of Texas. "The world is not one-or-the-other, and neither is gender. People who don't believe in change, or who can't tolerate change, ought not to be on a college campus."

Gender uncertainty, gender transition, gender dysphoria, and various suffixes attached to the word "trans" have captured more recent attention than any other gender issue since the peak of feminist activism in the 1970s, which itself was quickly followed by the Lavender Revolution that provoked nationwide gay "zaps" on those most hallowed of male residences, the football house. After a quarter century of dual feminist and LGBT activism, women are now a majority in most student bodies and make up 40 percent of college professorships. Both by law and by practice, discrimination on the basis of sexuality is illegal for institutions that receive federal funding, which is effectively all institutions of higher education; and being gay or lesbian is often an asset for a candidate under review by search committees seeking to expand gender studies programs. Yet *trans* continues to be among the most difficult of contemporary gender terrains (see Chapter 11) because unlike the more defined categories of gay and lesbian, transsexual cuts across physical (and physiological), social, and linguistic categories. Where gay and lesbian activists sought recognition for specific identities, *trans* covers multiple identities, not all of which are the same, have the same desires and behaviors, or want to be addressed by the same names. Many radical feminists denounce "transwomen" as false women out to use their male education to undermine feminist progress, while large numbers of gay males not infrequently dismiss transmen as "freaks of nature." Indeed, while the glamorous 2015 *Vanity Fair* portrait of sixty-five-year-old athlete Bruce Jenner reborn and recarved as a slinky twenty-five-year-old woman named Caitlyn gave a great boost to the trans movement, many born-women over sixty found her stock idea of womanliness insulting and degrading. Confusion over the difference between transvestite—conventionally gay men dressing as women—and transsexual—people born with male or female genitalia who feel themselves placed in the wrong body—has provoked campaigns to withdraw the T from LGBT. None of these internecine LGBT battles at all addresses an apparently small but growing body of humans who declare themselves as "asexuals," or "agender" people who feel neither male nor female and possess no desire for either.

Movements that find their launch on college campuses soon trickle down to earlier grades. The antiwar activism of the Vietnam era eventually spread to graduating high school seniors who found a double motivation to go to college in order to avoid the draft. The conflicts and anxieties surrounding gender have penetrated even more quickly into adolescence than the antiwar fever did among the Baby Boomers, accompanied by earlier and earlier onsets of puberty—eight to eleven years old for girls and nine or ten for boys—along with all the propulsions, compulsions, and obsessions that come with puberty. To note that crushes, attractions, and personal devotions are volatile in adolescence is far from original. However, the context for today's pubescent adolescents, almost universally attached to their smartphone-based social networks, is radically new, saturating their waking hours with unedited images, propositions, promotions, and declarations that were all but unknown a quarter century ago. The sex-ed offerings of Gen-Xers, much less the Vietnam generation, compared to what any fourteen-year-old can find now on the Internet, is roughly equivalent to how a Crusader in the eleventh century might perceive the aerial attack on the Twin Towers.

Aside from parental concerns about their children's safety, the conversation about adolescent sports has touched a number of deeper chords beyond the issue of transgender behavior. By addressing physiological issues like bone structure, musculature, and hormonal differences, conservatives opposed to the trans movement have found themselves entangled in the most elemental debates about sexuality, biology, and gender. Some states, like Kentucky and Alabama, have opened school sports to "transgender" students, but only if they have already initiated hormone and/or surgical treatment—procedures that doctors discourage before a child has reached at least age sixteen. Further, as mentioned, "transgender" and "transsexual" do not have the same meaning. Transgender refers generally to men who dress and "behave" like women, or women who comport themselves according to male styles and conventions. Transsexual refers to people who have or who are undergoing bio-hormonal-physiological changes. Beyond these "trans" questions, the whole discussion has steadily forced both children and parents to ask themselves what it is they mean when they speak of "boys" or "girls" and even further to question the way in which contemporary sex ed is taught in schools. In the not very distant past, the categories of sex and gender were simple. "Sissy boys" were still *boys* and "butch girls" were still girls. The omnipresence of boys or girls who are well on their way to reinventing themselves has not only challenged conventional categories, but it has equally upset the gay-versus-straight categorization that even homophobes rely upon to denigrate difference.

Uncertain sexual or gender display may well be one of the most destabilizing developments of the last half century, not only for cultural conservatives but for liberal-minded Americans and Europeans who have come to accept minority categories of sexuality. Lady Gaga's "Born

This Way," taken as an anthem for biologically based difference, including a category for transsexuals, still suggests that we are all created with a clear gender identity and that each and every one of us fits into that neat identity category. A closer eye and a more attentive ear, however, may come to understand trans-identity, trans-promotion, trans-discussion as signaling an ongoing state of transition that has no fixed endpoint but that reveals a near universal state of fluidity that we all—either as individuals or as societies at large—may or could inhabit from time to time. In that light *transition* is the norm that we primates collectively share as we transition through time, through attachment, through desire, and through self-discovery.

Even as I was writing these English phrases, news spun through the smartphone atmosphere that Mexico City, the world's fourth largest city—and the largest Catholic enclave on the planet—had just enacted a law enabling any person to declare herself different from the gender he or she was apparently born into. The cost: twelve pesos, no medical or judicial ruling required. And should that person's sense of gender change yet again, it will only cost twelve more pesos to reregister officially to a new gender . . . endlessly and without limit.

~

When *Lance Loves Michael* aired on the E! television channel in midwinter 2015, it made history as the first televised documentary of a gala homosexual wedding—and as the Supreme Court was awaiting oral arguments on the constitutional right for gays and lesbians to marry, Lance Bass and Michael Turchin were also doing their part in the long march by gay activists to strike traditional gender roles from the marriage pact. The wedding—hardly the down-home knot-tying sort that is celebrated every day in churches and county courthouses—took place in the extravagant elegance of Los Angeles's celebrity Park Plaza Hotel, three hundred of their closest Hollywood and Palm Springs friends in attendance. Bass, raised in a Mississippi teetotaling Baptist home, was a singer in the rock band *NSYNC. Turchin, raised Jewish, is a trendy pop art portrait painter. Both men were given away by their mothers. "We wanted it to have a royal vibe, and everything about the place is over the top and gorgeous. It was exactly the backdrop we needed," said Bass, the more voluble of the not-quite-young-marrieds. "It was less about getting married and more about showcasing our marriage and showing that a same-sex couple can get married to the rest of the world—especially to kids who are gay—but who feel there aren't any gay role models, or a life outside of what they're living," Turchin said, adding, "and, hopefully, to change other people's minds who were just ignorant about gay people."

The reruns and digital screenings of Lance and Michael's wedding had hardly calmed down when three million Irish citizens turned out to vote overwhelmingly (62 percent) to make the Emerald Isle, once little more than a subsidiary of the Vatican, the world's first nation to vote for same-sex marriage. The Irish vote, along with same-sex marriage's legalization in most of Western Europe and in six South American mostly Catholic countries, stands for its proponents as the culmination of the four-decade battle that officially began in 1969 in New York City with the Stonewall Rebellion, with landmark events including the national march for gay and lesbian rights in 1993 in Washington, D.C., the repeal of gay exclusion from the American military in 2011, and of course the 2015 ruling by the Supreme Court that states may not deny same-sex couples the right to marry because to do so would violate their Fourteenth Amendment rights to equal protection.

A significant minority, which in time may turn into a majority, have challenged the court's reliance on the Fourteenth Amendment to endorse same-sex marriage. However, juridical argumentation aside, the court's ruling in fact reflected a stunning reversal in popular attitudes toward homosexuality in general and the unfairness of same-sex couples' exclusions from the benefits of marriage—benefits that some two thirds of the country saw as both emotionally and fiscally valuable. Justice Anthony Kennedy, who wrote the majority opinion, said as much in his text articulating four principal justifications for expanding marriage. "The first premise of this Court's relevant precedents is that the right to personal choice regarding marriage is inherent in the concept of individual autonomy. This abiding connection between marriage and liberty is why Loving [v. Virginia, a 1967 case] invalidated interracial marriage bans under the Due Process Clause . . . Decisions about marriage are among the most intimate that an individual can make," which, he noted are "true for all persons, whatever their sexual orientation. A second principle in this Court's jurisprudence is that the right to marry is fundamental because it supports a two-person union unlike any other in its importance to the committed individuals. The intimate association protected by this right was central to Griswold v. Connecticut, which held the Constitution protects the right of married couples to use contraception . . . Same-sex couples have the same right as opposite-sex couples to enjoy intimate association, a right extending beyond mere freedom from laws making same-sex intimacy a criminal offense." A third basis for the court's ruling, Kennedy wrote, is for the protection of the children who live with same-sex parents and the probability that they would suffer ostracism and discrimination at school or on the playground if their parents could not marry. The fourth and essentially conservative principle cited in the ruling identified marriage as a keystone to the nation's stability—no less for same-sex couples than for heterosexual couples. "There is no difference between same- and opposite-sex couples with respect to this principle, yet same-sex couples are denied the constellation of benefits that the States have linked to marriage and are consigned to an instability many opposite-sex couples would find intolerable. It is demeaning to lock same-sex couples out of a central institution of the Nation's society, for they too may aspire to the transcendent purposes of marriage. The limitation of marriage to opposite-sex couples may long have seemed natural and just, but its inconsistency with the central meaning of the fundamental right to marry is now manifest."

In a word, Kennedy argued that because American society—and most of European societies as well—no longer regards the traditional gender roles as the only basis for marriage, then simple fairness, simple justice—to use an earlier court's ruling concerning racial relations—cannot any longer allow the states to discriminate against and penalize same-sex couples.

Yet even if same-sex marriage seems to have swept the Western world (holdouts Germany and Italy notwithstanding), nothing better illustrates how deeply the battles over gender and justice have reached into contemporary life. Moreover, despite the decision by the *New York Times* to include same-sex unions intermixed with straight ones in its wedding announcement columns, the fervor is far from unanimous—even from within the ranks of gay and lesbian militants. No less a figure than Masha Gessen, the best-selling Russian-American author and longtime lesbian activist, dismisses the gay marriage campaign as built on outright lies. "Fighting for gay marriage," she said in one widely reported speech, "generally involves lying about what we're going to do with marriage when we get there." Gessen famously added in a radio interview that she looks forward to the day when conventional marriage will not exist. "It's a no-brainer that [homosexual activists] should have the right to marry, but I also think equally that it's a no-brainer that the institution of marriage should not exist ... I have three kids who have five parents, more or less, and I don't see why they shouldn't have five parents legally . . . I met my new partner, and she had just had a baby, and that baby's biological father is my brother, and my daughter's biological father is a man who lives in Russia, and my adopted son also considers him his father. So the five parents break down into two groups of three . . . And really, I would like to live in a legal system that is capable of reflecting that reality, and I don't think that's compatible with the institution of marriage."

An Irish friend and his American mate of a decade wrote me triumphantly one day after the Irish referendum that "we (secretly) are going to transform or destroy marriage from within." The object for Gessen and for my Irish friend is not merely a call for simple justice and equality but a drive to bring about the collapse of the marriage pact as we have known it for most of Judeo-Christian history, along the way unraveling the remnants of the traditional gender roles upon which conventional marriage has been built. That is almost exactly the argument made by Brian Brown, who led the famous 2008 Proposition 8 ban on gay marriage in California; Brown remained one of the key opponents to gay marriage in arguments before the Supreme Court. "The notion of the uniqueness of men and women is not some side thing in Scripture, it's a key part of our view of humanity: that there are two halves of humanity, male and female, and that we complement each other, and that complementarity bears fruit in children," he said in a highly publicized debate with gay columnist and marriage advocate Dan Savage in 2012.

Marriage, anthropologists and archaeologists tell us, is the oldest of human institutions, as present among our Stone Age ancestors as it was among the Roman emperors as it was between Mao Zedong and Jiang Qing or between Paul Newman and Joanne Woodward. Or Ellen DeGeneres and Portia de Rossi. When traditionalists worry about cracks in the foundation of marriage, their worries are little different from the worries expressed by critics of divorce in classical Rome. What is different—and what has varied across the centuries—is what "marriage" means, how it happens, for what reasons and with what consequences. When the classical historian John Boswell wrote a deeply researched—and deeply flawed—book about the roots of Christian marriage, he argued as a self-interested gay man that the earliest of Christian monks had exchanged marriage vows. Official Vatican scholars were scandalized. Later more prudent scholars criticized Boswell for confusing the ancient Greek vows of solidarity with vows of domestic fidelity. The same issue rests at the core of gay marriage campaigns today.

Radical feminists of the 1970s saw traditional marriage as a soft prison used by men to trap women into relentless servitude changing diapers, peeling carrots, and nursing the elderly. Traditional Protestants, Mormons and evangelicals, whose numbers are all growing, understand marriage as the ancient loving compact through which the muscular male defends and nourishes the tender womb that will bring forth his progeny. Neither reading of marriage addresses its origins or its historic function, writes marriage historian Stephanie Coontz; marriage prior to the late eighteenth-century doctrine of love and romance existed to transform strangers into relatives and relatives into stable cooperatives through which states and nations could prosper in peace. Individual attachment from the beginning has played but a minor role. "Marriage," Coontz writes, "became a way through which elites could hoard or accumulate resources, shutting out unrelated individuals or even 'legitimate' family members. Propertied families consolidated wealth, merged resources, forged political alliances, and concluded peace treaties by strategically marrying off their sons and daughters," a theme that pervades Thomas Hardy's most successful novel, *Far from the Madding Crowd*. Among the wealthy, a wife brought a dowry with which her husband could pay off debts or expand investment. Among the poor, mostly marginal farmers, the question was similar but simpler: "Can I marry someone whose fields are next to mine? Will my prospective mate meet the approval of the neighbors and relatives on whom I depend?"

Generating successful progeny may be a marginal, if growing, motivation for Jack and Jerry to marry, but the mostly childless nature of same-sex unions has reopened underlying tensions about desire, what it means, how to use it, how to manage it, and how it can transform individual solitude into (with luck) lifelong collaboration in the greater society. In a world where having a thousand Facebook "friends" is more or less routine, social researchers tell us that there has never been as pervasive a sense of solitude as the Western world faces today. Where once the extended families created by organized marriage were the chief reprieve from personal solitude, new sorts of marriages have arrived, sometimes conventionally gendered on the surface but far more complex within the compact.

~

Shirley Royster's first marriage ended after she came home early one day to find her husband in conjugal delirium with two women and the bedroom door chained shut. He had fathered her first child. She had a second by another man in Philadelphia and started using hard drugs. When the second relationship ended, she gave up on men and moved north to Massachusetts, physically and culturally far from her childhood home in a small mostly black town outside Richmond, Virginia. It was at a barbecue party in Jamaica Plains, Massachusetts, that she met Catharine, her wife, a quarter century before our conversation. "Catharine was laying in a hammock with her girlfriend when I met her. She was gorgeous. Still is gorgeous. I said to my friend Debbie, you know what, that girl's gonna be my girlfriend. And she said, how you gonna . . . that girl's married! I'm like, I'm gonna wait for her." A year and a half later Catharine and her girlfriend broke up. When Shirley found out, she asked a mutual friend to invite Catharine to a circulating card game that included both gay and straight, mostly black, friends.

"So we invited Catharine. I'm all up on her. If she's sittin' on the couch, I'm right there on the couch. She's standing up, I'm standing up. I'm all over her. Later she said, 'I just thought you were being nice.'

"'Nice?' I said. I was trying to get in your underwear! What do you mean, being nice?

"I can be nice to anybody.

"She said her girlfriend came home one day and said I don't want to do this anymore, and moved out.

"I said, 'Poor baby, if you was with me, that would never happen.' She was two years younger than me. I asked her out [to a club]. I didn't drive at that time. Somebody gave me a 1978 Pinto and the floorboards in the back were all rusted out. The kids would say, 'Ma, we got to put our feet up like this.'" She drew her feet up. "'They be touchin' the ground.' Catharine had patience enough to show me how to drive a standard shift 'cause that's what she drove. A Toyota. She showed me how to drive and we been together ever since."

Shirley, who works in social service, and Catharine, a glassblower, got married a few months after Massachusetts approved same-sex marriage in November 2003. Shirley said they married for love, but they also found solidarity in raising their children together. When Jean and Barb married, their two sets of children were already grown and living with or married to men. Jean is an international health care consultant; Barb is a doctor in general practice. Each had a secure income and a wide variety of gay and straight friends. They married each other on November 3, 2003, the day the law passed.

"Why did we get married the first day? Because you say to me I can't get married, you bet your sweet bippy, I'm gonna be there the first instant it's possible. Oh no, you say all these things about the construction of my life and who I am that could hurt my kids, you bet I'm going to be married . . . even if I don't believe in that form."

"So you mean marriage is a trap either way?" I asked her.

"You can't compare what marriage means in terms of my relationship to authority and the state in such a contested time, where marriage is actually an act of resistance, not simply an act of acquiescence to the state. You can't make the same arguments that you will be able to make in a generation."

"Yes," I answered, "but isn't it also about people's need for some sort of symbolic ritual?"

"Okay, but that's not the argument," she persisted. "You can't simply say I am happy because I found a great love, and it shaped and reordered my life. The fact that I could marry that person, yes, I'm not saying it's a bad thing. But, the act of our marriage was an act of resistance as much as a reclamation of our relationship. We can't simply assess it from its conservative component [citing] the difference between us and single people who are uncoupled because they don't have a great love. My argument is not about single people and that marriage makes people better or arguing that the institution is beneficial for the relationship. I don't think you can do that in a time when marriage is so contentious. I don't think it's clearly true. Maybe it's true."

Over the quarter century that I had known Jean, first when I was an NPR health reporter, she had always blended analysis with a sense of playful sentiment. Barb has always been fiercely rigorous in her arguments about how access to privileges like state-regulated marriage is mostly about recognition versus erasure of a minority.

"It's not at all clear to me," Barb continued, "that the people who are twenty years younger than we are have themselves never experienced issues of discrimination. Look at young lesbian doctors. There's a set of people who have the same set of privileges as they would have had as heteros. So marriage for me is a totally different experience. Sort of like having been with the Wright brothers and then seeing the Concorde. People around me—privileged—don't get it! They aren't different in many ways than their privileged hets . . . so if you're doing a study about what marriage means to them, it probably isn't so different than what marriage means to their buddies. But it's very different for us."

As an example, she cited the case of Jean's son, Daniel, when he was away at college. "He'd call and say he was coming home for dinner. We thought, Oh God, he's failing something or some other bad news. But no. It took about four times before we realized that each time there had been something in the news that was bad for gay families. Every time. We were his family."

Jean's practicing Catholic family bears uncanny resemblance to the ancient family structure that Stephanie Coontze writes about. It is both a child-rearing institution and a social institution that has historic roots in the community, whereas Barb's evangelical Protestant parents were more similar to the fire-and-brimstone Holy Rollers I had known in Kentucky. Jean frequently defers to Barb in dinner table talk, as she had on the evening we discussed their family life, but then Jean broke in. "I've been very moved by the fact that most of Daniel's girlfriends have been working class or first-generation immigrants from Lebanon. The thing I find interesting is those are particular places where who we are is contested. I don't know how he gets them to understand us, but he never doesn't bring the girls home."

"I remember going to a Lebanese church outside Lawrence when his girlfriend's grandfather died, and he wanted us there," Barb added. "She wanted us there too."

"The family was moved by the fact that we came," Jean said.

Jean's parents had praised them about how they were raising their kids, but they also drew a line about their marital status. "They said, 'You're not welcome in our house.' Then later they set up a double bed for us, after we went to a family wedding," Jean recalled. "When my brother's wedding came up six months later and he invited me and the children, I sent the children. I didn't go. My parents called up afterwards and said, 'Barb's welcome here.' If my parents hadn't been clear, and we hadn't been clear, we would never have gotten to the place we got to in terms of the quality of our relationship. It was like you flipped a switch."

The two Jerrys are among the most famous gay couples in Kentucky, and by chance their organic farm, where they plow with mules instead of tractors, is only a half hour from the apple orchard where I grew up. Neither Jerry Hicks, who does most of the physical labor, nor his husband, Jerry Neff, who commutes to an electronics factory, were married when we met. Kentucky is one of the states that banned both same-sex marriage and civil unions. The Jerrys met in a Walmart parking lot in Winchester, about twenty minutes east of Lexington, in 1998. Jerry Hicks had just returned from a fishing trip on the river and had his aluminum job boat wedged in the back of his pickup. By chance Jerry Neff pulled into a space just next to him and commented on Hicks' fishing tackle. Great loves can launch themselves in parking lots.

A few passionate months later, Hicks took Neff along for a weekend visit to his grandmother's house on the edge of the mountains. She showed the two young men to a bedroom with two beds, which they sometimes used. Once the Jerrys could marry, they straightaway set upon organizing the event, Jerry Hicks told me: a quiet celebration among friends out in their hay barn "with plenty of good food and Guinness." While they both regard themselves as spiritual Christians, no ministers were invited. ("I talk to the Lord whenever I need to," Jerry Hicks told me, "whether I'm in church or behind the plow.")

Seventeen years had passed since they met when the Supreme Court ruled that Kentucky, Ohio, and twenty-seven other mostly red states could no longer block two men or two women from marrying each other. Unlike the groundswell in Americans' overall approval of same-sex marriage, a majority of Kentuckians remained opposed to it—just as a majority of white Southerners had opposed the Brown versus Board of Education of Topeka ruling in 1954 that ended segregation between blacks and whites in public schools along with other rulings that had blocked interracial marriage. Even if a minority of couples in the 646,000 same-sex households (2010 U.S. Census) say they want to be officially married, Jerry Hicks and Jerry Neff had waited a long time to be able to take the legal step. "First of all," Hicks said, "is public recognition of our relationship. Our relationship is as important to us as heterosexuals' relationships are to them." For Neff, who grew up Catholic, getting married was not only about formalizing personal bonds. It was equally about reinforcing the separation of church and state. Condemned by the Vatican for the sex he has with Jerry Hicks, he says he could care less what churches say or do. Public marriage, he said, "nails it all the way down to the floor for all the bigots out there. It says 'Look, you can believe whatever you want to believe inside your private little church, but when you go into the public sphere, there's a religious marriage that you all cherish so dearly that you can exclude gay people from, but there's also a civil marriage, and you need to get that damned idea into your head finally. Marriage in the eyes of the state has nothing to do with marriage in the eyes of the church."

There were of course more pragmatic reasons they wanted to be married: insurance contracts, hospital visitation rights, health and retirement benefits. "I pay quite a lot of money into Social Security," Jerry Neff pointed out, "but if I kick the bucket, Jerry Hicks will get none of that." Jerry Neff's father had encouraged them to get married in West Virginia, where he lives and where same-sex marriage was legal. But both Jerrys wanted to wait until marriage became legal in their own state. "I don't want to come home with some certificate from somewhere else, Japan or somewhere, that people in Kentucky can turn their noses up [at] and say that's not real here. I want it to be real in my home." Jerry Hicks cut in, "And it wouldn't be recognized here on the state level," where they also pay several thousand dollars in taxes and other charges.

Marriage, more than any of the other quasi-cinematic convulsions on the contemporary gender stage, may appear to be the final battle in unraveling traditional social values, a crossroads where sex, sexuality, and daily life converge, where gender as most of us grew up understanding it has either disappeared or been fundamentally redefined. So it may seem. The flagrant sexual display celebrated by 1970s gay liberation, complete with the bump-and-grind floats in pride parades and S and M whips and chains, appear to have gradually but steadily given way to conventional domestic routines. Ozzie and Harry squabble over who will walk the dog while Gail and Gracie trade diaper duty and grocery shopping. The backroom bars and all-night clubs that once defined the sizzling quarters of San Francisco and New York are now dominated by chain drugstores and mini-marts supplying the needs of aging homo husbands and lesbian wives. Marriage, that oldest and most conservative of human institutions, seems to have tamed all and, on the surface, with the Supreme Court's blessing, it has won the approval of a clear majority of Americans.

Surfaces, however, are often misleading. Public health researchers are often among the first to report subterranean social currents—be they rising rates of disabling allergies despite improved sanitation or newer varieties of sexually transmitted infections (STIs). While the epidemic of sexually transmitted human immunodeficiency virus (HIV) has shrunk into the shadows since the 1980s, another marker of what the French call libertinism has flourished in the form of a potentially more devastating virus, human papilloma virus (HPV). HPV is the tiny beast that has infected an estimated 70 percent of adult Americans and presumably was the source of actor Michael Douglas's famous case of throat cancer, which he proudly admitted (and later denied) came from his addiction to applying his tongue to a vast number of women's clitorises. Thanks for the explosion of heterosexual cunnilingus goes to Larry Flynt's *Hustler* magazine ("*for those who think pink*") and the late Bob Guccione's Vaseline-lensed soft-porn *Penthouse*—both of which in an earlier epoch I wrote for. Both *Hustler* and *Penthouse*, however virulently heterosexual they were, owed much of their success to the blatant libertinism that accompanied homo liberation, for in the popular mind the most stereotypical image of oral-genital engagement was embodied in the denigrating term *cocksucking*. Cocksucker in the 1950s and '60s was about the worst epithet that could be hurled against a sissy-boy outsider. With the sweeping triumphs of gay liberation, cocksucking and "muff diving" came out of the closet of shame and paraded themselves as the bedroom activities that any hip child of the sixties had to perform regardless of the sex of the players. The behavior once shrouded by social and psychological taboo turned Flynt and Guccione into megamillionaires as their slick magazines pushed aside nearly all their competitors and their editorial pages defended every sort of sexual freedom including gay liberation.

As *Hustler*, *Penthouse*, and their imitators flourished, they of course brought out their enemies, most notably Jerry Falwell and his Moral Majority. Later in his life Falwell spoke out in favor of gay civil rights and even of same-sex "civil marriage," but at the peak of the battle he denounced homosexuals as "brute beasts" in service to a "vile and satanic system [that] will one day be utterly annihilated and there'll be a celebration in heaven." Falwell and millions of his followers were not only concerned about the sexual acts associated with HIV and other STIs. Far graver, he preached, was "God's punishment for the society that tolerates homosexuals." Chief among those punishments were epidemic sexually transmitted diseases (STDs), including acquired immunodeficiency syndrome (AIDS). But disease represented only the beginning of God's wrath. "We will see a breakdown of the family and family values," he intoned, "if we decide to approve same-sex marriage, and if we decide to establish homosexuality as an acceptable alternative lifestyle with all the benefits that go with equating it with the heterosexual lifestyle."

What marriage represented to the Moral Majority remains bedrock faith to hard-core conservatives throughout the Bible Belt, notably in

Arkansas, Mississippi, and Alabama, where solid majorities of the population still staunchly oppose the Supreme Court's same-sex marriage ruling and often still refuse to issue marriage licenses to same-sex applicants. At the same time major corporations now lobby hard in favor of gay and lesbian equality, not least because childless middle-class couples today represent a major chunk of the consumer market. For the moment the tide of history appears to favor welcoming same-sex couples into the marriage tent. Yet what forms the fabric and shape of that tent? Barb, Jean, Shirley, Catharine, the two Jerrys, and my Irish activist friend all favor opening the marriage laws regardless of gender, yet none of them even vaguely embraces the meaning that marriage has carried since Abraham fled Ur with his wife and half-sister Sara for the green pastures of Canaan.

For nearly all same-sex parents, some version of that complexity is the reality, a reality that the Hollywood star couple Lance and Michael declared in their marriage video. Strict opponents of same-sex marriage, who almost always see homosexuality itself as evidence of moral degradation, of course have no sympathy for Masha Gessen's position. Many liberal-minded parenting groups also find such a model deleterious for child raising, but as a child of the semi-Appalachian South, I see nothing especially radical in her viewpoint. Large rural extended families in eighteenth- and nineteenth-century America nearly always included multiple older generations that functioned as parents to assorted siblings and cousins, and sometimes even technical aunts and uncles were raised as siblings. Few middle-class Europeans and Americans live any longer in such arrangements, having opted instead for the standard nuclear-family model under the influence of everything from Protestant ministries to housing costs to family insurance policy premiums. Yet one of the places where such arrangements do persist is in Australia, among the Aboriginal population. Nearly all children are raised collectively with clear obligations across the kinship group. Mayan communities in Mexico continue to raise their children collectively as do many Maori in New Zealand and several ethnic groups of Central Europe. And indeed as the divorce rate approaches 50 percent in both America and Western Europe, the nuclear-family model favored by conservative traditionalists appears to have a very uncertain future.

Within all these Occidental family formations the stability of conventional "marriage" is again undergoing profound transformation, which, as Jerry Falwell accurately warned two decades ago, is concretizing even more fundamental changes in the greater gender roles that define what it means to be male or female. However startling and even bizarre it may seem that students are now demanding to be addressed by their own self-crafted pronouns, the inescapable reality is that whether in the nursery, the classroom, the ball field, or the marital mattress, an increasingly fluid sexual and social terrain needs to be addressed.

CHAPTER 2

From Homemakers to Nation Builders

When India Mitchell first joined her local police force, she was not alone (she prefers not to identify the town), but she was in a very distinct minority. Far fewer women served as active officers in American police departments in the early 1980s than the 55,000-plus who serve today. In recounting her experiences, she restricted the conversation to her work life and left aside how being a cop altered her domestic life. But she, like many others, wanted people to know that, as for women crashing the software code-writing barriers, the effective strategy was not to leave her womanliness aside and try to imitate her presumably bigger, tougher male colleagues.

"I tried that," she said, "and it got me nowhere." Instead, she used her reality as a woman. "One shift I was driving down the street of my district and a young man 'cat called' me and whistled. It irritated me as I felt it disrespectful to my profession and to me. I spun my cruiser around, got out, and walked up to this young guy and began my lecture. I told him how hard I had to work to just get hired, then get through the academy of forty-plus men and five women and three years on the street with people who didn't believe in me."

The guy apologized. A far greater problem, she said, is the assumption that women can't handle the physical challenges as well as men can. "Interestingly," she wrote in a widely circulated personal essay, "most women are better at calming people down with verbal techniques so they don't often have to be as physical. But when the adrenaline hits, most women can get that superhuman strength they need, to contain a suspect when necessary."

Fellow officers were more difficult, at least in the beginning. "The first three years I worked patrol (and even later at times) when I would get a radio call with a male officer, I knew another male officer would come to back *him* up to protect him in case I didn't. It was very annoying to realize that the accepted thought process was that because someone had male genitalia, he was automatically qualified for the job, but no woman ever was. It was the same for minority officers. They also were considered (but not as obviously) less competent than the average white male officer."

There are, of course, biological differences in men's and women's work in the field—some fairly banal, as in where to find a place to pee. "Men can still get behind a tree or down an alley," she wrote. "Female cops have to take almost all their gear off, not to mention get somewhere to go! The uniform and gear can weigh around twenty-two to twenty-five pounds. On a two-hundred-pound person that's one eighth their body weight." For a woman who weighs 125 pounds, it's about one fifth. From Mitchell's point of view these differences, including the challenge of wrestling a larger male armed suspect to the ground, may be annoying, but they shouldn't become barriers to the work. "You are expected to run as fast, jump over the same fences, and wrestle the same people and not hurt them and then arrest them. That's why the smart women learn to use their brains when dealing with volatile people."

Women didn't become standard fixtures in urban police departments until the early 1990s, and even now, a quarter century later, many of the same anxieties continue in what remains an essentially male world. Laws passed to curb gender discrimination and reward diversification in traditionally male workplaces have made real impact: Women on American police forces have risen from just over 2 percent in 1970 to slightly more than 12 percent in 2010—a result both of Title IX and of the reorganization of family roles to accommodate the pressure for dual incomes. As much as those changes worry cultural and religious traditionalists—be they Alabama evangelicals or Saudi clerics—it is a worldwide phenomenon.

Policing is one of the most extreme jobs where women crashed the gates. Yet the steady increase of women in the postindustrial workplace is only a small marker of how drastically the landscape of gender and work has changed since the mid-twentieth century. Surely auto work is one of America's signal industries. In 1970, slightly more than one hundred thousand people, mostly men, worked under United Auto Workers union contract at the River Rouge assembly lines of Ford Motor Company. By 2015, the UAW's total membership barely tops one hundred thousand—30 percent of whom are women. Moreover, the UAW has long since expanded beyond automobile plants to include hospital workers, bicycle builders, casino staff, legal service workers, museum employees, and even writers. Increasingly, the future for unions who want to survive is with women. Little surprise then that as the global economy relocates traditional industry to low-cost sites in Asia, Africa, and South America, men are facing unprecedented challenges, or, as a major 2015 report in the *Economist* headlined, "Badly educated men in rich countries have not adapted well to trade, technology or feminism."

The *Economist* inquiry focused not on devastated Detroit, where a minimum of three carjackings take place every day. Instead their reporters went to the heart of butch male America, the tiny Mississippi town of Tallulah, Louisiana, where until not long ago even high school dropouts could find a reliable job in a car muffler factory. Orlando Redden used to work there operating a forklift for $10.95 an hour—about two thirds of McDonald's' new minimum wage. Then the factory shut down. Now the main employers in Tallulah are the town's two prisons and a local jail. In the county, or parish as they're called in Louisiana, 53 percent of working-age men have no steady work. Most of them have high school grade point averages on the bottom slope. Says Tallulah's mayor, Paxton Branch, "If you don't have an education, what can you do? You can't answer a phone if you don't have proper English."

Men's test scores in high schools and colleges continue to fall across the developed world along with their graduation rates while women's scores are rising as they collect a majority of diplomas. In a seminal study of Texas and Florida universities, Dylan Conger and Mark Long report that men's failure is rooted in high school, starting in tenth grade, when, contrary to conventional perception, boys began falling behind girls in *both* math and reading classes. Low grade point averages in high school, they found, predict poor performance in the first semester of college, which in turn leads to higher college dropout rates for boys than for girls. Key to both high school and early college decline, they argue, is a depressive attitude, higher among males than females, toward the value of further education. The steady decline in grades and the rise in dropout rates among males leads to the sort of dismal social prospects the

Economist found in Tallulah. Not only are the men shut out of the workforce. Forced into any temporary low-paid jobs they can pick up, their sense of self-worth plummets as well and their prospects of finding a compelling mate in the marriage market falls still farther. As jobs disappear, the prisons, filled mostly with young men, grow fat.

Another major study about the male grade deficit published in 2013 in the *Journal of Human Resources* focuses far earlier than high school. What researchers found after examining 5,800 students from kindergarten through fifth grade was that the old category on report cards called "comportment" matters enormously in grades for reading, writing, and arithmetic. They found no particular evidence of inferior cognitive capacity among the boys; in fact on standardized tests, the boys and girls at that age scored equivalently. The boys were simply more fidgety, less attentive, and less "eager to learn," and their teachers, stressed by ever larger class sizes, graded them down for their comportment—a track that followed them on through high school (see Chapter 3 on neurodevelopmental differences between boys and girls).

All the while, in America and across Europe, women's test scores and employment rates continue to rise, and because employers value brains and stability above muscles and braggadocio their hiring rates are also rising. Little surprise as well, the women who are filling professional ranks are less and less interested in hooking up with either poorly educated or poorly employed men. A key study by the Pew Research Center in 2014 found that 78 percent of never-married American women want their male mates to have a "steady job." Women's superior education, linked to rising though still unequal pay rates, has made them ever more skeptical about entering into marriage with a low-wage male or a male with a shaky job history. But the likelihood of finding one of those well and reliably employed males falls every year. More than 95 percent of men held good jobs in 1970 compared to 84 percent in the 2010 census.

As services and technology steadily replace brawn in the labor market, the number of jobs available to poorly educated men keeps falling. In her apocalyptic book *The End of Men*, Hanna Rosin cited employment projection data that only looks worse for men who do poorly in school. Of thirty professions slated to grow in the next decades, *twenty* are occupations mostly held by women, including childcare, food preparation, nursing, accounting, and medical technology.

In short, poor performance by males in grade school and lack of adequate parental attention in dual-income households followed by early dropout rates in high school and college appears to have contributed to the most radical transformation in gender roles and work. Conservative Christians attribute these gender convulsions in the workplace, also accompanied by a growing rejection of marriage, to moral laxity. But a similar trend has also been tracked in Asia, notably in China, which, despite a recent slowing, still leads the world in economic growth.

~

Connie Y works in the Chinese division of a major American-based outdoor outfitter. From her sixth-floor office window she can see the necks and crowns of the skyscrapers that crowd together along Shanghai's Bund, but on Sundays she is also only a twenty-minute stroll from the ancient marriage market where parents still post scrolls on park walls promoting the assets of their sons and daughters.

Connie (not her real name) was born and raised in a working-class family in northern China, her father a mechanic, her mother a bookkeeper. Connie's parents scraped together enough money to send her to a private university in Henen founded by an American businessman. Then she moved to Shanghai looking for work and personal independence. Fluent in English, she advanced rapidly through a series of management jobs until she was named merchandising director for the apparel company. Her husband, who was born in Shanghai, worked off and on as a real estate site manager, but it was Connie's income that covered most bills—including the high health costs, retirement contributions, and property charges that Shanghai residents must pay.

The particular details that women like Connie face in the workplace are profoundly Chinese. They reflect centuries of tradition that have favored male dominance even as today women in China, like women in the United States and Europe, are bypassing men in business schools and lower levels of management. She explained that no matter how much she earns as a senior manager and how much she pays into the public retirement system, her eventual benefits will always be far less than her husband's because benefits in China are linked to an individual's birthplace rather than where they work. "It's one of the most corrupt things in China," Connie said. "People with money from the provinces come here to buy some property [so-called phantom apartments] to qualify for better health care or get their children into better universities."

Professional women in China face an additional barrier to marriage. "Chinese people often think males should be higher in a relationship in every sense including height, age, education, and salary," a prominent television matchmaking host explained to a Reuters reporter. The result: So-called A-grade men look only for B-grade women, B-grade men for C-grade women and so on, which means that both at the top and the bottom of the scale there are not enough women to go around. One researcher estimated that in Beijing alone in 2013 more than a third of young women were searching for qualified partners without success. Again, qualified or "quality" men are the problem. While the one-child policy established by Deng Xiaoping has sharply favored boys—female fetuses are still much more often aborted than male fetuses and rural families have been permitted a second child if the first is a girl—the surplus of boys and men is largely in the countryside or in poorer cities where their wages are lower and their schooling has been worse. Consequently the great majority of men don't meet the "mother-in-law" standard. The problem is especially acute in Shanghai, and the city organized a series of "matchmaking" fairs in 2013. Tens of thousands of men and women showed up, but one young language teacher who went to the fairs told a Reuters reporter that she could find no one who interested her who wasn't a "playboy" or a "momma's boy" (meaning one who was sexually suspicious). "Twenty thousand people and I can't find anyone I like?" she said. "I sometimes wonder if there is something wrong with me."

~

Nowhere in the world has gender equity in the workplace won as much attention as in Norway, where 74 percent of women are employed, publicly financed childcare is offered to any child over age three, and national law requires that corporate boards be at least 40 percent female. Norway has also famously opened its frontline military defense forces to women, among them Henriette Hummel, who wakes up every day in a dormitory she shares with three young men. She and the guys are part of one of the world's toughest military postings: They serve as border guards on Norway's barren 125-mile northern frontier with Russia, a sensitive assignment as tensions between NATO and Russia have mounted over the fate of Ukraine.

Hummel told ABC's Eric Campbell in a lengthy interview broadcast in 2014 that she actually prefers cohabiting with men to "being segregated with other women." Cohabitation, she explained, enables them to get to know each other quickly, pass through typical gender anxieties, and develop stronger unit cohesion. When it comes to one of the classic territories that divide men and women—housekeeping—"they understand I'm not their mother," she said.

By eight A.M., the unit is out in the rocky forest dodging reindeer with their sniffer dogs to spot illegal border crossings. Peder K, one of her military housemates, says the initial anxieties about sharing quarters with a woman disappeared quickly, adding, "I don't really notice it that much anymore. It's part of our daily routine now and she's one of the guys so . . ." Being "one of the guys" still doesn't carry quite the same implication as describing a male soldier as "one of the girls" in a majority female unit, a gender balance that's not likely to arrive soon. Norway has committed to sharply raising the number of women in its military forces, most of whom are currently young recruits taking a year off before going on to university studies, from 13 percent in 2014 to 20 percent in 2020.

Norway's approach to changing the nature of gender roles and dynamics in the military has won worldwide attention as reports of rape and sexual harassment have risen in other sexually integrated forces, notably in the United States, France, and Australia. "We would like to choose from the most motivated men and women, because we think that we cannot afford in a modern Armed Forces to not use the competencies that both genders have," said Norwegian defense minister Ine Eriksen Søreide, the country's first female defense minister and a leader in the country's Conservative Party.

Norway is the global leader in cracking workplace gender norms, but it is far from alone. Even in Saudi Arabia, where official Wahhabi doctrine decrees that a woman's place is in the home, female participation in the workforce reached 15 percent under the late King Abdullah; and it has risen to 25 percent across the Middle East. Women make up more than 44 percent of the workplace in Brazil, the world's largest Catholic nation, despite a pay gap between men and women of nearly 25 percent in equivalent jobs. Still, the rise of women in the workplace appears to be invincible no matter how many fundamentalist bishops and jihadists cite sacred texts to the contrary. Certainly feminism in its diverse forms has helped fuel what may well turn out to be the most profound social transformation of the twentieth century, but the reconstitution of marital roles or the reorganization of gender in the workplace cannot be attributed to moral and ideological claims alone. As report after report from World Bank economists has shown, globalization and the development of multinational markets have both depressed family incomes as the cost of living steadily rises. With few exceptions, single-breadwinner households simply cannot survive, especially in countries where child labor restrictions and ambitious parents aim more than anything to keep their children in school. That is as true in São Paulo as it is in Tokyo as it is in Cincinnati.

Activists on the left blame "family disintegration" on the exploitative depredations of the workplace under the force of a global economy; their counterparts on the right denounce the moral depredations of feminism and the homosexual agenda for the remaking of "traditional" families. Both betray a profound misunderstanding of how those romanticized traditional families really functioned. It would be hard to find a better case study for traditional family values than the rural hilltop in the Appalachian Kentucky of my youth. All the families, save ours, had lived there for generations and nearly all the adults had at least a half dozen siblings. Ours was the only family that didn't attend church on Sunday morning and Sunday evening and often on Wednesday night. But in no case were the women relegated to strict homemaking and childcare. All the women worked in the fields alongside their husbands or their neighbors' husbands during planting and harvesting seasons, and as often as not it was the wives who collaborated in or directed the business planning that any small enterprise, including small farms, depended upon for its survival. The point is that even in deeply traditional cultures, the workplace has historically been far more mixed than it was in the model families presented to the Baby Boom generation of the 1950s and '60s.

~

Tradition, of course, still has its defenders—be they in Confucian China, Hindu and Muslim India (where obstreperous women are still burned alive), or the Southern Baptist Bible Belt. Twenty-five years have passed since Susan Faludi published *Backlash* (1991) detailing American men's resentment of women's then still minor progress in public life and the workplace. Presidential candidate Hillary Clinton, by most international measures more a neoconservative than a militant liberal, has been the subject of an unprecedented number of misogynist denunciations on social media sites. And of course there is the still growing sector of evangelical Americans who argue that when women leave the home for the office, everyone suffers. In a widely circulated 2013 *Washington Post* video interview, Mississippi governor Phil Bryant blamed boys' poor classroom behavior on their mothers' absence at home. Dual-income families, he said, echoing others, "just don't have the time" to properly parent their children, which in his view has led to the failure of young men to compete with women in the new postindustrial workplace.

Feminists, both men and women, may snort at remarks by red-state politicians like Bryant, or by Louisiana governor Bobby Jindal, who cites the Old Testament in his fight to save marriage from the homosexual lobby, or former Arkansas governor and subsequent presidential candidate Mike Huckabee, who claimed that the only reason women need contraceptives is because they are "unable to control their libidos," leading to the new "American holocaust—abortion." But beneath Fox News's daily pandering to the enemies of contemporary feminism, a deeper anxiety does exist among many educated Americans and Europeans about the radical shift in gender roles. Several sociological studies, including a key report on college students by Caryl Rivers and Rosalind Barnett in their 2013 book, *The Truth About Girls and Boys*, have tracked growing anxiety among young, well-educated males. Boys and young men, they found, see women's rise from short-order cooks to business professionals as a direct threat their fathers never faced.

No less a figure than the very liberal Massachusetts senator Elizabeth Warren warned that the flattening of men's wages linked to women's steady gains have forced both dads and moms to enter the workforce, "a strategy that has left them working harder just to try to break even," and that the smallest "misstep can leave them in crisis" as prices rise faster than wages. In just one generation, millions of mothers have gone to work, transforming basic family economics. "The typical middle-class household in the United States is no longer a one-earner family, with one parent in the workforce and one at home full-time. Instead, the majority of families with small children now have both parents rising at dawn to commute to jobs so they can both pull in paychecks." Buffeted by a tumultuous global economy, industries have been forced to make layoffs that have disproportionately affected men, while women's pay in the growing service sector still only averages three quarters of men's pay.

All those anxieties feed the followers of millennialist evangelicals who argue that the global upheaval in gender relations is a direct affront to natural law and sacred preachings. That was the core argument one Saturday afternoon in February 2014 when drums, whistles, and chants began rattling our apartment windows in the calm, respectable neighborhood where we live. February is not normally the season for marches and demonstrations in winter-gray Paris, but clearly there was mischief afoot in the streets, and not far away. We pedaled on our bikes toward the noise to find out what was happening. We arrived just in time to see Cardinal Philippe Barbarin, the archbishop of Lyon, accompanied by his personal entourage, walking in all his finery before a huge banner that read MANIF POUR TOUS, or the March for Everyone. It was a play on words aimed at mocking the 2013 march of several hundred thousand calling for *Marriage à Tous*, or marriage for everyone, in support of same-sex marriage, which in fact did become French law in 2013. Here in Paris, which Americans and other Anglo-Saxons have long regarded as the world capital of libertinism, several thousand *intégrist* (fundamentalist) faithful had come to raise their angry voices, but this time they were not focused on condemning same-sex marriage. These radical opponents of strict gender equality had already demonstrated multiple times against legalizing homo-unions. On this chilly afternoon, they had come to target a proposed change in the national school curriculum that was to be called "The ABCD's of Equality." A proposed new law prepared by the Women's Rights Ministry had been introduced in the National Assembly; it promised a sweeping across-the-board reform in the school curriculum intended to promote equal opportunities for boys and girls, and men and women, throughout France. To that end, textbooks, classroom assignments, sports programs, and field trips would be reimagined to break the gender stereotypes that tend to track girls and boys into different life patterns—all these changes presented as consistent follow-ups to the 1944 law that gave French women the right to vote and the 1975 law guaranteeing women the right to control of their own bodies and have access to abortion through the national health care system. Despite its reputation as a fervent proponent of human rights, France in fact was ranked forty-fifth in the 2013 World Economic Forum scale of gender equality—far behind Norway, Iceland, Sweden, and Germany, even behind Kazakhstan. The new law aimed to bring France at least up to the level of its neighbors concerning a long list of rights: equal pay for equal work, equal access to all professions from brain surgery to rocket design, or equal respect for men who choose childcare over corporate lawyering.

For the most part these intentions provoked little public resistance. Two other elements in the proposed law, however, did prove upsetting. First, for many of the fiercely nationalistic French, the gender language in the law seemed to be an invasion by American feminist rhetoric, a gender equivalent to McDonald's displacing neighborhood cafés (which happened decades ago). Much worse were the curricular changes aimed at promoting gender equality down to age six in primary schools, changes that not only would address stereotypes but would question directly what it means to be a boy or a girl. This element was not particularly American; it has been standard in Nordic schools for decades. But for the men and women pushing their baby strollers behind Cardinal Barbarin this new law promoting the ABCDs of equality constituted a radical perversion of what it means to be human. One particularly alarming telephone text message they had sent to thousands of parents read: "The national education system is going to teach your children that they are not born a girl or a boy, as God intended, but choose to become one." Other messages bombarding social media sites conflated sex—the biology of male or female marked by XY or XX chromosomes—with gender—the term long used by sociologists and psychologists to describe the social roles taken by men and women.

Most of the Manif leaders protesting "gender theory" came from conservative Catholic and Muslim sectors, but many on the secular left were also quietly alarmed. The right of any two people to marry each other was one thing, but part of the campaign for equality also touched on parenting rights for same-sex couples. No one has a *right* to have a child, one leftist journalist I'd known for decades told me. Why should same-sex couples then ask the state to intervene in their self-chosen biological sterility? Wouldn't the paid maternal surrogacy that American gay men were using—and that was still outlawed in most of Europe—just codify another dangerous abuse of poor women, rendering them as nothing more than rent-a-wombs? A market-driven libertarian approach to child making and child rearing based on laboratory procedures, the leftists argued, represented nothing but rank individualism and constituted yet another attack on the social solidarity inscribed in the French constitution. A gay movement that had turned sex into little more than ego-centric pursuit of orgasm, or *jouissance*, would not reform families; it could destroy them on the perverse notion that any individual has a state-guaranteed *right* to a child.

Back across the Atlantic, in Louisiana, one of the last American states with a whiff of French culture, Governor Bobby Jindal, a converted Christian and the first non-white (Indian) American to be elected governor there since Reconstruction, has dedicated himself to reversing the Supreme Court's same-sex marriage ruling by constitutional amendment. Jindal would also outlaw abortion except in certain limited cases of rape and would generally restrict access to contraception. He has fought hard to bring Louisiana alongside twenty other states that have enacted "religious liberty" laws that would protect Christians and Muslims from lawsuits if they refuse services to gay men or lesbians. Similar "religious liberty" laws were retracted or severely weakened in 2015 in Arkansas and Indiana after major corporations, including Walmart and Eli Lilly, lobbied hard against them, fearful of losing market share from gay customers and upsetting gay employees. In a notably vitriolic op-ed essay in the *New York Times*, Jindal said he would resist soulless corporate pressure and declared, "I'm holding firm against gay marriage." Musicians, caterers, photographers, and others "should be immune from government coercion on deeply held religious convictions," he argued, adding, "I hold the view that has been the consensus in our country for over two centuries: that marriage is between one man and one woman." Consistent with his increasingly conservative Christian views, Governor Jindal signed a state law upholding teachers' rights to offer supplemental "intelligent design" curricula opposing Darwinian evolution.

A parallel federal religious liberty law sponsored in 1993 by congressional Democrats, including the late senator Ted Kennedy, was ruled unconstitutional by the Supreme Court. The new state laws, most enacted since 2010, may or may not survive judicial review, but their supporters' objectives are not purely limited to passing laws about same-sex marriage. The point, as Southern Baptist minister Tim Overton of Muncie, Indiana, explained on National Public Radio, is to nurture a much broader movement that would go beyond protecting priests and preachers from being forced to violate their faiths. Overton's followers aim to bring public policy back in line with fundamentalist religious values, which they see as under threat from the whole array of gender liberation movements. "As a Baptist pastor who believes the Bible, I believe God made us male and female. And embracing God's will is embracing our gender and acting accordingly. And I don't think people like myself are going to abandon the biblical view of gender and God's plan for the family. And I would hope that society would make allowances for traditional Christian theology and belief and allow us to practice our faiths in the workplace and in public as well as our houses of worship."

Defenders of same-sex marriage and LGBT rights compare the so-called religious liberty legislation to laws that once existed in nearly every state south of the Mason-Dixon line that first outlawed interracial marriage and then defended county clerks and other officials against discrimination suits for refusing to issue marriage licenses based on their religious convictions. Any rearguard action that has Walmart as its enemy is unlikely to succeed. Survey after survey during the last decade indicates growing majorities of Americans support the whole array of Title IX civil rights provisions, including protection of gays, lesbians, and transgender people and antidiscrimination laws in public hiring and commerce. But even so, all but one of the leading Republican candidates for the 2016 presidential election opposed same-sex marriage. Many conservative leaders have also spoken of weakening Title IX protections related to gender discrimination.

Social liberals may feel comfortable supposing that these more and more vitriolic critics of gender realignment are only poorly educated red-state religious fundamentalists. They are not. Bobby Jindal graduated from Brown University with an honors degree in biology and went on to study at the University of Oxford. Yale-educated Camille Paglia has been a brilliant if somewhat strange antagonist to much of contemporary gender radicalism after her disenchantment with the philosopher Susan Sontag. And even the scholar Elizabeth Fox-Genovese has written serious critiques of feminist and gender theory.

Backlash and resentment run deeply through middle- and working-class white America, evidenced not least by the surge in misogynist messages that surfaced across social media as economic growth stuttered following the Great Recession of 2008. Amazon was forced to cancel sales of T-shirts that read "RapeALot." An explicitly antiwoman movement flying under the name Gamergate—presumably made up of snarky adolescent boys—caused another site, Gamasutra, to lose major advertising clients after the Gamergaters flooded the site with campaigns aimed at driving women out of the online gaming world. After a barrage of hateful tweets flooded Twitter in 2013, including death threats made at several women prominent in Britain, Twitter felt itself forced to install software that would alert its managers to hate speech and physical threats. The usual response to social network nastiness is that the sites' anonymity encourages outlandish behavior that the (mostly male) writers would never express face to face. That may or may not be true. But what is certain is that across Britain and America, real threats against women and girls have risen dramatically in recent years, and it is hard to imagine that there is no relation to the rising roles of women in the workplace and in public life matched with the explosive media attention given to multiple gender minorities.

~

Hanna Rosin argued in *The End of Men* that the convulsions rattling the foundations of family and workplace life are only the first stages of an emerging—and not universally welcome—global matriarchy. Her argument was intriguing: Women surpass men in college and medical school enrollment as well as in many bar associations; male unemployment following the 2008 recession was more than twice the level of female unemployment; women's pay in a third of the households in Catholic Brazil topped men's wages; women consistently score ahead of men in foreign service exams—all leading to a coming "gender apocalypse." Were it all true, that might spell good news for a globe well on the way to broiling itself to death; but, as many more sober critics quickly pointed out, the titans of industry remain overwhelmingly carriers of Y chromosomes. A mere 3 percent of the people who run Fortune 500 companies are women, the *Economist* magazine noted in 2015, and then there's high tech: At Apple only 20 percent of the tech jobs went to women in 2015 and at Google the number was 17 percent. Nationwide, only 14 percent of engineering jobs are held by women, according to a 2015 report from the Congress's Joint Economic Committee. In China, often cited as the coming economic master power, 40 percent of businesses are believed to be run by women, but Chinese social regulations still overwhelmingly register the properties and the benefits in their husbands' names. Even in blessed Norway, world leader in gender equality, women are paid 15 percent less than men for the same work.

Public perceptions, especially during periods of loss and pain, are often in conflict with cold data, whether they appear in the middle chapters of Hanna Rosin's book or on the people pages of *USA Today*. Gender power is shifting, if slowly; yet while fear of a gender apocalypse may have been grossly overblown, even slight slippage in what is frequently presented as a zero-sum contest is sure to provoke resentments. No one wants to be on the wrong side of an apocalypse. Anonymous fuming on the Internet, however, is not the only indication of workplace distress over gender equity. Far more pervasive and pernicious are the subtle judgments men make about women in the management corps, as New York University psychologist Madeline Heilman has illustrated in a number of recent studies of attitudes toward women in management. One study asked participants to evaluate an investment portfolio developed by a team with male and female names; although there was no information about the individuals on the team, the participants evaluated the women as having played only secondary or minor roles. Still more severe criticisms were made of women who have already succeeded in positions of power thought normally to be undertaken by men. Women in those situations were consistently seen to be "brusque" while males doing the same work were characterized as "decisive." In another psychological study researchers sent out résumés to a number of elite universities looking for lab managers. The résumés were identical except that half bore female first names on the job application and half used male first names. The "male" candidates were consistently rated as more competent and deserving of higher salaries than the "female" candidates.

"Those negative expectations are lethal," says Heilman. "You're not going to pick somebody for a job if you think they're not going to do it well. And if they're in the job, it's going to affect how you view what they do." In yet another review of job performance evaluations at a powerful New York law firm, junior attorneys characterized successful female attorneys as failing to demonstrate the "interpersonal warmth" traditionally expected of women. Such women, Heilman says, are consistently regarded both by other women and by men as "out of line, breaking the rules, violating the 'shoulds' of gender stereotypes." Much more overt biases and exclusions continue to plague women in police departments despite—or perhaps because of—their growing presence in the nation's police forces. Kristen Ziman, who fought her way up through the ranks at the Aurora, Illinois, police department, has recounted how the women at her police academy were consistently evaluated as inferior by male officers while the young male recruits were readily hired and promoted. Later in the Aurora department her field training officer, a woman, was subjected to "unmentionable" insults by male officers and regularly excluded from meetings and other office activities because it was clear that the men "didn't want her to be there." Ziman, a former president of the National Association of Women Law Enforcement Executives, says that bias and resentment diminishes among higher ranks but remains present.

~

Many thousands of gender-anxious Europeans continue to march through major cities intent on repealing same-sex marriage in campaigns they are unlikely to win. Though the opponents have scored few solid victories, they did succeed in watering down France's gender-equality curricula targeting the programs proposed for primary schools. Same-sex adoption reforms also remain tied up in political jockeying as the extreme right French National Front and its analogues in neighboring countries spread their influence—on top of which came the jihadist attack on the French satirical weekly *Charlie Hebdo*, and the jihadist slaughter of 130 people later in November 2015, as well as ongoing fundamentalist Islamic threats in Denmark, Germany, and Sweden. None of these assaults directly targeted "gender theory," women's pressure on the job market, or the media celebration of transsexuality. Yet as the feminist sociologist Phyllis Chesler has written, gender relations are at the core of fundamentalist Islam's war on modernity. "What else can we expect from a religious-terrorist culture in which both life and the life force is mocked, feared, hated, and destroyed? A pregnant woman with young children was recently intercepted as a human bomb by the Israelis. Often, a suicide bomber will purposely stand right next to a mother with a young child. This is how Thanatos [the death force], in the most visually graphic and literal of ways, destroys Eros [the life force]. In the most recent instance, physicians, who are supposed to take an oath to save lives, were engaged in murdering innocent civilians—many of them ideally female. What clearer perversion of the life force can there be?" Chesler's essay was taken as a biased attack from an Israeli sympathizer. She has indeed defended Israel on many occasions, including Israeli attacks on Palestinian civilians in Gaza. But any close reader of jihadists' views of women, of Salafist treatment of women, and of the reasons why they denounce Western societies that encourage women to go "naked" in the streets—that is, to display themselves with their arms and faces exposed to the public—will be hard-pressed to deny that the global movement for gender equality is one of the core reasons for their own apocalyptic threats and actions. Careful biographies of the men who succeeded and nearly succeeded in launching the armed attacks in France and Denmark in 2013, 2014, and 2015 reveal that they also came from the class of young men who have seen employers choose women over young men for even menial jobs. Faced with entrenched working-class unemployment, they have seen their status and prospects slip steadily behind the girls in their schools who have shown more resilience and flexibility in finding work.

Many years before the current spate of jihadist terror attacks, the Middle East specialist Fawaz Gerges spent several years talking with members of an earlier generation of Islamist militants in preparation for writing his book *Journey of the Jihadist*, which was published in 2006. Among the several young militants Gerges met in Egypt was a young man named Kamal. They met in Liberation Square in the heart of Cairo. The general atmosphere was relaxed as young couples walked about and sat together on public benches much as they might in Paris or New York. Kamal, worried about Egypt's ever-present security forces, came alone, but even without fear of being surveilled, he would never have gone out in public with a woman. The role of women in society was high on Kamal's list of outrages in the modern world. "No one can dictate that there should be equal inheritance rights," he said. "Women must not be permitted, like men, to marry more than one husband at a time. I can accept a woman judge as long as her authority is limited to women. I reject a state ruled by a woman because women are not psychologically equipped to lead men." A true Islamic state, Kamal insisted, could never accept these rules imposed by the ancient texts of the Qur'an.

But Kamal and his associates went farther. Not only the shameless display of women's bodies in cities like Paris, Rome, Copenhagen, San Francisco, and almost everywhere in the Western world were at issue. The combination of such "wanton displays" with the rising campaigns for gender equality constituted a clear imperialist encroachment on Islamic culture by the West. "I will do everything in my power to prevent women from becoming judges," said one of Kamal's friends, an Egyptian lawyer. "They belong at home with the children." Both these young Egyptians have doubtless become more secretive since the 2013 military coup that banned the Muslim Brotherhood and sentenced the previous president to death; they had been well-educated college students who saw strict Sharia law as the only alternative to the corrupt, Western-influenced dictatorships that have dominated Middle Eastern governments for decades if not for centuries.

Westerners, including Americans, regularly shake their heads in dismay at what they perceive as the "medieval" outlooks and condemnations of men like Kamal. Yet the core of Southern Baptist preaching, as articulated by Indiana pastor Tim Overton, is only slightly softer. Southern Baptist churches count more than 16 million members who, when added to the slightly larger general Baptist congregations make them the largest Protestant denomination in America. Not all Baptists subscribe to the hard-line articulated by Overton, but a growing number do, as journalist Kathryn Joyce detailed in her book *Quiverfull: Inside the Christian Patriarchy Movement*. Probably the most extreme of Christian fundamentalists, the Quiverfull members take their name from Biblical doctrine that argues that real Christians—like real Islamicists—are today in an all-stakes state of war against the infidels of modernism. They believe that they must follow strict Old Testament laws commanding the true Christian to breed as many warriors as physiologically possible and then to send their sons to war to slay the infidels. The movement, of course, is strictly patriarchal. "They advocate a very extreme version of wifely submission to male headship," Joyce says; "wives are submissive *in everything* [emphasis added] to their husbands, and before that, to their fathers. The women are never out from under the covering of the men, and this is very important, because getting women back to the submissive state is the first step towards a Christian revival." Some of the Quiverfull sects even forbid women to speak in church and subject them to hour-by-hour schedules imposed by their men throughout the day.

By comparison, Kamal's Islamist arguments that women must stay at home with other women seem almost reformist. Many will protest against associating hateful misogynist tweets with the broad array of Christian fundamentalists, including the Southern Baptist Convention, that oppose same-sex marriage and openly call for women's strict submission to their husbands—positions embraced by both presidential hopefuls Governor Bobby Jindal and former Arkansas governor Mike Huckabee. Tweeters, however upset they may be over women's growing independence and power in the workplace, are blessed with anonymity: They may be Quiverfull militants or simply angry atheists. But what both represent is the extent and diversity of rage and resentment that exist across the American and European landscapes far from the battlefields of the Islamic State.

PART II

Nature, Nurture, and Society

CHAPTER 3

Science and Society

"Why can't a woman be more like a man?"

That was the question posed by the irascible linguist Henry Higgins in the world famous Broadway musical *My Fair Lady*, based on George Bernard Shaw's 1913 London play *Pygmalion*, itself based on the classical Greek poet Ovid's story of a sculptor who fell in love with a statue he had carved. *My Fair Lady* was the first piece of professional theater I ever saw, a roadshow version playing in Cincinnati, then known as the Queen City of the Midwest. It was also undoubtedly the first time I was brought face to ear with our era's shifting and ever more uncertain notions of gender, of what it meant to be a man or to be a woman. Addressing his doughty housekeeper, Mrs. Pearce, Higgins runs through all the presumed superior qualities possessed by those humans who carry both an X and a Y chromosome. Men, he avers, are inherently decent. They are always ready to help another fellow in trouble, ready to cheer you up whenever you're down. Mrs. Pearce goes about her work silently rolling her eyes as Higgins rattles on, asking why women are so incapable of logical reasoning, more obsessed with curling their hair than uncurling the messiness of their brains. Finally, he concludes, "Why can't a woman behave like a man?"

By that age, I was already old enough to hear Shaw's irony; all I had to do was look at who were the real, sensible, pragmatic problem solvers on the farmsteads along our hilltop. Had he lived a hundred years later,

Shaw's Higgins would surely have been baffled by today's framing of the question: Why can't men be more like women? Or, for that matter, why must a man be only a man and why must a woman be only a woman? Neither musical comedies nor classical Greek poetry generally qualify as profound social or scientific analysis, but deeper questions about the differences between males and females, aside from obvious reproductive functions, do fascinate contemporary investigators—especially brain scientists. Scientists have long dismissed earlier assertions that the larger size of male brains (on average male brains are 10 percent larger than female brains) explained men's overwhelming dominance in science, mathematics, and other intellectual endeavors. But as MRI scanning of living brains has advanced, along with molecular tracking of the relations between hormones and gene function, other differences do show up, especially in boys' and girls' developmental years. Take, for example, the classroom problem of inattentive, "fidgety" boys versus sensitive, "empathetic" girls. Parents and pediatricians have long observed that from infancy forward girls tend to do better at quiet concentration than boys, and they tend to outperform boys in emotional expression and in forming close friendships.

Two neurologists at the University of Iowa, Peg Noupolos and Jessica Wood, wondered if there might be some bioneural basis that could explain these male-female differences; they wanted to know if they were innate (a result of nature) or a consequence of silent cultural influence (a result of nurture). They undertook two studies published in 2008 and 2009. In the first they used functional MRI imaging (fMRI) to look inside the heads of thirty men and thirty women. As expected they discovered that the ventral prefrontal cortex (called the SG for straight gyrus), a narrow neural ribbon that runs along below the frontal cortex well known to relate to social awareness and interpersonal response, was in fact about 10 percent larger in the women than in the men. Women organize parties; men write the checks. But further, those men who did score higher on sociability also had larger SGs than less social men. Noupolos and Wood wondered if indeed there might even be an evolutionary basis for these differences related to pregnancy and female nurture and protection of their infants across the mammalian world.

The researchers did not stop there, since, aside from not giving birth to their offspring, many male mammals share infant nurturing, and sometimes, as with penguins, the males undertake almost all the nurturing duties. Among our closer relatives, for example, male bonobos appear to be equally as social, if not more social than the females. So Noupolos and Wood decided to look inside the brains of a group of kids, ages seven to seventeen, to see if they found the same neural structure as they did with the adults. Oops! They found that little boys actually had larger SGs than the little girls but that this time *smaller* SGs correlated with greater interpersonal activity—exactly the opposite of what they had found in the sixty adults.

But that was still not the end of their investigation. In addition to comparing *biological* sex, they gave all the participants, children and adults, questionnaires aimed at measuring their femininity and masculinity based on their interests, their aptitudes, and their personalities. This time more feminine characteristics reflected larger SGs of the pre-frontal cortex. The women who had smaller SGs were also less conventionally "feminine." In short, their investigations showed a far muddier portrait of what makes men masculine and women feminine, and as they age not only do their interests, behavior, and mannerisms change, but so too can their neural biology change. Or, as neurologist Lise Eliot, author of *Pink Brain, Blue Brain*, commented in a review of their work, "Individuals' gender traits—their preference for masculine or feminine clothes, careers, hobbies and interpersonal styles—are inevitably shaped more by rearing and experience than by their biological sex. Likewise, their brains, which are ultimately producing all this masculine or feminine behavior, must be molded—at least to some degree—by the sum of their experiences as a boy or girl." Recast in terms of popular media interest, both biological and behavioral gender markers appear to be profoundly fluid across both time and personal experience. We are all of us both male and female, and the way we express our "masculinity" and "femininity" depends on the circumstances in which we find ourselves living—and moreover those experiences can alter our neurology and physiology.

Other observable differences in male brains and female brains have also surfaced with more sophisticated MRI scanning. Most male brains tend to have as much as seven times more "gray matter" associated with concentrated attention on a specific action or task while female brains can have ten times more white matter—associated with coordination between gray matter centers and, hypothetically, with women's alleged greater capacity to switch between tasks and to multitask, advantages that can be beneficial in infant nurturing. (See also Chapter 15, Gender and the Techno Mind.) In nearly all individual cases, the proportions vary, and more importantly, lifetime tracking suggests that balances of white and gray matter shift over time, and in extreme cases of deformation can be related to senility and Alzheimer's disease.

Still more importantly, global changes in fashion, design, advertising, culinary work, and even childcare matched with the arrival of women in positions of corporate and political power have drastically changed modern perceptions of what it might mean to be either masculine or feminine, whether we're talking about the selection of hair styles or the manner of running a corporate board meeting. Take, for example, the Australian designer Gabriel Ann Maher, who in a 2015 interview promoted her *ambisexual* coiffure "[that] allows me to be several people." When her hair is "up" and the tight trim revealed, she's easily taken to be a young man, but when she lets her hair down, "someone always says, 'Oh, you look so feminine.'" A transplant to Holland, where gender fluidity marks everything from coffee stands to furniture design, Maher joins millions of others who insist that they are neither male nor female, or at least not always one or the other. Aside from biological distinctions (which, as the neurologists tell us, are far less fixed than what I was taught in high school biology), male and female are nothing more than abstract concepts rooted in centuries of cultural storytelling, painting, sculpture, and the rigors of politics and war. For Maher and her mates, daily life is constructed around a spectrum of personal performances that depend and rely on the circumstances and situations in which she finds herself, situations that may vary even across a single day as she addresses one set of clients or another.

Gender traditionalists fume about the attention given to apparent gender radicals like Maher. They warn of a dark alliance between feminists and queer sex radicals that is promoting a culture of decadence and libertinism resulting in the collapse of gender reliability and the fundaments of social stability. Even some feminists have argued that the long-established gender norms may have resulted from biological coding to give male animals the larger, sturdier frames and stronger muscles that were once (but are no longer) needed for protecting broods, families, and clans nurtured by the females of the species. Hence the common refrain among fundamentalist Catholics in France, evangelical preachers and politicians in the American red zones, and tribal jihadists in the Middle East that the betrayal of gender roles is at once an attack on God and on Nature. The fundamental trouble with that perception, as the French scientist and philosopher Denis Diderot pointed out in the eighteenth century, is that nothing within nature is either fixed or stable. Diderot was continuously hounded by both church and state for his rejection of any presence of God's hand in the work and display of nature. Any close reading and experience of the natural world demonstrates just the opposite: that there are "no fixed limits in nature"—neither for man nor for animals nor for trees nor the lilies of the field that are always and forever spinning toward transition. Male rams hump each other. Adult bulls will demonstrate a variety of "sexual" gestures toward both male and female offspring. Goats will hump anything that seems to be warm and alive. Tomcats will lick kittens. And many male birds will perform nurturing roles more actively than their female cohorts.

Farmers and zookeepers, like many artisans and craftsmen of his age, fascinated Denis Diderot, for while most were illiterate in the eighteenth century, he found their intimate, practical knowledge of the natural world was often as useful as the abstract, mathematical discoveries then giving birth to modern laboratory science. Among the many statements that made Diderot controversial was his assertion that what we think of as fixed genders are rarely fixed at all: that all men have female elements and, he suspected, other less visible female characteristics, and vice versa. He was fascinated by more and more widely cited cases of hermaphroditism in rural families. France, then still essentially a peasant society, apparently found hermaphroditism less alarming than did the already industrialized British, who did their best to root out all manner of human "aberration." Similarly, in isolated pockets of Appalachia, grandmothers and aunts not infrequently were called on to speak to and comfort the unconventional adolescent boys or girls, advising them that all families from time to time had lifelong "bachelors" or "spinsters" and that there was nothing wrong with them being so. (That, however, did not mean that they should take up and mate with their likes in other families; the Bible still weighed heavily on these special children.)

Fishermen and foresters across the globe have long made similar observations about the pervasiveness of sequential hermaphroditism in plants, trees, fish, and animals. Certain species of fish are famously hermaphroditic. The California sheephead, a bright blue, green, and yellow fish that swims in waters between Monterey Bay and Mexico, starts her life as a female bearing eggs; then after four years her gonads atrophy and she becomes a fertilizing male. Orange, red, and white belted clownfish breed across the Pacific and in the Red Sea, but they start life as males and later become female. Scores, if not hundreds, of other fish species change both their sex and their gendered behavior as fighters, nurturers, and protectors.

Fish are not alone. One of the most common urban decorative trees, the gingko, fairly frequently changes its sex to the dismay of the people who have to trod the sidewalks beneath them. Because month-old rotting eggs compare favorably to the odor of the freshly fallen gingko fruit, nearly all gingkos planted along sidewalks carry male pollinating flowers, but as they age and are subjected to urban stresses, a fair proportion undergo a variety of floral sex changes and begin bearing and dropping their sticky, stinking fruit. More pleasing to the nose and the tongue, certain avocado trees change their sexual formation from evening to the next morning. Travelers through Amazonian rain forests frequently settle in at sunset to watch giant water lily pads open their succulent white petals, which in turn draw a species of beetle that descends deep into the fragrant flower, becoming trapped when it closes itself up at dawn. By the next evening the nectar-drunk beetles wobble out; by then the flowers have been fertilized, their petals have turned pink, and they have transitioned from female to male packed with fertilizing pollen that the beetles carry on their backs and legs to the next unsuspecting virgin lily.

In Turkey and Bulgaria, botanists have discovered the appearance of yet another transsexual plant—the pistachio tree—that produces one of the most popular and nutritious nuts in the Western world. The discovery, in the early years of the current century, concerned two trees in a commercial pistachio plantation. Normally, growers must plant one male flowering tree for every eight female to achieve effective pollination, but the botanists discovered that two of the theretofore male trees had in fact become self-pollinating: transsexual hermaphrodites. The discovery sent pistachio specialists all a-tizzy. They began scouring wild pistachio forests all over Mesopotamia, and before long they discovered an entire patch of transsexual pistachio trees, some of them fifty years old. By studying the flower formations on younger wood and older wood, the scientists determined that as these particular trees matured, male blossoms were regularly replaced by female blossoms, thus rendering the trees transsexual. Pistachio growers might no longer need to waste land and expense dotting their fields with useless males.

Somewhat closer to humans are the favorites of animal researchers, guinea pigs, which, when treated prenatally with testosterone, often behave later like castrated males. Closer still to us within the primate world are rhesus macaque monkeys. A near half century of research on captive macaques has shown how prenatal injections of estrogens or testosterone, especially early in gestation before the fetuses develop sexual formation, can produce dramatic changes in how genetic females or males play, fight, or mount or otherwise engage in sexual behavior. Estrogen and testosterone are of course the two fundamental hormones that distinguish female from male animals, though we each contain both hormones in varying degrees. Females treated with testosterone are frequently more aggressive than their untreated siblings, and males treated with estrogen frequently appear more docile or submissive. Even pattern baldness in men appears to be related to higher levels of testosterone in addition to genetic tendencies inherited through the mother. Genetic heritage alone, however, does not determine gender appearance or behavior.

Which brings us back to boys and girls. Since hormonal experiments on human fetuses have long been considered unthinkable (aside from Nazi Germany and certain labs in Russia during Stalin's era), parallel research on human fetuses is scant. Hormones and hormonal expression remain especially mysterious substances in all animals, humans included. Explained simply, hormones are messenger molecules governed generally but not exclusively by our brains that are sent out throughout our bodies to instruct other organs how to perform—be they processing organs like the liver, the pancreas, the ovaries, or the prostate, or, earlier in life, muscle tissue and bone composition. Yet hormone production, including but not limited to testosterone and estrogen, responds directly to exterior conditions, notably to flight-or-fight responses, to erotic caresses, or to the way we digest different foods. The sad news, well known, is that the two key erotic and tissue-building hormones, estrogen and testosterone, both begin to disappear with age. Recently developed sophistication in molecular tracking of fetuses and amniotic fluid in relation to maternal stress has also begun to indicate effects of hormones on subsequent childhood maturation and development. In 2008 biologist Lauren Ellman published a study in *Developmental Psychobiology* that showed how high levels of cortisol in pregnant mothers' blood correlated directly with both emotional and neurological development of their children—but the effects were different between boys and girls. High stress during pregnancy appeared to quicken maturation among the girls while it slowed down boys' later maturation. Or as Ellman wrote, "Insults or disruptions of normal fetal maturation can lead to long-lasting neurobiological and health outcomes that persist across the lifespan."

The particular effects of diet, stress, or even birth order may have no certain effect on any individual child, but studies like Ellman's do illustrate how hormonal levels in the womb, which are clearly affected by external circumstances, can create dramatic differences in subsequent behavior among brothers and sisters raised in the same household. Midlife stress in fathers also can have clear consequences on their sperm quality and count and on disease resistance of their subsequent offspring. As noted earlier, even birth order, one major Canadian demographic study suggests, appears to affect sexual orientation among boys. Anthony Bogaert at Brock University studied 944 heterosexual and homosexual men with multiple brothers. He found that the likelihood that the first boy in the family would be homosexual was 3 percent, roughly the general prevalence of male homosexuality in North America; but the probability that a fourth boy born of the same mother would be homosexual doubled to 6 percent even when there was a different father, suggesting some sort of "biological memory" within the mother's body. Bogaert had no clear biological explanation for the phenomenon; still, one strong but unproven hypothesis suggests that since all women automatically produce immune responses, or antibodies, to the presence of the foreign male proteins contained in semen in their bodies during pregnancy, the accumulation of those antibodies may affect the neurology, hormones, and sexual orientation of male fetuses and thus of male babies. Critics of the research ask why then there was not more evidence of homosexuality in the much larger families of earlier centuries—to which today's social critics answer that even if there were more homosexual sons in the eighteenth and nineteenth centuries, severe social and religious sanctions forced them to hide or to lead secret double lives.

Another example of the variance in nature concerns the prevalence of intersex births, which were once considered extremely rare. Medical researchers in Australia and the United States now say that at least one in every 1,500 children is born either with ambiguous genitalia or with other less visible sexual characteristics, including differences between their chromosomal identity and the visible genitals. Until recently, most babies born with intersex characteristics were "sexually reassigned" surgically within days of their birth. Following mounting outcries by intersex advocates, who frequently claim that one in every 150 births can be categorized as intersex, sexual reassignment surgery among neonatals has sharply declined. Following the banning of the surgery in Malta in 2014, the World Health Organization now lists sterilization as a consequence of forced reassignment surgery as a human rights violation. Transsexual rights groups, which have also won unprecedented sympathy and support in major media (notably the *New York Times* digital site), have also pressed for greater official recognition of nontraditional gender and biological identities. On the surface at least social liberals appear to have embraced not only intersex transsexual people, but equally people whose genitals don't conform to their internal feelings of masculinity and femininity, or gender. It is a worldwide movement—save for Russia, the Middle East, and parts of Africa—but it is also a movement that has left the majority confused. Many of the activists themselves argue that transsexualism is a *biological identity* while human rights activists insist that sexual identity should be understood as the right to *self-determination,* or gender expression. And again, as the biology of sexual differences grows fuzzier and fuzzier, so do old certainties about the roles and capacities of males and females.

Diane Halpern, long recognized as one of the world's leading cognitive psychologists, has also tracked what appear to be male and female differences related to verbal and spacial skills—which often change across a lifetime. Halpern is always quick to point out how apparent biological and neurological differences are mischaracterized as deficiencies, but she does not back away from describing differences in verbal and spacial skills. One difference that has long been observed, even across different primate species, is males' greater ability to rotate a picture of an object in their minds, a capacity even seen in infants as young as three months. Another suggests that males across cultures and age perform better at following cardinal directions—north, south, east, or west—while women do better at tracking directions based on specific landmarks. Neither method, however, suggests any superiority. "You can get there using both," Halpern reminded one journalist; "there is not a smarter sex." One of the most frequent and misleading assertions in popular media claims that boys in school are *innately* better at math than girls. In general boys do tend to score higher on standardized math tests than do girls though the difference is only very slight; and, as Halpern notes, in Nordic societies that enjoy greater gender equality, "the male advantage virtually disappears."

One of the most popular gender clichés concerns men's presumed greater obsession with sex. Pop surveys often assert that men think about sex nearly twice as often as women and consistently say they would prefer to have more sex partners than women want. University of Michigan psychologist Terri Conley looked a little deeper into those claims, including one that suggested men think about sex every seven seconds. False, Conley found. Instead, in a series of controlled surveys published in the *Journal of Sex Research* in 2011, she found that what men think about is their bodies, including hunger, fatigue, aches and pains, and sex. Men and women were each given charts on which they recorded a broad array of thoughts throughout the day; men recorded thinking about sex an average of eighteen times a day while women recorded thinking about sex ten times a day. Men do seem to think about sex more often than women do but not every seven seconds. Similarly, when men and women were asked orally how many sex partners they would like to have per year, young college-age men reported many more than young women did. Conley also noted that college-age men's concern about appearing to be good sexual performers may have distorted their answers, while young women's concern about being discrete may have also influenced their responses. However, when both were attached to lie detector machines, the number of desired partners per year turned out to be about equal. Other studies that count the number of orgasms men and women have per week suggest that while men do ejaculate more often than women climax, the numbers depend on whether the contact is in a longer-term relationship, where women report more orgasms, or in "quick hook-ups," in which men reach orgasm more quickly.

In short, as Halpern has frequently written, behavioral differences between men and women are deeply dependent upon context and how context affects everything from external societal judgment to hormonal response to fear and pleasure, each of which again can reflect a society's moral and cultural norms. Even boys' superiority in mathematics, when evaluated across class and economic strata—schools in rich neighborhoods versus poor neighborhoods—changes sharply, and those differences can reflect how each student's personal experience provokes highs and lows in testosterone and estrogen expression.

Or again to recall Denis Diderot, little in "nature" is fixed. The more we learn about the uncertain dance between nature and nurture, the more public attitudes toward supposed masculine and feminine values are also in continual flux. One remarkable shift in attitudes suggests that increasingly people want men to behave more like women. It is a shift in human consciousness that has received only the scantest of public note but is one that a team of social researchers has detected on every continent and increasingly with those born after the peak years of the Baby Boom.

In 2012 John Gerzema and Michael D'Antonio surveyed 64,000 men and women in eighteen countries ranging from South Korea to Germany to Brazil as well as the United States about behaviors and attitudes normally considered masculine or feminine. They did not directly address the sex versus gender (or nature versus nurture) question. Instead they wanted to understand how popular attitudes toward masculinity and femininity are shifting throughout the world. Their findings undoubtedly proved distressing to gender traditionalists. Two thirds of the people in Gerzema's and D'Antonio's survey said that "*the world would be a better place if men thought more like women.*"

The obvious next question, for radical feminists, male supremacists, or transsexuals, is what it means to think like a woman. Clever researchers, Gerzema and D'Antonio did not pose the question directly. First, they asked half their subjects to label 125 different behavioral traits—among them selfless, trustworthy, rugged, generous, dynamic, agile, understanding, curious, and down-to-earth—as either masculine or feminine, or neither. Then they gave the other 32,000 participants in the study the same list of behaviors, but instead of asking them to categorize the behaviors as masculine or feminine, they asked the participants to rate the importance of those traits to certain universal values: leadership, success, morality, and happiness. "By comparing the two samples," they wrote, "we could now statistically model how masculine and feminine traits relate to solving today's challenges." Regardless of age, gender, or culture, "people around the world feel that feminine traits correlate more strongly with making the world a better place . . . Our data," they concluded, "show that many of the qualities of an ideal modern leader are considered feminine."

Their research, compiled and rendered readable in the 2014 book *The Athena Doctrine*, covers a wide array of human issues that lurk quietly beneath the headlines—be they about massive laundering of drug money by the world's leading banks or how corrupt autocrats and dictators have been toppled. Accumulating wealth was far lower in popular estimation than achieving happiness for their children or building communities—despite (or perhaps in response to) the ever greater concentration of wealth in fewer and fewer hands. As surprising as anything were responses to questions about success and failure: "[Eighty-six] percent of people," they wrote, "believe that having some personal failures is critical to one's overall success." Facing difficult hurdles and failing early in life, as gerontologists have begun to find (see Chapter 17), explains to a significant degree how it is that women in almost every society live longer and healthier lives than men. To survive failure, be it a consequence of nature or nurture, requires resilience; and in a world of intensifying challenge and complexity, resilience appears to be central to enjoying a long and healthy life.

CHAPTER 4

Who Is Woman?

During my teenage years in eastern Kentucky at planting time I often found myself wedged into the back of our two-person "tobacco setter," an iron-wheeled contraption that had a fifty-gallon drum of water mounted on top. Tobacco setters were used to insert tender young tobacco seedlings into the earth. Two people sat side by side inches above the ground, both with a twenty-pound load of the freshly pulled seedlings piled on their laps. Most times, my tobacco-setting seatmate was a woman who worked on the farm. The rig was pulled by a red Farmall tractor that was always driven by a man; the faster he drove, the quicker the water spurted out. The women were as a rule quicker and more adept than most men at smoothly sliding those fragile *Nicotiana rustica* plants into the ground without breaking them, thereby setting them on their mission to become sticky six-foot-tall sources of lung cancer.

Women who seeded and weeded the fields or pruned the fruit trees seldom attracted much comment for wearing the same sort of pants and flannel shirts and jackets as the men. They were never taken to be sexually unusual or seen as gender radicals when they were carting around thirty-pound crates of apples during harvest. Wearing conventional "city" or "Sunday" clothes in the field or the orchard would have seemed simply absurd for such outdoor work. The contemporary notion of shipping off these tough *and* sexy young women to behavior modification was unimaginable. By the time they had reached age twenty-five or thirty, the majority had already borne two or three children. They were in most people's eyes—mine included—simply part of the "gender spectrum" that accommodated a wide array of masculine and feminine behavior—or gender performance, as social theorists would express it half a century later. (Neither, I should add, did I ever hear dark comments made about the willowy married gentleman who sold ladies' garments at the town's sole dress shop.)

If rural life, which in the United States is usually considered to be deeply conservative, regularly confounds the roles, dress, and actions that define standard womanhood, it is just as often that the metropolitan elites have turned to "science" and religion to create straitjackets on the meaning of womanhood. Women are more "patient" than men—and are therefore more competent at childcare. Women are designed by "nature" to be receptive—and are therefore less competent at managing other people. Women are "designed" to be smaller than men—and therefore require less sustenance. Women are "hormonally" more emotional than men—and therefore less capable of rational argument (said Henry Higgins). When I was growing up in a rural area and surrounded by women who were generally the most competent adults, none of these tele-reality notions of womanhood made much sense to me. At the same time, this was the era when Grace Kelly, Ava Gardner, and Marilyn Monroe epitomized sultry femininity, while Harriet Nelson (of *The Adventures of Ozzie and Harriet*) exemplified the model of perfect motherhood and Rosie the Riveter, the wrench-wielding heroine of World War II, had faded from public remembrance. After having taken over the wartime assembly lines where they bolted together cars, trucks, airplanes, and battleships for the "boys fighting overseas," these Rosies found themselves dismissed from their jobs as soon as the armistice was signed. They were expelled from the industrial lunchrooms where they had forged camaraderie and they were erased from the textbook accounts of national heroism. Dispatched to the suburbs, they were told to stay home, cook dinner, cuddle their veteran husbands, and change the diapers of the billowing baby boom that would restore the demographic imbalance created by the half million young men sacrificed to the war effort.

In America, a quarter century would pass before a new, fierce, college-educated generation of women would fight back for the social and sexual independence their mothers had found during the war and their grandmothers had known on the farms. But in Europe, where everyone, male and female alike, went to work to rebuild war-ravaged cities, the churches faced a mass exodus taking traditional Catholic teaching about gender with them. Social democracy began to take root and a new language of gender began to emerge. No single "feminist" voice of the last hundred years has been cited so often as Simone de Beauvoir's declaration, deep into her postwar masterwork *The Second Sex*: "One is not born but becomes a woman." The 1953 American translation of Beauvoir's book stripped out most of her deeper philosophical discussion, reducing her work to a simple feminist liberation treatise that denounced society's treatment of women as second-class creatures. In fact, Beauvoir saw American-style feminism in its popular expression as philosophically wrongheaded and dangerous insofar as it appeared to strip men and women of their essential physical and sexual differences. No, women and men are not the same, Beauvoir insisted, and it is as degrading to women to insist that they are as it is to imprison them in a second-class existence.

The emerging sentiment of gender rebellion was not, of course, universal. As I look out from my dining table in Paris, one of the greatest monuments to male domination overwhelms the horizon: the gigantic dome of the Panthéon, the decommissioned eighteenth-century church of Sainte Geneviève that long ago was transformed into a mausoleum for the bones of France's *grands hommes*, or great men. The Panthéon was constructed by the architect Jacques-Germain Soufflot of seemingly impregnable limestone and marble, its façade a reference to the pantheon of Rome and its dome larger than that of Saint Peter's Basilica. Now, however, the Paris Panthéon is bathed in aluminum latticework bright in the morning sun, full of air, as though with the right breeze it might flutter off into the heavens. The latticework is the scaffolding on which masons are working to save the dome from imminent collapse. The monumentality of the building commissioned by King Louis XV and finished under Napoleon was too heavy for the space it occupied; fissures in the stone led to cracks and then to leaks and then to a structural fragility that the French government has now committed ten work years and one hundred million euros to correct.

Within the gossamer scaffolding are enormous steel stanchions installed to support the dome while new sturdier walls are constructed beneath it, designed to prevent a total implosion. The metaphor has its limitations, but it also raises a number of issues parallel to Simone de Beauvoir's own questions about the *grands hommes* deposited below it. Defenders of the phrase have always insisted that *hommes* refers to all French persons, as *man* refers to all mankind. Nonetheless, of the seventy-four sets of bones residing beneath the dome of the Panthéon, only two once belonged to women: Marie Curie, who was shuttled over along with her husband, Pierre; and Sophie Berthelot, who hopped into the crypt to keep her chemist husband, Marcellin Berthelot, company. None of the dozens of corpses of singular French female writers, philosophers, scientists, Resistance fighters, or revolutionary heroines had been invited in. Only in 2015 did President François Hollande choose two women and two men to be reinstalled in the Panthéon. As the aging rebel of 1968's student rebellion and later trendy philosopher Bernard-Henri Lévy has remarked, "the Panthéon is a kind of assembly. An assembly of ghosts, perhaps, but one that represents French values and legitimacy as much as or more than any political body. And the lack of women there is flagrant."

Yet inclusion of female remains in a patently male tomb addresses little more than the surface of things. Beauvoir herself dismissed the Panthéon as a banal affront to gender equality and, still worse, an erasure of female existence on the earth. She made it very clear that having her cinders hauled over there would constitute an insult to everything that she and her companion, Jean-Paul Sartre, had said, written, and lived. The terms of inclusion in the category *grand* or great—whether in the Panthéon or Washington's Tomb of the Unknowns (formerly called the Tomb of the Unknown Soldier) or Russia's Memorial to the Heroes of the Motherland—have been conceived according to desperately male ground rules. Aside from being patriotic and faithful to each nation's inherent values, the candidates must have demonstrated personal strength, courage, fortitude. But how to measure each of these? Beauvoir asked. If physical strength is to be one of the categories, should it be measured by virility in battle or by the duration of life, in which case female physical endurance is plainly superior to that of males. If endurance is to be estimated by perseverance in the face of challenge, women's resilience in sustaining families in the absence of men who abandoned them or were killed in battle again trumps the male record in almost every instance. And, as more and more data on family violence have demonstrated, if personal resilience is the arbiter, the capacity of women to survive brutal assault by their male mates and go it alone with little or no promise of financial security has long outdistanced men's. So much for courage and fortitude.

Even more important, Beauvoir argued, is the necessity to reconfigure the terms and parameters of what we mean by fidelity to national values.

Courage in battle, the necessity to defend peace and equity when they are under threat—even through violence if necessary—is never to be denigrated. My personal freedom is only defensible as long as, in exercising it, I extend you the ground to pursue your own freedom, knowing that neither of us can ever fully comprehend the other's internal condition or dreams. Or, to address the ongoing deep conflict between secular values and faith, only by acknowledging the importance of apostasy *and* the daily rituals of believers in a multicultural society can freedom flourish. Only then can either of us not be erased from his or her personhood by the force of the other; only then, by defining ourselves as nodes in a force field defined by the network of other existences, is it possible to live in a free and secure human community. The Panthéon in Paris, like Saint Peter's in Rome or the Tomb of the Unknowns, stands as a stolid bulwark against everything that Beauvoir argued for and represented, just as the Vatican hierarchy itself remains the world's greatest monument to male supremacy.

Admission into the male gender temple represented for Beauvoir the worst of bad faith: It amounted to a new submission to conventional male paradigms, rendering all other ways of being as outside and "other." It would constitute, as she wrote in *The Second Sex*, a reenactment of Plato's famous argument for equal access of men and women to the classical army, a force whose icons, structure, training, and battle techniques were strictly defined by then conventional male rules and hierarchies. Women admitted into such a structure would change nothing essential about that structure, its history, or its symbolic power. Instead they would be converted at the threshold into nothing but "lesser" men, not only because of their smaller frames and musculature but, even more importantly, because of their manifestly secondary role in the master history of men and their works. Similarly, Beauvoir saw opening the now structurally frail Panthéon, with its unchanged terms and categories for admission, as in fact reinforcing—rather than reforming—this bastion of ghostly male authority.

While Beauvoir and small bands of mostly European intellectuals were at work in cafés and seminar halls reimagining the parameters of gender, thousands of American women were directly refusing to go gently into that good night of the 1950s. Well before the feminist movement associated with Betty Friedan in the sixties, women who had held jobs of importance and authority—a quick scan of ads in *Time*, *Newsweek*, *Life*, and *National Geographic* in the 1940s and early '50s reveals women doing everything from rescuing fallen aircraft victims to directing large businesses—fought back with fervor at their dismissals and displacement. For their resistance to being banished they found themselves labeled as the new *hysterics.* Although my father was already beyond the draft age when World War II broke out, and though my mother never worked outside the home, she found herself swept up in the collective diagnosis, a mild "hysteric" whose "female troubles," my father explained, led her to act in ways that she could not control. She suffered, he said, from what medical schools were still labeling as "hysteria": anger, yelling, depression, withdrawal.

A quarter century would pass before Phyllis Chesler's landmark 1972 book *Women and Madness* appeared, chronicling in painful detail the ancient and near-automatic assumption that women in their essence are uniquely subject to an illness of the mind and spirit labeled "hysteria," after the Greek word for uterus. Since Plato's era, and for some of the Greek physicians writing under the collective name Hippocrates, women had been seen as secondary humans, created first in the form of Pandora for the amusement of the male Gods. When Pandora opened the wedding jar given to her by Zeus, she let loose multitudes of evil, vengeful spirits, or *daimones*, that would ever after plague mankind—and specifically men. Myth aside, physicians continued to see women as uniquely possessed by uncontrollable spirits. The symptoms of their hysteria remained unchanged until the middle of the last century. But for the Greeks and the Romans they were frequently diagnosed as suffering from "wandering uterus" syndrome. The uterus, from which physical life springs, was believed to be in continuous search of humidity, of blood and other fluids, and when denied those fluids, this "wild organ," likened to an alien animal, would roam uncontrollably through the female body, to the liver, to the spleen, to the stomach, the lungs, heart, and brain, searching with such ferocity that the frail female creature herself could not control it, in which circumstance she suffered *hysteria.* Even the eighteenth-century Enlightenment rationalist philosophers barely altered their perceptions. Voltaire, the great defender of free thought, and Rousseau, the tribune of personal liberty and author of the social contract that gave birth to the French Revolution (liberty, equality, fraternity), barely conceived of women as belonging to the same human race as men. Even Denis Diderot, the creator of the idea of encyclopedic knowledge, argued for the protection of women (rather than the equal treatment of women) because, his studies told him, women are totally and completely subject to the irrational demands of "the muscles of the uterus," the contractions of which, being vastly more intense during orgasm than men's contractions, rendered the female captive of her lesser body and incapable of reliable rational, physical, and spiritual self-control.

By the mid-twentieth century, the uterus had mostly ceased to wander through the male psyche, but hysteria remained at the bedrock of medical diagnosis of women's identity and illness. Today at the U.S. National Library of Medicine, which is run by the National Institutes of Health in Bethesda, Maryland, there still hangs one of the great paintings of the nineteenth century, André Brouillet's depiction of Dr. Jean-Martin Charcot presenting his "pet" hysteric, "Blanche." Charcot holds onto Blanche as she contorts her body into a backward twist, her large eyes out of focus, her white blouse pulled open from the top of her breasts to the side of her shoulder. A nurse, the only other female present, stands at the ready, her arms extended in case Blanche should fall. Curious middle-aged men from the neurology team, suited in black, accompanied by a seated priest, look on as the French doctor describes Blanche's case history. In one of his original lectures on the nervous system, the doctor described what happened to Blanche: "The patient suddenly falls to the ground, with a shrill cry; loss of consciousness is complete. The tetanic rigidity of all her members, which generally inaugurates the scene, is carried to a high degree; the body is forcibly bent backwards, the abdomen is prominent, greatly distended, and very resisting."

There is little doubt that "Blanche" was suffering some sort of seizure, but from what? There is no answer except that she was female. Doctors and social analysts, including many feminist writers, have since the 1960s sought to understand what was going on in images like Brouillet's painting, but even more importantly they have sought to understand what evidentiary medical science was about during the last two centuries. Phyllis Chesler herself skirted close to the argument raised by some feminist critics that madness and hysteria must have been a normal reaction to the unbearable conditions that denied women political participation, meaningful careers, and respect for their intellect despite Western society's laws supposedly guaranteeing them equality with men. "We also learned that it was mothers'—not fathers'—genetic predisposition, . . . and/or poverty [that] caused neurosis and psychosis," Chesler wrote. "None of my professors ever said that women (or men) were oppressed or that oppression is traumatizing—especially when those who suffer are blamed for their own misery and diagnostically pathologized . . . we were taught to view women as somehow naturally mentally ill. Women were hysterics ... malingerers, child-like, manipulative, either cold or smothering as mothers, and driven to excess by their hormones. We assumed that men were mentally healthy." Controlled masculinity was assumed to be the norm, while genuine emotional reaction to existential abuse was seen as aberrational, or as a measure of illness. Chesler specifically avoided describing "hysteria" as a form of protest. Rather, she argued, hysterical responses arose specifically because conventional society provided most women no venue for protest or even a language for expressing their circumstances.

Not long after *Women and Madness* was published, another subtler argument recalling the ancient Hippocratic texts began to emerge concerning the nature of female hysteria diagnoses. Descriptions of hysteria in the nineteenth-century medical literature began to create evidentiary case studies of actual individuals suffering illness. Though he was not the first doctor to present case histories of the linkage between mental and physical troubles—shaking, a sense of suffocation, the inability to walk or move hands and arms—Sigmund Freud's accounts, mostly of women, provoked a radical break in how hysteria was seen and analyzed. Doctors quickly began collecting accounts of hysteria across Europe and America. A century later, when medical historian Edward Shorter began examining these case histories, he was struck by how the waves of hysteria diagnosis seemed to shift across the decades. At first, in the early stages of industrialization, they concerned primarily young middle-class women in cities; almost none appeared among farm girls in the countryside. Socially minded psychiatrists began to argue that these young women were under assault by the stress and pressure of modern urban life, symbolized by the power and speed of the new locomotive steam engines. New York, symbol of the money-grasping, capitalist economy, emerged as an epicenter of hysteria—for three or four decades. Later, as high-rise urban life became emblematic of twentieth-century progress, hysterical paralysis shifted to the countryside, where the iconic yeoman farm families were rapidly disappearing. Across all the waves of shifting hysteria, however, young and middle-aged women of child-bearing age seemed to suffer most.

Edward Shorter's tracking of female hysteria epidemics offers many possible interpretations: stress from economic transition, demographic displacement following waves of immigration followed by quintessentially American religious upheaval, disintegration of family ties linked to the relentless westward march toward new opportunities. Men of course also suffered displacement anxieties, but for males, movement was mostly tied to the dream of new opportunities and escape from old oppressions. As much as women may have shared in those dreams, women continued to fulfill all their historic roles as nurses, nurturers, and family counselors with one great exception: With each displacement there came a severing of the social networks that they and their mothers and grandmothers had always relied upon for their own psychic and social support. Nowhere in a woman's life was that peculiarly female social networking more important than at the moment of childbirth, from which men were mostly excluded. Given that many women found themselves largely alone at the very moment when their own survival and that of their baby was at risk—the probability of a newborn baby's survival in 1900 was barely above 50 percent—there's little wonder that hysteria diagnoses were clustered around early adulthood. Moreover, giving birth as well as suffering a miscarriage were both very dangerous for young women, especially for the majority who gave birth in their homes with no access to quick medical intervention. Clean water and improved general sanitation surely improved survival rates, but the relative circumstances of all but the richest of women changed little from the age of Enlightenment to the turn of the twentieth century.

Hysteria has at long last disappeared from the *Diagnostic and Statistical Manual* (DSM), which is the fundamental handbook of psychological diagnoses. But traces of its influence still linger even in modern history. Only since the rise of the second-wave feminist movement of the 1970s has "feminine" ceased to signify a lesser condition. Examples pepper the work of Freud. When he first reported a case of male hysteria to his Viennese colleagues, they were at once shocked and dismissive. How could a person lacking a uterus possibly suffer hysteria? After Freud explained that the male hysterics were Jews, his Austrian colleagues began to nod their comprehension. These hysterical Jews were of Eastern origin, particularly Polish Jews. Unlike the Ashkenazi, who were more or less integrated into European secular life, the Eastern European Jews had long been treated as, at best, "feminized men" by Western elites. To be "feminized" was not merely to be less but also to be weaker. These Jews' faces and bodies were categorized as weak and feminine by no less a physician than the psychiatrist Richard von Krafft-Ebing; their weakness was ascribed to centuries of shtetl inbreeding. Edward Shorter's 1986 essay surveying the diagnoses does not deny that hysteria was more frequent among Jewish men than among other males. For European Jews suffering the virulence of vicious Gentile anti-Semitism in Austria, Germany, and France, who still remained largely confined to marginal urban neighborhoods and who until the 1950s continued to be shunned by major public and private institutions, a "hysteric" response seems hardly shocking. But that Jewish males continued to be stereotyped not merely as outside "others" but as feminized males speaks even more brutally of what it meant well into the twentieth century to *be* feminine.

The image of the Jew as a feminized male runs deep through European history and still persists in some quarters. My friend and colleague Steve Weissman, a sharp critic of recent Israeli policies, once explained his own contradictory feelings about Israel's 1947–49 war of independence and its subsequent 1956 invasion of Egypt, known as the Suez Crisis. Both wars in his view fundamentally changed both Jewish self-perception and global perceptions of Jews, despite ingrained European and American anti-Semitism. "I was in high school when the fifty-six war broke out," he told me. "Though I didn't believe in any religion really, I could feel that this campaign [in the Sinai] was important for all of us." But if it wasn't about religion for you, what was it? I asked. "It was about being 'a mensch' and about standing up for ourselves, about ridding ourselves of the old stereotypes." To be a mensch in both the German and the Yiddish usage means standing as a forthright man, free of any feminine frailty. For the shtetl Jews of Catholic Eastern Europe and even for their children, the idea of degraded manliness was often deeply internalized. (A new book by the Euro-Moroccan art historian Bruno Nassim Aboudrar tracks parallel portrayals in painting and photography of Arabs characterized by their French rulers as *both* feminine and savagely brutal.) One of the clearest statements about the gendered image of the Jewish diaspora appeared in 1904 in an obituary of Theodor Herzl by a young Russian writer, Ze'ev Jabotinsky, who would later become a founding member of the fierce paramilitary Zionist Irgun and a mentor to the eventual Likudist Israeli prime minister Menachem Begin:

> Our starting point is to take the typical Yid of today and to imagine his diametrical opposite . . . because the Yid is ugly, sickly, and lacks decorum, we shall endow the ideal image of the Hebrew with masculine beauty. The Yid is trodden upon and easily frightened and, therefore, the Hebrew ought to be proud and independent. The Yid is despised by all and, therefore, the Hebrew ought

> to charm all. The Yid has accepted submission and, therefore, the Hebrew ought to learn how to command. The Yid wants to conceal his identity from strangers and, therefore, the Hebrew should look the world straight in the eye and declare: "I am a Hebrew!"

Herzl was the symbol of the new Jewish man whose powerful appearance embodied "everything that Jews were not but sought to be." The distinction between the proud, forthright manhood of "the New Hebrew" and the weak, fearful victim of the Pale of Settlement was equally echoed by no less than Israel's founding father, David Ben-Gurion, and the Zionist Labor militant Nachman Syrkin, who described the old diaspora Jew as "puny, ugly, enslaved, degraded and egoistic . . . when he forgets his great self; great, beautiful, moral and social is the Jew when he returns to himself and recognizes his own soul."

That deeply gendered notion of femininity as insufficiency, incompleteness, and lack of self-worth surely persists in today's world, not least in the Middle East and North Africa, but the linkage to ancient notions of hysteria has not survived. Likewise, death during childbirth and infant mortality have both declined to the fringes of the human mortality watch, taking with them two of the key markers distinguishing men from women. Biology—chromosomal, hormonal, physiological—does continue to distinguish what it means to be male or female or, for that matter, transsexual; but these historic definers of gender are withering fast, as we shall see across the chapters to come.

For Élisabeth Badinter, who has spent her life examining what distinguishes manliness from femininity, the game is far from finished even if she and others argue that apart from the work done by testicles and ovaries, there is nothing else in our gendered bodies that makes much difference between men and women: no cognitive difference, no endurance difference, no esthetic capacity, and, increasingly, less difference in physical size or strength once diet and exercise are made equivalent. Increasingly most neuroscientists and psychologists argue that despite our biological and generative equipment, what we call gender is nothing more than the consequence of many millennia of power struggles between the bio-types that up until now have been controlled by males.

CHAPTER 5
Show Us What You're Made Of

"Show us what you're made of!" is one of the oldest taunts young men have faced to demonstrate their masculinity. On the battlefield. In the boxing ring. Or inside the football stadium. Despite forty years of high-profile feminism and twenty years of "masculinity studies," popular conversation persists in characterizing battlefield heroes, boxing champions, and bull-shouldered quarterbacks as "real men." Car mechanics, architects, and barbers are seen to be real men. Hairdressers, interior decorators, and florists are not.

Nothing quite so clearly defined the form of real men for me as the image of a painting in one of my high school English texts, entitled, "Men Are Square" by the once-popular painter Gerrit Beneker; it depicted a broad-shouldered sort with his arms crossed to form a square with his shoulders beneath fierce eyes and barely tamed whiskers. An accompanying quatrain, its lines sifted now into the dust of memory, lauded the value of tough, durable fidelity as the measure of a real man. Beneker found his fame producing similar World War I images of invincible patriots who "got the job done" before making his fortune painting illustrations for Ivory soap. As for myself, I'd just taken up painting watercolors.

Real men, more especially boys who wanted to be seen as real men, didn't do watercolors—no matter the masterpieces painted by Dürer, Whistler, Homer, Turner, Sargent, and Hopper. Among high school boys, watercolors were for maiden aunts and little sisters ... or boys whose wrists weren't stiff and who had never worn cleats or helmets, and didn't know what to do in the back seat of the borrowed family Chevy on a Saturday night. I never told a soul in high school about my watercolors and the emotions I attached to them. Masculinity, of the square-shouldered variety, was about silence and resolve.

Resolve. In itself the word seems far removed from anything concerning gender. Mothers are surely as resolved to care for, defend, and properly raise their children as Gerrit Beneker's square men were to win the war and roll out steel. Yet once we step beyond the frontiers of family discourse, resolve remains an overwhelmingly masculine trait—as former Harvard president Larry Summers discovered when, in a speech in 2005 to a conference on diversifying the science and engineering workforce, he applied the notion offhandedly to explain why it might be that men are more present than women in the upper echelons of science, high tech, and engineering. Here's the passage that cost Summers his job:

> The most prestigious activities in our society expect of people who are going to rise to leadership positions in their forties near total commitments to their work. They expect a large number of hours in the office, they expect a flexibility of schedules to respond to contingency, they expect a continuity of effort through the life cycle, and they expect—and this is harder to measure—but they expect that the mind is always working on the problems that are in the job, even when the job is not taking place. And it is a fact about our society that that is a level of commitment that a much higher fraction of married men have been historically prepared to make than of married women ... Another way to put the point is to say, what fraction of young women in their mid-twenties make a decision that they don't want to have a job that they think about eighty hours a week. What fraction of young men make a decision that they're unwilling to have a job that they think about eighty hours a week, and to observe what the difference is.

A firestorm of rancor rained down on Summers—mostly but not exclusively from radical feminist quarters. Did Summers really mean to say that only men have sufficient resolve to face standards of scientific research? Did he really mean to imply men alone possess the intellectual rigor required of frontline science and technology? The more he tried to explain his statement, the deeper he dug himself into his own trench. Frontline science and engineering design of the sort that takes place at institutions like Harvard, MIT, and Stanford is limited to a very tiny percentage of human beings, and, since it's widely accepted that males are far more diverse in their intellectual capacities than women—far more men score at the bottom end of IQ tests *and* at the top end [Wai et al, *Intelligence*, July–August 2010]—it shouldn't be much of a surprise that the scarce handful of positions at the top end in science currently go to men. Perhaps they always will.

Summers, who quit Harvard within a year of his pronouncement, fell prey to one of the most profound debates about what separates masculinity from femininity: innate biology—sex—or social conformity. The reality that men dominate the empyrean heights of bench science was never in question; top science and technology have always been a boys' club and for the most part they still are. But whether young women at the peak of their child-making capacity are doomed to step aside from a world that demands a minimum of seven twelve-hour days a week of concentration is a much hazier issue. Pregnancy lasts nine months. In most cases only the last three present possible reasons to reduce a rigorous workload, and in the Nordic countries, kindergartens typically accept children beginning between ages one and two. Home husbands, though far from a majority, are no longer so rare as to raise immediate questions about the male capacities. Further, the question of whether exhausting eighty-hour workweeks, of the sort that Summers identified, constitute the best application of intellectual talent raises profound issues concerning the essential paradigms of masculinity and femininity.

At its simplest, of course, men—biologically—are defined by possession of a Y chromosome. With it you're male; without it you're something else. But possessing a Y chromosome tells us nothing about "manliness." For the twentieth century, the world's single most famous model of manliness was likely the Brazilian soccer great Pelé, while in North America Sean Connery as Agent 007 or Muhammad Ali might have claimed the title. Regardless of the heroic profile, Western manliness owes its origins, its form, its character, its display to the most ancient of Western ideals, Achilles, the reticent yet invincible warrior of Homer's *Iliad*. Achilles, recall, took himself to his tent in protest following a quarrel with the leader of the Greek army over access to a captured woman; it was only upon learning that his genuine beloved, the young warrior Patroclus, had been killed and degraded by the encroaching Trojans that Achilles exited his tent and roared in such rage that the Trojans cowered. Achilles then slashed his way through the surviving Trojans until he reached Hector, the Trojan leader, decapitated him, and dragged Hector's mutilated corpse through the dust behind his chariot. (One of the abiding debates in classical scholarship concerns Achilles' sexual predilections; in Homer's version the bond between Achilles and Patroclus was a bond of brotherhood; when recounted several hundred years later by Aeschylus, their relation was plainly homoerotic.)

I might have been twelve when my parents gave me a child's version of *The Iliad* and *The Odyssey*. These two texts have been bedrock tales of masculine heroism for more than two millennia, re-rendered across centuries of Christian interpretation but consistently cited as vital guiding models for the hallmarks of manly virtue: justice, courage, self-restraint, physical prowess, and wisdom. Following Plato, within all of these virtues is contained a binding notion of ideal form to which a man must strive. (Women, being regarded mostly as incomplete versions of males, were seldom addressed.) To attain the magnificent physical form of those perfect Greek warrior bodies meant that from early boyhood, the would-be man of quality must work endlessly and set aside childish attachments. So it was that we were also encouraged to undertake serious sportsmanship, to replace "childish games" with popular competitive sport—baseball, basketball, and football—herein we would presumably learn deeper rules of honor, sacrifice, and courage. Linked together, the achievement of manliness emerges as a variation on Simone de Beauvoir's axiom: One is not born a man; one is made a man through resolve and relentless cultural learning.

Back when "libraries" meant books on shelves, entire rooms were devoted to philosophical treatises about the roots of war. Hobbesians and Malthusians argued that war is essentially an eco-biological phenomenon whereby one set of genetically superior males prunes away their genetically inferior victims; the Rousseauians maintained that war is purely a consequence of state power bent on aggrandizing itself, or essentially of nurture, however ironic the term may seem. Either way, warfare has long played out as emblematic of male force and male reason. By establishing territorial boundaries and frontiers that may not be breached, the preparation for and exercise of warfare has been from Greek mythology forward the ultimate expansion of inviolable space. To become the loser in warfare, therefore, represents a collective demasculation of the warrior and the warriors' state—just as a male who has been sexually violated and penetrated by another male has been in popular parlance "unmanned." (Never mind that contemporary medicine regularly counsels prostate massage followed by ejaculation as a physiologically healthy activity valuable in preventing the onset of prostate cancer—something gay men learned decades ago and that their straight brothers feared to discuss.)

Learning masculinity starts early and in little ways. One June afternoon in 2014 I took a midday break for a walk into the botanical park not far from my apartment in Paris. At the northern edge sits a circular tower made of earth and stone with a trail spiraling to the top, rather like the mythical Tower of Babel. The top ring is flat and lined by ironwork rails on which small boys were climbing about. The little girls were playing giggling games. All were between two and four years old. I asked a friend who had joined me on the walk why the girls weren't climbing too. "Look at their shoes," she suggested. The girls were all wearing lace-less slippers or sandals. The boys had on tightly laced sneakers. To run, climb, and jump a three-year-old, boy or girl, needs a sturdy shoe or no shoe. The girls were being taught, consciously or not, not to climb. A day or two later, I dropped by a children's shoe store in my neighborhood to take a look at what was on sale. "Do you have sandals for little boys?" I asked the clerk. "What age?" she asked. "Three," I answered. "No, no," she answered. "Only for girls or toddlers."

I never saw a boy wearing sandals in my grade school or in high school. When I went away to college, I was initially shocked to see guys in sandals; almost without exception—this was the 1960s—they also had long hippie hair that could provoke redneck yells of "Faggot!" if they drifted very far from campus. Shoes, clothing, and hairstyle were and remain markers of correct masculinity, indicators of internal male character. Those markers shift with the times and fashions, but the distinctions remain. One weekend, when I returned back from college for a visit, I took along a newly purchased umbrella. My father noted the umbrella and asked simply, "Don't you have a raincoat and a hat?" Even when he had been a young man in Berlin and Paris during the 1920s, he had never seen a man carrying an umbrella. Umbrellas, sandals, necklaces—even Indian bead necklaces—were not indicators, or signifiers, of correct masculinity.

During the last quarter of the last century there surfaced one of the new hot zones in university social science: masculinity. From Berkeley and Cambridge to small community colleges in the Midwest, classes on masculinity—or more properly *masculinities*—flourished. In large part the emerging fascination with maleness sprouted in gender studies programs that were themselves born of feminist activism in the 1960s and '70s. As documentation steadily mounted illustrating how women had been subordinated or outright excluded by law, religion, and political tradition from key roles in business, government, and even the household, it became clearer and clearer that the relations of dominance, or hegemony, would remain opaque if one only examined "femininity." Gender, in whatever way it is formulated, is a dynamic notion. By concentrating only on who cooks dinner, who cleans the toilet, or who keeps the books and answers the phone, the other half of the human equation was left shielded from scrutiny. Men and maleness needed to be examined too.

Language, terminology, iconography, and storytelling style both obscure and illuminate how we understand our basic notions of who and what human beings are. Among the first terms, which certainly trickled down from antiquity, is *virility*. "Real men" then as now exude their virility. But what is it, this virility? Formal definitions trace the etymology to the Latin word *verilis*, meaning "of a man," which in turn is derived from *vir*, the Roman word for both man and hero. (By Shakespeare's time a virile man was one who had a functional penis.) Etymological citation, alas, tends to lead us into tautology. A famously cited passage from the quasi-classical, profoundly popular novelist Dan Brown asserts that the "thumbs-up" gesture owes its origins to an earlier Roman gesture indicating phallic readiness, which, with only modest reflection, requires little explanation. Today, the thumbs-up gesture suggests little more than success or good luck in a contest, even if it's more often used among men than among women. Forgotten in all this symbolic reference to virility, however, is its perhaps oxymoronic application to women. Today the word has also been applied to women, especially young and fertile women possessed of an unyielding life force. And potency, at least in biological terms, speaks directly of the male capacity to produce semen—an ability that declines sharply with age. (While 90 percent of the seminiferous tubules within the testicles of men under age forty contain sperm, the proportion drops to 50 percent for males between forty and seventy.) Historically, males who could not accomplish reproduction had plainly lost their virility. More recently, as the economic imperative to raise many children has declined, and as effective family planning has become universal in the West, virility has instead come to imply social potency or the exercise of power. The Cambridge University dictionary currently characterizes virility simply as "strength" and applies the term even more broadly to a nation's "economic virility"; while in Catholic parlance virility draws on the parallel definition of the Latin *vir* meaning virtue, implying purity and virtue in young men and chastity in women. Like masculinity, virility has grown steadily more confusing if not mysterious.

But what of female virility today? Are purity and virtue only masculine values? The argument would surely seem bizarre to most of Judeo-Christian or even pagan history when female purity was held among the highest of values, particularly in cultures where a woman was often regarded as little more than a vessel for patrilineal succession. Other traditions, especially in the Amazon, have understood women as humanity's elemental *force vitale*. Claude Lévi-Strauss's student Chris Knight explored a wide array of indigenous beliefs and rituals relating blood, vitality, and virility in North and South America in his book *Blood Relations: Menstruation and the Origins of Culture*. Menstrual blood was and to some extent still is regarded as an outright threat to male strength, or virility, among some Plains Indians. That broader sense of virility—classically masculine—appears in the writer Marguerite Duras's wartime diaries when she writes of a sexual encounter with her companion Dionys on an Italian beach.

That broader sense of virility—classically masculine—appears in the writer Marguerite Duras's wartime diaries when she writes about the "virility of maternity" following a sexual encounter with her companion Dionys on an Italian beach. "None of the most acknowledged aspects of virility can touch that one, if by virility one means the brutal exercise of freedom." She describes it as a brutal virility that "roots around" deep within her being. "I feel that freedom live, and my own, just as free, containing it." Rereading her diary description of those moments with Dionys many years later, Dionys seems to actually return to her, the two of them bonded together in complete freedom.

Throughout her work Duras beautifully and famously sought to sabotage and reconstruct conventional gender notions of frailty and power, passion and freedom. Neither a mystic nor a spiritualist, she, like Simone de Beauvoir, sought—a generation before the rise of feminism and two generations before "gender studies" came into vogue—to question the ordinary assumptions and daily language that define masculinity and femininity. Standard notions of male vitality would come under still greater question at the end of the last century as both biology and epidemiology began to track differences between boys and girls, men and women, in intellectual development and susceptibility to disease. Indeed a near avalanche of pediatric, adolescent, adult, and geriatric research leaves little doubt that males, human and animal, are not only more fragile across their lifespans; they are also consistently more subject to disease.

Male fragility begins in the womb and persists through the much shorter lifespan that men face compared to women. To take an extreme example, boys born prematurely are 1.7 times less likely to survive than premature girls. Boys develop verbal skills on average two years later than girls do. A large British study of young school-age children born very prematurely found that slightly more than half suffered cognitive and other learning disabilities—and the vast majority of those were boys. A Canadian study of mothers living in a chemically polluted area found that male embryos were far less likely to survive through gestation than female embryos. Child psychologist and author Susan Pinker collected a vast amount of demographic and epidemiological data showing parallel results from around the world. "Over twenty years of clinical practice and teaching as a child psychologist," Pinker wrote in her 2009 book *The Sexual Paradox*, "I had seen mostly males. Boys and men with learning problems, attention problems, aggressive or antisocial boys, those with autistic features, those who didn't sleep well or make friends, or couldn't sit still, dominated my practice—and that of every other developmental psychologist I knew." Cognitive and attention deficit disorders, she said, were from four to ten times more common in boys than in girls. A raft of cross-cultural child psychology studies confirm her own experiences.

The reasons for these striking markers of male frailty are diverse. Some neurologists and endocrinologists have focused on the differential effects of male and female hormones generated in utero. A number of studies have suggested that exceptionally heavy levels of testosterone in the fetus may reduce immunity to diseases, while other research has also suggested that too little testosterone can provoke other developmental disabilities later in childhood and adolescence. Household and social surroundings also can play a role; one recent study appears to link early exposure to digital toys to heightened attention disorders. On the positive front an early intervention project beginning with hyperactive kindergarten boys in North Carolina reduced levels of testosterone over a period of eight years, sharply reducing aggressive and antisocial behavior compared to a control group. The children's overall health profiles also improved. As children move through adolescence they experience much stronger flushing of either estrogen or testosterone, and still more issues emerge that appear to distinguish male and female health. But heightened frailty for men persists throughout their lives. Men develop cardiovascular disease on average seven to ten years earlier than women do. Men have strokes much more often than women—even though women's strokes seem to be more severe. Cancer numbers are still worse: 4.5 to 5.5 times more throat and mouth cancers in men than in women and 3.3 to 1 for bladder cancer; 2.3 to 1 for lung cancer deaths and about the same for liver cancer. The notion of males as the tougher and sturdier to the two human animals is highly suspect.

Beyond biology, however, no one has cracked the conventional assumptions surrounding male identity more sharply or more subtly than the Australian scholar Raewyn Connell in her book *Masculinities.* Drawing on history, anthropology, sociology, and psychology, Connell argues that no single notion of masculinity exists across all cultures or across all history; then she illustrates her work by drawing on actual human stories.

Connell begins with a clipping from an Australian newspaper about men who have lost their way. It's an experience I've often had that has often separated me from many male friends and mates: Why are so many men loathe to ask for directions when they are lost? "Women are more likely to stop someone in the street and ask for directions than men—simply because the sexes think differently," the Australian journalist states. She then proceeds to interview several experts on why that might be, and on how men and women use language differently (women being more pragmatic information seekers, men being more protective of the knowledge they possess and consequently more reticent to expose their lack of knowledge and authority). The "investigative journalist" hiked herself over to Sydney University to inquire of biologists and neurologists about whether inherent physiological differences between male and female brains might explain why the male brain speaks differently from the female brain. Somehow, alas, she forgot to inquire of historians how it came to be that the keepers of most sacred truths throughout history—pharaohs, popes, rabbis, even Buddhist priests, among others—have also guarded the paths into and through their sacred temples, or what relation these sacred temples have played in launching wars, issuing political decrees, or minting the coins of their realms. Men and women, of course, have both formed private, often secret, circles to look after their own security, but those circles and the secrets guarded within them have always existed within hierarchies of power, creating vast and all-embracing "hegemonies." He who holds the map holds immeasurable advantages over the inquisitor who does not know the way. A mere three decades of gender scholarship and activism has sought to decode the maps of power and privilege that men have used for multiple millennia to organize the world.

Connell tracks the rich history of masculine definition across the West—from Freud's subtle and intricate analysis of the essentially feminine impulses—and conflicts—within the male psyche to the later and far more conservative forms of psychoanalytic argument current in the 1950s that saw almost any nonconventional male activity as evidence of a disturbed boyhood generated by bad parenting. Real boys shouldn't wear sandals and real men don't wear pink—at least not until pink dress shirts became all the rage at the end of that decade, drawing immediate wrath from the psycho establishment of the time as a threat both to male identity and to social stability in general.

~

My closest French comrade recalls how a slightly older, more sturdily built family member repeatedly taunted him for his size and interests, saying, "You're just a girl. You're a girl. You're a girl." What did the bullying cousin mean? In her treatise on the formation and nature of masculinity, *XY*, Élisabeth Badinter goes to the womb where all children were once functionally a part of the female body and in significant ways remained bound to the female body throughout their nursing months. In classical psychoanalytic language, it is only when the testicled child insists on separating himself from the feminine other, in negating his sameness with the female, that his masculinity emerges. Aided of course by the testosterone bath he received in utero, he embarks on making himself into a social male. Badinter recounts the broad array of mostly punitive initiation rites ingrained in premodern, indigenous cultures, from the Plains Indians to the Sambia people of New Guinea (who engage in a rite that includes bloody flagellation to rid the boy of his "female blood" followed by fellatio with older boys to imbibe real masculinity). In East African practice boys are separated from the nurturing mother and placed with the males of the group for exposure to collective fatherhood in sleeping huts. Michel Foucault famously detailed the parallel same-sex rites described by Plato in the formation of the fierce fighter. By the opening of the industrial age in Britain, northern Europe, and the United States, those rites had mostly been suppressed—to be replaced by the schoolyard playing-field rites and the "dirty games" of preadolescent Little League boys described in painful detail by sociologist Gary Alan Fine.

Back in my own two-room grade school in eastern Kentucky, versions of the "dirty games" were fully present in the 1950s and '60s. Our village schoolhouse was divided into two large rooms, each with its own cloakroom. In the "big room" for grades five through eight, large blackboards covered one wall while five windows filled the opposite wall, looking out to a field where a farmer's cows munched their meals. A water cooler stood inside the cloakroom. A coatrack stretched from one wall to the other behind the cooler. Behind the coatrack in the winter the pubescent seventh- and eighth-grade boys hid out during recess and lunchtime, giggling, squealing, and sometimes emitting strange sighs. Being a "good boy" from a "good family" and already something of a loner, I was seldom invited into this makeshift clubhouse, but I could hear the excited giggles and smell the sulfur from matches being lit and extinguished. Once I found crusty nasal paper left on the floor. It was obvious what those "bad" boys were up to . . . in what the sociologist Michael Messner labels collective manhood formation, or, in popular parlance, "circle jerks."

The cloakrooms were loci of more than their apparent function. They were separate destinations where both sexes could create their separate solaces. The girls, significantly, kept their wraps in another cloakroom attached to the classroom used by younger students. The boys' cloakroom bench behind the winter coats was plainly a no-go zone both for little boys and for any girls, or even for the teacher; it was a place apart dedicated not only to priapic pleasures but even more to mutual male observation and comparative measurement, a testing ground for twelve- and thirteen-year-olds to establish hierarchy and dominance. One of the boys, a bit brighter than the others, once boasted to me on the playground swing about the immensity of his high-school brother's physical equipment: "Glenn's are so big he has to wear a sack to hold them!" he insisted with filial admiration and evident hope that one day he would develop the same evidence of virility.

If the "dirty games" in the cloakroom created one kind of secret turf for boy-bonding and hierarchy, the ball field that had been lent to the school out behind a red barn at the edge of the playground established another more competitive zone of male testing and performance. As small as our school was, and despite the fact that its two teachers were generally women, we somehow managed to field a baseball team to compete with the other country schools around our county. I was one of the tallest boys in our school. It was assumed I ought to be good at baseball. I could run. I could bat fairly well. I couldn't catch much of anything. The way I threw the ball was to all eyes appalling, so much so that word got back to my father, who in his youth had been a talented athlete.

One day a young man who was the son of our bus driver showed up after classes.

"You Frankie, aren't you?"

"Yeah."

"Well, my daddy told me to come over and learn you how to throw right."

I must have looked at him like he was from another planet.

"You got a [baseball] glove here?"

My parents had bought me a fielder's mitt for Christmas that year, which I kept in my desk.

We went off behind the school building where the other kids wouldn't see us. Thankfully. For half an hour he showed me how I was supposed to hold my shoulders, pull back my upper arm, and twist my right hand to hurl the ball forward hard like a bullet. His lessons had little effect. I still continued to throw with my arm arched overhead "like a girl."

"Well, you doin' better," he lied to me. "When you go home you practice it."

A rich literature has documented the critical function of competitive group sports for the formation of "proper" masculinity. In America it usually starts with baseball, then moves on to basketball or football, while in South America and Europe, soccer provides the standard ladder to manhood. Tennis, my father's sport, barely passes since girls and women also excel at the game, and it therefore fails to advance the necessary gender distancing expected of sport. Tennis's association with upper-class dandyism and the uniform of tennis whites further degrades it as the sport of real men. No sport, however, compares to the most hyper-masculine of games, the slogan of which is "You have to have leather balls to play rugby." One of several sorts of football that emerged between the tenth and nineteenth centuries, rugby pits two teams of fifteen males against each other on an open pitch. They wear no helmets or protective foot, knee, or shoulder gear. Dozens of books have recounted the game's evolution into a nineteenth-century upper-class British university sport that sought to distinguish itself from the "soft" football practiced notably in France, a nation denigrated by the captains of the British Empire for raising soft, feminized males. A more recent examination by the French anthropologist Anne Saouter, *Être Rugby: Jeux du masculin et du féminin* ("Being Rugby: Masculine and Feminine Games"), looks at both English and continental rugby culture as one of the few zones wherein men openly express physical intimacy, grasping each other's groins and asses and kissing mouth to mouth, while in the locker room they play with each other's penises and testicles in much the same way as my grade-school buddies did. The brutality of rugby frees them to break conventional male rules and become publicly affectionate, bearing the facial scars of the field scrum to prove their manliness.

American football has developed as a marginally safer version of the same masculinity test; the teammates are outfitted in ever more high-tech protective gear. Dan is one of my few ex-footballer friends. He grew up in Texas, where he was a minor star on his high school gridiron. When I met him in San Francisco he was a nationally known political cartoonist with a ribald sense of humor. Football for Dan and his adolescent teammates was the crystal prism through which masculinity defined itself. "If you were a real man," he told me, "you were supposed to risk hurting yourself in pursuit of a manly goal. We were working-class kids. We all had jobs, and a lot of them were dirty, hard jobs. Working in factories . . . working in filling stations. My first job was in a filling station. The whole male cult of it was that you never complained and you really, really did your job hard. It was a point of pride that you got more done. You washed more cars than the other guys did. You made more tackles on the football field. It was all a manly art." Sex, work, and ambition were always intricately tangled. But above all three came performance. By your performance you would be judged and aggressively so, no matter the risk. "It's what you had to do." Like drag racing on empty country roads. "In football," he explained, "tackling can be a very scary thing. Racing your car was a similar kind of very masculine thing to do, and it was very scary. Very scary! But it's what you had to do. You had to prove yourself. That set in again a little later when I was a telephone man. I was scared to death of climbing those fucking telephone poles. Without a college degree I dropped out. My family needed money. I took a job as a telephone man and did it for a whole year. Including using those spike things you strap into your shoes. Terrifying. But I did it; it's a manly thing, then you have all this internal pride because you've managed to tamp down your fear."

Fear bore two faces: direct visceral fear of falling and breaking your neck, and fear that you might not be man enough to meet your family's needs. Though Dan described the second fear in vital working-class terms as his father's health had begun to fail, the psychological literature is rich with the confessions of young lawyers and rising corporate executives who hold no particular attraction to their work. They excel solely to demonstrate their "professional virility," still no better exemplified than by Budd Schulberg's *What Makes Sammy Run?*, the popular rags-to-riches story of Sammy Glick, an ambitious Lower East Side Jewish immigrant boy who must both demolish the image of the emasculated Jewish victim and propel his family into the American success myth—all of it a barely veiled portrait of Schulberg's real father, the Hollywood mogul B. P. Schulberg. Sammy lies, cheats, and steals his way to the top, bedding starlets and a banker's daughter and even hires the Lower East Side tough that in childhood used to beat him up as his personal fixer. Libido and demonstration of libido are inseparable from money and power, as they famously became decades later with Donald Trump's rants about the normalcy of forced sex in Hollywood and the U.S. military.

Only by exposing themselves to dangerous, risky challenges were Dan or men like Sammy Glick and Donald Trump able to prove themselves to others . . . and to themselves. Whether it's a function of evolutionary development or inherent genetic disposition, a growing body of psychological research suggests that risk and masculinity have long been intimately intertwined. The convenient cliché often repeated in the popular media recalls early man as the tribal hunter and early woman as the nurturing gardener. Large amounts of archaeological and ethnographic research have shown us significant flaws in that outlook. Females across the mammalian panorama have frequently been the toughest and most effective tribal hunters, while many males have excelled as primary litter keepers and gatherers. Social and religious barriers to both training and employment have also skewed the gender balance in risky work—from life savers to military marksmanship—where male muscles play only minor roles. Nonetheless, the propensity for risk taking does at the moment appear to be a masculine hallmark. British psychologists Geoff Trickey and So Yi Yeung took three years to survey business leadership styles among two thousand individuals in twenty occupational sectors across four continents. Presenting their work to the British Psychological Society in 2012, they concluded that men are far more prone to make risky decisions than are women in equivalent positions—very often to the detriment of their companies or organizations. Referring to early humans' survival threats, Trickey declared, "It's easy to see how the balance between prudent, cautious, long-term decision-making of females would have married up very effectively with the impulsive, carefree, adventurous approach of males."

MRI scanning of adolescent brains has also suggested that the earlier development of girls' prefrontal cortexes, the part of the brain thought to be most important in reasoned decision-making, may lead them to take fewer obvious risks than boys. At the same time the notion of risk itself is very frequently fuzzy. Cornell University developmental psychologist Valerie Reyna distinguishes between known and unknown risks when she studies adolescent risk behavior. Adolescents of both sexes, she found, are more risk averse when they are aware of possible negative outcomes, and indeed they may even overestimate negative outcomes. Yet all adolescents, but especially boys, appear to be less hesitant to take risks when the outcomes are murky and the rewards promise excitement. On average, boys—and to a lesser extent adult men—tend to be innately curious about unknown futures and open to taking risks solely in the pursuit of discovery. The same also appears to be true of adolescent laboratory rats and mice where young males tend to be more exploratory and compete for territory.

Risk-taking, of course, brings both penalties and rewards. Stresses associated with risk taking are directly associated with a variety of the illnesses that men suffer more than women. But at the same time, as Susan Pinker illustrates in *The Sexual Paradox*, men far more often land at the extreme ends of the curve on a broad array of measures—or, more plainly stated, men are much more likely to be exceptionally stupid or exceptionally bright on most measures of intelligence. An oft-cited IQ ranking of eighty thousand Scottish schoolchildren born in 1921 demonstrated more or less equivalent intelligence between girls and boys. However, while most kids' scores clustered in the middle, boys were far more represented at both the lowest and the highest IQ quartiles. Parallel and more recent data compiled in the United States by the Scholastic Aptitude Test consistently confirms that old Scottish test. Pinker doesn't fail to acknowledge the obvious societal barriers that block bright women from succeeding in such traditionally male territories as physics, engineering, and high-tech design. Nor does she hesitate to note men's propensity to undertake extreme risk either in the research laboratory or in the marketplace. But when she began speaking to psychologists and social scientists about these apparently innate differences between the sexes, she found doors quickly slamming in her face, and her phone calls went unanswered. Intimations of inferiority and superiority in matters of intelligence, like the parallel evidence on readiness to undertake risk, provoke intense anxiety in an era when gender equality has become nearly an article of faith among right-thinking people.

There are other caveats never to be forgotten as well in assessing shifting gender differences. Until very recently, girls in junior high and high school have been regularly steered away from the sort of preparatory classes in mathematics that are generally essential for success in the new and very risky world of high-tech start-ups. (See Chapter 15.) Similarly, until the last quarter century very few women were ever admitted into leading European or American business schools, and the senior professors in those schools remain overwhelmingly male. Only since the turn of the century have women begun to edge men aside in student management classes or in the hard sciences. Several more decades will likely pass before we can know whether the projected preponderance of women in public and private management will alter the gender profiles that distinguish male and female risk taking. One peculiar indicator, however, has emerged: the incidence of peptic ulcers. The two largest recent studies of ulcer incidence between men and women were conducted in Denmark and Southern California toward the end of the last century. In each case, men's susceptibility to ulcers was significantly higher than women's, as is true for cancer and cardiovascular diseases. But graphed over time, men's ulcer diagnoses have slowly and steadily declined while peptic ulcers among women continue to increase.

CHAPTER 6
Gender War

While the image of the wandering, insatiable uterus haunted the offspring of the secular Enlightenment well into our parents' middle age, today's gender battles are wandering toward a world divided over continuous gender transition, and the roots of the battle reach far deeper. The traces of ancient gender eclecticism reveal themselves in hieroglyphs and stone monuments from southern India to the Mayan highlands, but today's two great monotheist religions—Islam and Catholic Christianity—continue to insist on a fundamental cleavage between the genders, each underwritten by unyielding male supremacy. In the Islam of Malaysia, southwestern Russia, and parts of the Middle East, male hegemony is so absolute that women accused of "aberrant" behavior continue to be subjected to the lash far more often than men. Yet it is in the cradle of Western civilization, Rome, that the largest force of Christian expression continues its absolute embrace of male domination—expressed in softer language than that regularly used by hard-line Islamicists, but very little different in its essence.

Official Catholic doctrine on gender remains what Pope Benedict XVI articulated in his 2012 Christmas message fiercely denouncing any notion that either sex or gender should vary from the dictums of the Old Testament. "The profound falsehood of this [gender] theory and of the anthropological revolution contained within it is obvious. People dispute the idea that they have a nature, given by their bodily identity, which serves as a defining element of the human being. They deny their nature and decide that it is not something previously given to them, but that they make it for themselves. According to the biblical creation account, being created by God as male and female pertains to the essence of the human creature. This duality is an essential aspect of what being human is all about, as ordained by God. This very duality as something previously given is what is now disputed. The words of the creation account: 'male and female he created them' (Genesis 1:27) no longer apply."

Benedict's position is clear and unequivocal and while his successor, Pope Francis, has softened his language on the roles of men and women, his fundamental gender message has not changed—either in regard to women's access to the priesthood or to divorce, same-sex marriage, or transsexuality. Indeed the violence committed against women and sexual minorities in predominantly Catholic countries remains as intense today as in many Islamic nations. Mexico, while offering protection and recognition of transsexual people and same-sex marriage in its capital, ranks sixteenth in the world, according to Human Rights Watch, in the level of violence committed against women. In upwards of 60 percent of marriages in Mexico, depending on the state, women are frequently beaten. The Vatican, of course, regularly denounces any form of domestic violence, but human rights workers argue that it is the underlying teaching of the church in the light of the gender equality movement that continues to fuel what can only be seen as an intensifying gender war.

The drumbeats of that war are by no means limited to poor and third world nations where the Vatican's troops go largely unchallenged—as evidenced by the *Manif Pour Tous* in February 2014, cited earlier, led by the archbishop of Lyon, Philippe Barbarin. Barbarin is no church simpleton. He holds advanced degrees in philosophy and psychology, was born in Morocco, and has come to be deeply involved with France's far-right Catholics in their campaign to ban birth control, abortion, and same-sex marriage. This time, however, their target was not abortion but something they saw as an even greater threat to humanity: gender theory. These *intégrist*, or fundamentalist, Catholics drew their energy directly from Pope Benedict's preaching and writings. Though officially secular, France at its cultural roots remains Catholic. Seventy-five percent of French adults have been baptized by a Catholic priest even though church attendance hovers around 10 percent.

"When your house is on fire, you don't ask each fireman to show his identity card," remarked Béatrice Bourges, the effective organizer of the

Manif demonstration and its umbrella group, *Printemps Français*, or French Spring, a not so subtle mockery of the Arab Spring demonstrations four years earlier. Bourges, a child of France's colonial past in Algeria with close connections to the French oil industry, rose steadily as an advisor to former president Nicolas Sarkozy's conservative UMP party. A divorced Catholic no less and mother of two, she drew herself steadily closer to France's small but increasingly vocal religious extreme right, including the notorious *Action Française*, which had not only supported the collaborationist Vichy regime during World War II but was founded during the Dreyfus Affair in support of French anti-Semitism. *Action Française* continues to deny the legitimacy of the French Revolution, calls for the restoration of a symbolic monarchy, and remains militantly opposed to France's separation of church and state.

Church teachings about gender have led to a state of near panic in many sectors of France, especially in working-class suburbs, where unemployment can run as high as 50 percent and a general anxiety about Muslim immigration grows more intense by the month. The morning daily *Libération* published a collection of anxious comments soon after the Manif demonstration from parents across the nation:

— (Caen) I live in Caen and my children are in a private school and saw *The Kiss of the Moon* [an animated film] that presents all sexual orientations. But two men together, it's not the same as a man and a woman.

— (Seine-Saint-Denis) What bothers us is that the National education wants to kidnap our kids, take them into a pre-determined kind of family . . . Our children belong to us and to themselves. My girls don't feel inferior to the boys. Gender is not a social construction.

— (Seine-et-Marne) My son was telling me about all this, he was born biologically a boy, he told me, "it's not gender he's searching for but a place in society." We're headed toward something very serious, where kids are going to be deeply troubled; they're going to question what they are . . .

— (Noisy-le-Grand) School exists to teach kids how to count, to read and to write . . . My boy likes to play football and now they're going to stop him and teach him to tap dance and jump rope.

— (Suburban Paris) When I received this SMS, I was not at all surprised because France is changing—worse and worse.

> Marriage for homosexuals has already become law despite most people's opposition; today they want to teach kids anything. What's next? They're going to tell kids that God doesn't exist?
>
> — (Paris) The government is completely crazy and lies to the people ... Right now everything is normal, but with the first doubt I'll keep my kids at home and if I see that gender theory is introduced ...

The alarms came not only from conservative prelates but also from poor and working-class parents who were racial minorities, and who had received anonymous text messages on their portable phones spreading rumors about the imposition of "gender theory" in their children's classrooms. For many it was the first time they had ever heard about or read the phrase, just as they had never been exposed to the dense philosophical tomes of writers like Simone de Beauvoir, Michel Foucault, or Judith Butler that form the bedrock upon which contemporary gender discourse is based. The leadership of the Manif movement was not, however, terribly interested in sponsoring community seminars for parents to tease out shifting notions of gender, sexuality, identity, and equality—any more than they were willing to expel the even fringier ultra-ultras from their ranks who had taken to the streets a week earlier calling for the expulsion of Jews and for homosexuals to be burned at the stake.

Hardly a week had passed after the march before Bourges and the other Manif leaders, thrilled with their success in the streets and having provoked withdrawal of a new family law concerning adoptions, launched an even angrier multi-prong attack. The conservative Catholic group *Civitas*, allied with the reactivated *Action Française*, blasted the Franco-German public television service ARTE for airing the 2011 film *Tomboy*, which recounts the story of a young girl who dresses like a boy and plays boys' sports. *Tomboy*, they said, was advancing "gender ideology." An ad hoc group of sixty conservative members of Parliament announced an investigation of "gender ideology" in the schools and denounced "gender theory" as a degradation of the human body based on "an ideology fabricated in America and imported into French schools." Still more broadly, Béatrice Bourges's group launched an attack on the kind of children's books stocked in school and neighborhood libraries. High on their target list were *Tango a deux papas* ("Tango Has Two Daddies"), *Jean a deux mamans* ("Jean Has Two Mamas"), *Tous à poil* ("Everybody Naked"), and *Mademoiselle Zazi a-t-elle un Zizi* ("Does Miss Zazi Have a Pipi?"). All these short kids' books are well known in French kindergarten and primary schools—and they score high on French Amazon's list of children's book sales. *Tous à poil* led the Amazon list in 2013. Parents were urged to overwhelm libraries and schools with daily phone calls and to survey the book shelves daily. Rumors ran rampant. Six-year-olds would be taught how to masturbate. Playtime would pressure boys to dress like girls and girls to act like boys. Boys would be forced to cut out paper dolls. Girls would be taught to play with trucks and become neo-Soviet mechanics. Behind this new reform, the warnings suggested, lurked a secret cabal of lesbian and gay propagandists who were not merely bent on destroying the foundations of family but were planning to launch a state-sponsored biotech program to reengineer the fundamentals of human biology much as Monsanto and its multinational allies were propagating their genetically engineered pantry.

Bourges and her comrades saw them all as emblematic of France's deepening moral degradation, symbolized by broad public acceptance of homosexual relationships and the changing perception of gender identity. As Bourges said to one of the few, generally rightist, journalists with whom she agreed to talk, "gender theory" is "a threat to humanity." By gender theory, she was referring to the view, credited to American feminists but in fact first articulated a half century earlier by Simone de Beauvoir, that one is "not born a woman, one becomes a woman" through the influence of society. For a person who would only identify her profession as chief officer of a commercial venture, Béatrice Bourges's statement seemed odd for someone who insisted that she is not on the radical fringe. Radical fringes, of course, shift through time. Conventional, mainstream notions of men's and women's roles in the nineteenth century, even among France's most revered liberal philosophers, would today be seen as rank misogyny. Hardly a one of the eighteenth-century Enlightenment thinkers imagined giving women the franchise. A half century ago, open same-sex parenting would have drawn prosecution for child abuse, while today it is priests who are more likely to be so prosecuted. Bourges draws deeply on classic Catholic teaching and metaphysics, which is internally profoundly logical and consistent. Gender and the roles assigned to one gender or another, as they see it, are neither fungible nor a function of human invention or construction. They are the immutable gifts of God—and therefore same-sex desire and marriage can only be understood as perverse betrayals of God's gift.

Gender battles, however much they may clothe themselves in the trappings of current-day politics, are essentially metaphysical. They cut to the core of what traditionalist Catholics understand as the relationship of the human soul to the human body, and the individual body as the basis of individual rights. That sacred essence, which Bourges calls "humanity," therefore derives not from individual human choice or action. It arrives as a gift, or in some versions an infusion, from God in the form of the individual soul at the moment of conception; it is as inviolable as the sun and the stars. Biological sex, determined visually or in utero by ultrasound, is a fixture of that sacred essence. Discriminatory actions do exist in that cosmology. Traditional believers, unlike secularists, understand such discrimination as rooted in the eternal spirit; for them a rejection of one's God-given form is an insult to the sacred soul as much as it is to the body. The bodies of men and women are nothing less than sacred, living receptacles, the actual manifestations of God's handiwork. Consequently the notion of creating "the New Man" or "the New Woman," whether framed in Marxist language from the Communist era or in the language of science and libertarianism, represents more than an insult to the human body: It constitutes a frontal assault on "God's body" and all that is sacred.

Gender theory insists on the absolute opposite. In a secular society dissociated from religion, the language of rights relies exclusively on individual and group freedoms that are formulated and negotiated collectively. The rights of man and woman in secular metaphysics are never "God given." God is nothing but an idea created by man; rights—or protection against stereotypes—are "sacred" only in the sense that free democratic debate, discovery, and negotiation are "sacred" to the creation of a free society.

Abstract and theoretical as the metaphysics may seem when set against bullhorns and banner waving, the metaphysical surfaces quickly and often in direct human encounters: The most obvious in my life took place when I was called for my physical examination for the military draft during the Vietnam War. It was a February day in Detroit. Several hundred boy-men between eighteen and twenty years old had been ordered by the Army examiners to strip to their briefs and carry their clothes in a bag. We stood in long serpentine lines in a huge and not very warm National Guard armory. Most of us were students looking for any possible justification not to pass our physicals. Many carried dubious doctors' notes attesting to physical or psychological maladies that they hoped would exclude them from service. Some of the guys would be inducted that very day and sent off to basic training before being dispatched to the deadly jungles of Vietnam. Others of us, still in university, were forming other evasion strategies. As I approached the table of military medical examiners, one tall, skinny boy just ahead of me addressed the chief examiner.

"I'm gay," he said.

Being homosexual normally resulted in immediate rejection, but the medical examiner was tough. He looked the shivering boy up and down, and in a voice loud enough for everyone to hear, asked, "Are you saying you're a homosexual?"

"Yes, sir, I am a homosexual."

The examiner pushed his face forward and narrowed his eyes.

"Don't you know that your body is God's temple?" he nearly shouted to be sure we all could hear. "If you are a homosexual you are profaning God's temple!"

"I am homosexual," the boy repeated, images of falling into the monsoon mud surely more powerful than the risk of being thrown into a lake of eternal fire. The military examiner continued to spit out vile insults, but finally he marked the examination card 4-F—Not Qualified for Military Service.

Assuming that the examiner was not merely using bullying tactics, he surely believed that the young man before him was committing the same sort of assault against God that Pope Benedict XVI and the French *Manif Pour Tous* leader Béatrice Bourges cited almost fifty years later: Secular gender freedom could only be understood as "a war against humanity." Or worse. If the rumors were true that the French education ministry intended to create a new curriculum aimed at converting boys into girls and girls into boys; if same-sex married women could ask science to help them create babies; and if married gay men could fly to Texas and California and openly purchase human eggs made by God, then inject them with sperm and hire women to bear those fertilized eggs—then the whole gender tech enterprise had elevated the idea of creating "the New Man" to unprecedented heights. Divine creation would be replaced by living robots devoid of soul. Little surprise, then, their shock, their panic, and ultimately their rage at finding primary schools stocked with handsomely illustrated books raising questions about whether little girls can have penises or whether little boys and girls might have two mothers.

Their rage and their militance led them to spread out across France and beyond—although, mostly with the aid of the Vatican, they concentrated on predominantly Catholic lands. They demanded the withdrawal of so-called "gender theory" books, or failing that, their followers were advised to steal and destroy the books. Yet if these fundamentalist Catholic militants were driving the campaign against gender studies, gender research, and more broadly "gender freedom," they were not the only people pushing their baby strollers through the battering winter wind of that February afternoon in 2014. Many who joined the *Manif Pour Tous* demonstration were not at all religious—at least not in conventional terms. For them God remained far away in his heaven. These secular opponents saw artificial insemination of same-sex lesbian couples and surrogate maternity for same-sex husbands as an affront to Nature—with a capital N. Likewise any notion that gender itself—the way we act as boys and girls, men and women—is a social construction or a result of centuries of social habit simply denied the law of "the birds and the bees." For them all the gender babble constituted a betrayal of Natural Law.

Natural Law is a remote concept for most contemporary Americans. If it's discussed at all in school, Natural Law is usually traced to the Founders, not least the Deist Thomas Jefferson, author of the Declaration of Independence: "We hold these truths to be self-evident, that all men are created equal, that they are endowed by their Creator with certain inalienable rights, that among these are Life, Liberty and the pursuit of Happiness." Or, more simply, our fundamental rights are inscribed in our nature as human beings.

Partisans of Natural Law—including many contemporary biologists—reach much further into the past. For the most part they do not draw directly on religious doctrine even though the term "Natural Law" dates back to the thirteenth-century Dominican Thomas Aquinas or still earlier to Aristotle's argument that all beings and all objects in the universe possess a specific function and that the job of human reason is to discern the laws that govern that function. Aquinas, as much philosopher as theologian, following Aristotelian logic, saw Nature as the expression of divine creation. He concluded that by studying Nature's forms and underlying laws scientifically, man would come into the presence of God. The understanding of scientific method in the thirteenth century surely bears little semblance to how we perform science today, but it did demand patient, detailed observation of the natural world. (Several centuries later the Austrian School of Economics would employ the same approach in arguing that certain inescapable "laws" of rational human behavior reveal the unvarnished, and mostly unregulated, market as the foundation of human good.) Natural Law, in itself and at its best, sidesteps the origins of things or references to the divine. Like the Austrian economists, Natural Law proponents look to Nature and extract immutable underlying "laws," applying all the tools of contemporary physics, chemistry, and biology. As Texas philosopher and theologian Janet Smith writes, "Natural law operates on the premise that nature is good . . . it holds that the operations of things and parts of things contribute to the good of the whole. The wings of different birds are shaped in certain fashions because of the particular sort of flying that they must do to survive; different digestive systems work in different ways because of what each creature eats and must digest. Indeed, natural law holds that the natural instincts of natural things are good."

Nothing is more important to Natural Law than the process and function of sexual reproduction. Humans, being a part of nature, are therefore also subject to Natural Law—with the exception that we have the apparent capacity to exercise free will and therefore to "disobey" or "ignore" the law much like drivers who drink too much or exceed speed limits. Regarding sexual reproduction, Natural Law begins with short, detailed observation. Since the sexual organs of male and female mammals appear to have evolved to be joined with each other, and each primate species's sexual organs have evolved somewhat differently, their natural purpose must be used exclusively for procreation. Janet Smith, however, goes still farther. She asserts that we human animals derive more than species survival from sexual union: Sexual union also provides humans emotional bonding and mutual fulfillment. (She does not speak of sexual fulfillment among other animals, though naturalists have carefully documented multiple sorts of sexual fulfillment among other species and in manners unrelated to procreation; nor does she acknowledge the emotional bonding and fulfillment that comes with the various forms of homosexual union.) There lies the crux of the Natural Law opposition to nonconventional marriage among the genders as well as an assumed biological opposition to same-gender procreation and child rearing. If Nature had been designed for women to procreate without men, or men without women, their procreative organs would not have evolved in the forms that they have. But Smith does not stop even there. Contraception as well, she declares, is "one of the great evils of modern times." Contraception is responsible for promoting a sexual revolution that has led to "millions of babies born out of wedlock, millions of divorces, tens of thousands dying of AIDS." All these grim realities, she argues, are the consequence of contraception, which in effect acts as an "abortifacient" within the woman's body, causing her not to release the egg or to render it impermeable to the sperm by coating it in mucus—neither of which is natural to the body. Finally, she argues, barrier contraceptives—condoms or vaginal screens—block the essential union that is equal in emotional importance to the reproductive function.

She takes the case of a heterosexual couple who want to make love but must first be sure their "barriers" are in place. Those barriers may be a spermicide to kill the sperm as it approaches the ova or a physical device to prevent fertilization. Either way it promotes discord, she argues, saying in effect, "I want to love you and give myself to you and to receive you, but I want to kill any sperm that may penetrate my being." Is there not a discordant note of hostility now in an act that is meant to be a loving act? she asks. Does not the rejection of one's beloved's fertility also mean a rejection of one's beloved as well, at least to some extent? All of contraception, she insists, says, "I want to give myself to you and to receive you but I reject completely your fertility; it is not welcome here."

Were Margaret Sanger still alive, Smith would surely have campaigned for a new prosecution against her for fomenting all the presumed abuses of gender that birth control, and particularly the pill, have let loose.

Karol Wojtyła (later Pope John Paul II), Smith notes, spoke even more directly to his Catholic adherents about an essential betrayal provoked by contraception because it is through the sex act that we "make ourselves whole by giving ourselves to another . . . an act that is meant to express the deep commitment and desire for union that we feel and wish to express." Any attempt to "thwart the fertility of the sexual act means that one is withholding one's fertility from the other—one is withholding something that belongs in the sexual act." If contraception equals subversion and betrayal of Natural Law in human relations, it follows by the same Natural Law logic that a mechanical intervention aimed at creating fertility between two humans who together are infertile must surely then violate "Nature" even more violently since the simplest observation of animals demonstrates that coitus between two members of the same gender can never be reproductive. In each case Natural Law is subverted and betrayed through what most moderns now regard as the strained logic Thomas Aquinas brought to his students at the University of Paris.

Natural Law arguments owe their pedigree to Aquinas, but their "logic" continues to reach far beyond the Catholic faithful and, not always consciously, into the discomfort and suspicion that permeates New Age and other secular objectors to the use of laboratory science and technology for procreation within and between genders. Many of the placards carried by non-Catholics at the *Manif Pour Tous* demonstration proclaimed that the proposed family reforms pervading Europe constitute a "war against humanity." One Parisian friend I've known for decades, an American whom I'll call E, has spent half her life in France. She identifies with no conventional religious practices. She abhorred the Manif "fachos" and she has built a wide following for her own quasi-pagan objects and rituals; nonetheless she expressed deep discomfort with what she described as the medicalized technology used by same-sex parents. "It feels creepy to me," E began. She was not speaking about the notion of lesbian or gay male couples raising children; she claimed several of each among her friends and even to have helped two of them become parents. What upset her was the sterile hospital setting for extracting ovaries from a woman, fertilizing them in a laboratory, and reimplanting the fertilized ovary in the donor or in another woman—described as ART (Artificial Reproductive Technology) by the U.S. Centers for Disease Control. The CDC reported more than 160,000 ART inseminations in 2011, resulting in nearly 62,000 live births. The numbers are roughly parallel in the European Union while in France, with about one fifth the population of the United States, some 50,000 babies are born each year through one form or another of artificial insemination.

By contrast E recounted the story of a woman named Christmas whom she had known in California in the 1970s. Christmas took it upon herself to help lesbian couples have babies. There were at that time few hospitals or clinics willing to provide, or capable of providing, ovarian fertilization. "Christmas would talk to the women and then interview a range of (usually gay) men who were willing to contribute their sperm. She would find out about the men's health, their personalities, how they lived and how they felt about sharing their sperm. I don't know how she collected the sperm, but after deciding on one or another man and presenting that information to the women, they would choose. Once she had the sperm, she would take it to the women and they really would use a plastic turkey baster to fertilize the woman who wanted to get pregnant. It didn't always work right away, but the women did eventually get pregnant. I knew several." Turkey-baster babies became something of a hip phrase in seventies-era lesbian circles—as well as with straight couples who couldn't get pregnant. E contrasts her sense of the "natural circle of human warmth" in those pregnancy procedures with the cold technological methods currently being used in fertility clinics. Further, she believes that "the body has its own natural biological memories and that all has an effect on those first very few cells that form the zygote. If there's been anger or violence, the body knows that and the mother's body's response to all that is going to affect the magic of how those first few cells join together to make a new person . . . This science and technology might be what you have to do, but it's going to have an effect on how that child develops and grows into a person." E does not use the language of Natural Law. She believes that each person's perception of what is "natural" may vary across time and place and cultural circumstance, but she is convinced of the evil of the sterile methods used in fertility clinics. She regards sterile fertility clinics as a subversion of ancient indigenous rituals used by traditional North American Indians or premodern Chinese that rely on collective celebration, drum beating, and vocal chanting that were once used to encourage fertility between couples. (And indeed outlandish as her notions may seem to many moderns, there is fair evidence that joyous communitarian celebration may have positive effects on hormone expression that in some cases can affect successful ovarian fertilization.)

While E has no use for Catholic-based Natural Law, she and many thousands like her feel profound distress over the cold laboratory mechanics and straightforward commerce in sperm and eggs that has replaced "natural process" in reproduction. Where that diversity of distress will go is far from certain. But throughout Europe or America wherever marriage has been legalized between two women, human rights law and equal protection provisions have become extremely clear. A fertility procedure available to women in one marriage cannot be denied to women in another marriage. There in the dark core of the fertile womb arises a deeper and wider protest that has stretched beyond the ranks of the French Manif demonstrators or philosophical treatises on Natural Law. Even among many who say they actively support same-gender weddings, when gender freedom and flexibility touch child rearing and schooling, resistance continues to find a fierce voice.

The principal problem with all the calls to gender traditions, especially when they refer to "Natural Law," is the complexity of biological reality. Even those who do not draw on religion for their distrust of gender equality very often rely on what they assume to be universal instinct separating maternal and paternal roles. One thoroughly open-minded male architect, the young father of two children, explained at great length why he believed inevitable problems would arise from two males rearing a child. "Females have more patience," he insisted, referring not only to dogs, cats, and wild creatures of the forest. "It's in their nature," he told me. Had he taken a course from one of France's world-renowned biologists, Frank Cézilly, at the University of Burgundy, he might have framed his argument differently. "Whenever I hear people talking about 'natural order,' I become exasperated with their ignorance," Cézilly said in a 2014 interview. "Political leaders ought to study a bit more the sciences, especially biology and sex. You cannot invoke Nature as the basis of human behavior. For if you do, then you might as well legalize infanticide too since certain animal species practice that! But seriously, these days when we very often hear references to what is supposed to be 'natural' it's very often a cover for people who oppose marriage and adoption for everybody." Cézilly then went on to describe his many years tracking "paternal instinct" across a broad array of bird and animal species, including seagulls and penguins, where the males are the fundamental caregivers of their young and the females mostly disappear, often engaging in multi-partner sex to produce more eggs that will be hatched and nurtured by groups of males. Among pink flamingos, males and females share incubation duties and both exude a nutritive white milky fluid to their young; the males of a certain cousin of the wild turkey gather tons of sand, earth, and leaves in which they bury the females' fertilized eggs until they hatch. In at least five species of toads the males are the ones that carry the fertilized eggs of female toads to gestation in a breast pouch. Cézilly has tracked a species of long-eared fox in which, after initial lactation, the females disappear and the males take over all the nurturing duties for their young.

In the human domain, Barry Hewlett, an anthropologist at Washington State University, spent time living with the Aka Pygmy people of Central Africa whose child-rearing methods are testament to a profound fluidity in the perception and performance of male and female roles. Aka men and women divide infant nurturing almost equally—even to the extent that the males succor their infants to calm them down at night while the women succor them for nutrition. "There is a sexual division of labor in the Aka community," he told a journalist for the *Guardian* newspaper, but, he emphasized, "there's a level of flexibility that's virtually unknown in our society. Aka fathers will slip into roles usually occupied by mothers without a second thought and without, more importantly, any loss of status—there's no stigma involved in the different jobs." Still more fascinating, endocrinologists during the last two decades have demonstrated the presence of primary hormonal changes in *both* sexes during the early years of child rearing. A large-scale longitudinal study of Philippine families conducted by Lee Gettler and his colleagues at Northwestern University have tracked heightened levels of prolactin, a protein necessary for stimulating lactation, in both fathers and mothers of newborns. Both parents increase their production of prolactin during early nurturing of children just as male testosterone levels decrease.

For French biologist Frank Cézilly, the message is clear: The natural world is replete with gender models of procreation and infant nurturing. While he acknowledges that among most mammals, females are the predominant nurturers, parental roles vary widely across the "natural" world as well as among humans—rendering calls to "Natural Law" increasingly ill-founded and meaningless.

Nature, a good friend who is a specialist in eighteenth-century thought has often reminded me, is the all-purpose excuse for defending both the status quo and revolutionary change. Nineteenth-century Romantics, like the poet Robert Browning, author of, among other works, the verse drama "Pippa Passes," found solace watching the lark on the wing in the dew-dropped glen follow her "natural destiny" far from God's intervention. The great French liberal Rousseau, like Aristotle, saw nothing wrong with denying women the right to vote or own property since, in their view, the law of Nature gave to females the roles of propagators and nurturers. Equally those who see in Nature the steady replacement of one life system by another, a socialized version of Darwinian succession, continually seek to redefine and reinterpret the roles of one gender or another assigned to humans across the millennia—each version fabricated and justified as the true reality for its own time.

PART III

Family Values: New Realities, New Complexities

CHAPTER 7

Start at the Very Beginning . . .

Birgitta sits at the head of a wooden lunch table. Two little girls are at either side of her. Three excited, raucous boys sit and stand a little farther down the table.

"I'm older than you are!" shouts one towheaded boy.

"No, I'm FOUR," retorts another on the other side.

"I'm four and a half," proclaims a third boy, supremely confident.

One of the little girls taps the teacher's elbow to get her attention but gets no response as the teacher tries to calm the boys a bit.

"Teacher, we're missing a knife," the first little girl says softly, but Birgitta, focused on the raucous boys, touches her arm gently and says, "Shush." The two girls draw their heads in toward their shoulders for a moment. One of them gets up and disappears; she returns a moment later with two lunch plates. Then the second girl follows suit, heading to the kitchen to bring in two more plates. All the children are between three and five years old.

The whole episode was captured on video. The first time I watched it, I didn't know what to think. So? Some kids are loud and aggressive and others aren't. People are different. I asked to view it a second time. Clearly the bigger, louder boy to the teacher's left was the domineering child and occupied most of the teacher's attention. When the video had run most of the way through a second time, I asked for a short rewind. Then something became clear. Both of the little girls had persistently tried to get the teacher's attention, and when they failed, they did what little girls typically do. They went to "the kitchen," as all the children were supposed to do, came back, and began setting the table for lunch. Girls work. Boys play. Girls sit quietly. Boys talk loudly.

The video has become famous in Norway, or at least famous among early childhood educators who argue that our most fundamental—and highly gendered—roles, attitudes, and assumptions are formed in the earliest years of our lives. The video and many others are key parts of a program that Norway's network of fifty-six non-profit kindergartens, called Kanvas, uses to train their teachers to become aware of how they are unconsciously imprinting gender expectations on children at a very early age—and how that unconscious imprinting meets or conflicts with Norway's fundamental commitment to gender equality between the sexes. If you want to genuinely change the society, they insist, you must start at the very beginning.

Gender equality in the workplace and in government has been law in both Norway and Sweden for decades, and along with Iceland and Finland the four nations top the World Economic Forum's ranking of gender equality among nations. That, however, does not mean that men and women have achieved equity in upper business management, on corporate boards, or in governance there. But gender equality in Scandinavia—and even in Ireland and the Philippines—ranks vastly higher than in the rest of Europe or in the United States, all of which have gender equality rules inscribed in national law. Indeed, even in Norway, as noted earlier, women in the top professions still earn from 25 to 30 percent less than do men with equivalent training and experience.

Pia Friis has worked with kindergarten children most of her life and also manages one of the Kanvas kindergartens in Oslo. She, like Robert Ullmann, the Kanvas Foundation's CEO, sees establishing real gender equality as a long-term, multigenerational proposition that can only be realized if it begins in children's earliest years. She has designed several internal research projects evaluating Kanvas's methods and pedagogical techniques, most of them focused on how teachers unconsciously reinforce gender stereotypes among children. It was at our first meeting in downtown Oslo that she played the video of Birgitta and the three loud boys and two rather timid girls.

The lesson Friis and the teacher Birgitta (who knew she was being taped) drew from the short video was plain: Like many teachers she hadn't realized how easy it is for adults to reinforce traditional roles between boys and girls. "We see that the girls have to shut up and help put the food on the table because if not, there will not be any food," Friis pointed out, adding, "Then the teacher serves the boys first. The boys learn they can get all the attention about who they are. Being loved for who they are is very selfish. The girls have to be quiet and help and do the work. So one of our basic questions always is how do boys and girls LEARN to be boys and girls in these situations?"

The following day at the Myrer Kanvas kindergarten I spoke with Birgitta, who some years later still remembered the episode clearly. "I didn't think I'd encouraged the boys to take so much room and left the girls behind," she said. "When one of the girls asked me if I could get something in the kitchen and I said, yeah, just a minute. I didn't think so much about it then."

"Why not?" I asked.

"Because the boys with their loud voices take so much of the emotional room, and I think at that time I was thinking about keeping it calm and keeping the boys under control."

Birgitta also noticed the nonverbal cues she had been sending with body language.

"I think I was more open to the boys the way I sat on the chair and the way I communicated. If you're talking to a boy, you sit more like this," she said, leaning forward and holding her shoulders back. "With the girls on sideline it was more like this," she said, relaxing her shoulders and glancing down. "Maybe the girls didn't have the same [emotional] space."

"But boys just are more physical, aren't they?" I asked.

She shook her head doubtfully. "Umm, in some ways, but some girls also are very physical. It's not black and white. With a lot of children at the table I was just focused on keeping it nice and calm."

There are no formal classes in the Kanvas kindergartens, but the teachers I met said that by the time the children turn six years old, nearly all of them understand English and Norwegian and many, depending upon their home backgrounds, can speak easily in both languages. How? I asked repeatedly. Through the games and close friendships the children form, they answer. The kindergartens are full of books, drawings, pictures, and letter charts, but the teachers never undertake organized instruction. If a child picks up a book and asks questions, there's always an adult ready to read it or explain it. When one or several children seem to want a break from the rough-and-tumble "soft gym" room, an adult will ask if they'd like to draw or read stories. But the central focus in the Kanvas schools is to follow the children's feelings, interests, and emotions—and never to assign them fixed desks or tables. Organized classes, they say, will come soon enough when they move on to primary school.

"We think today there's too much planning for children," said Rasmus, a young man who has two of his own children in Kanvas and directs another Kanvas kindergarten. He also conducts many of Kanvas's internal research programs. We were watching a troop of kids head out to walk in the forest nearby. Kanvas tries to send all the children, including the youngest, on forest hikes each week even during the coldest weeks of January and February. "When they come home it's television, or soccer, and with both parents working, the day is soon filled up. We believe the most important thing in kindergarten is having the space and the time to have a good childhood. So that means there's not so much adult planning. Adults should be where the children are, reading with them when the children want to read, so the children can also feel like they have their own life."

If it sounds like laissez-faire, anything goes, it's not. The Kanvas teachers seem to be far more engaged directly with the children than in, say, standard, often rigid French classrooms or even in the often highly structured American Head Start programs. The teachers, most of whom are under forty, and their full-time assistants, many of whom have no formal training, are expected to be triply alert—to what each child is doing, to how all the children are interacting or failing to interact with each other, and to their own body language and speech, all of it aimed at encouraging the children to become emotionally expressive.

"Here," Rasmus continued, "it's children being with other children, and our job is to support them, meeting their emotions. During the first six years they're only acting on their emotions. If they can express their inner feelings, it's important that adults be there with them on the ground and able to say, yeah, I can see what you want, I can feel your emotion now, so we must take them for real. This is the most important. Also, when they're having a difficult time, you can say, I see you're having a hard time, let me help you. And if they're having a hard time having friends, saying how can I help you make friends? Everybody needs a friend.

"Later in school, suddenly they must do what the adults want them to do. So if they're starting to ask, do I do this because the adults think it's good or because I think it's good, because I really like it? Going to the forest, yes, it's important. Reading, yes, it's important. Eating, yes, it's important. We do have some organized things, sitting together, like showing roles, doing role playing and talking about it. Teachers must have three things in our kindergarten: a good heart, a good knowledge about children, and good health."

Like most teaching approaches, the gender equality commitments in Scandinavia have developed their own terminologies. At the Kanvas schools, Pia Friis and Robert Ullmann speak about "gender acts" or the often unconscious ways in which adults say and do things that reflect certain gender assumptions. A gender act, Ullmann elaborated, "might be approaching a boy who is crying and saying, 'Oh, come on, that's not such a big problem, don't worry, you'll be fine' while picking up a girl [who is crying], putting her on your lap, and talking to her about how it feels when you hurt yourself. That takes away [the boy's] ability to get to know his feelings. And it will change girls' and boys' opportunities for the future."

What might be traditionally regarded as teaching children to be tough and self-reliant, Ullmann and the Kanvas teachers believe, too often sets social and psychological paradigms that both limit individual imagination and constrict men's and women's options later in life. "If you give the girl the opportunity to put words on her feelings," he said, "she will take that with her through the rest of her life. And if we interrupt the boys in the same act, they will learn from their role model that that is something we don't talk about. You block your feelings and that will go with you for the rest of your life—and this passes through generations."

(Some weeks later when I recounted Robert Ullmann's example to a French parent, she looked at me with wide eyes. "You can't do that in France [pick up the child and cuddle it]. It's forbidden to touch a child that way.")

One of the first kindergarten experiments Friis launched almost twenty years earlier directly challenged both the teachers' and the parents' notions about how to work with small children. Like preschools everywhere, very few Norwegian kindergartens employed men. Early childcare was almost automatically assumed to be "women's work," and there was an even broader assumption that women, by nature, were better adapted to caring for the young. Friis doubted both assumptions, but she had little data to support her notions. Her experiment was to put half the children exclusively with three male teachers in her school and to leave the other children with mixed male and female teachers.

Parental outcry was swift.

"How can I let my children only be with men?" she recalled them asking. "What if my daughter is tired? What if she falls down, how can she be pampered and be held? One mother said, 'I am pregnant with twins and my daughter is four years old, and when the twins are born, my daughter will need an extra mother in the kindergarten. How can she get that if there are only men working there?' Another said, 'It's an interesting idea but we don't like experimenting with our children.' Other people said, 'Why don't you put all the men across all the departments so they could all share the resources?' But we wanted to see if there was a difference . . . with the men, with the kids, and with the parents. We wanted to see if they [did] different activities during the day, whether they were painting pictures indoors or having a competition outside. What trips they went on. Where did they go? How did they use the rooms, how did they communicate with the parents and among them?"

As she recounted that long-ago teaching experiment, she harbored the slightest trace of a smile.

"The male parents especially asked if this was safe," Ullmann added, "to deliver my child to another man. That might seem crazy now, but that's how it was [in 1994]."

I asked if perhaps the parents weren't secretly afraid that the males would sexually abuse the children given the reports of near epidemic child abuse cases that began to surface in the 1990s. "No," Friis answered swiftly. "It was much more [what the men could do] if the children were sad or cried, their capability to show care, and to make the children feel comfortable. One mother said, 'Okay, if my child is three or four, but if my child is one year old, I wouldn't accept it.' They were thinking that women can do everything with children. They can care for them. *By their nature*. 'Maybe men can LEARN it,' they would say 'but women are born knowing how.'"

Friis worked for a year to prepare the parents, but then, just before the experiment was to begin, the Oslo city government got cold feet and cut off supplementary funding for the study, declaring it "too radical." But her school plunged ahead anyway with support from a sociology professor and a graduate student at Oslo University. Results of the study were at once surprising and predictable. "I found out the men were working very differently with the kids," she said. "For example, instead of standing up above the children, the men were always lying on the floor playing with the children. They were very, very relaxed but still fully attentive and very much in control. They also had other activities. They took an old model train system and put it together with the kids. They did technical, mechanical things." Or in short, the men felt more at ease reducing themselves to the children's eye level than the women teachers did.

But that was not the most startling difference. "The men also invited the parents to come to play [with the kids] once a week. *And nobody had done that ever before.* The parents were used to coming [to the school] for a meeting or for a talk or maybe to have a coffee. The fathers mostly thought, well, that is women's work. But when they came in there, they felt maybe that's my work too. I can do something here. It was an opener for the fathers to become more active in the kindergarten."

Another of the study's findings worried Friis. The men started initiating competitions with other groups of students in the school using the school's bicycles. "You know, women don't like competition. They think it's more important to join than to win." She rolled her eyes in self-mockery and laughed. But the men, they made it a competition between the different school departments, so that each group would want to be the best department in this kindergarten. Nobody had heard that before. I was very afraid what does it mean?"

"What were you afraid of?" I asked. "It's human to compete."

"I was worried that it would press the other children [the losers] down. That was my way of thinking then. I don't think that now."

"Don't forget," Ullmann added, "that men didn't exist in this kind of work at that time. The men teachers at Friis's school were almost the only men teaching in kindergartens in all of Norway at that time." Today the Norwegian education ministry has set a target of 20 percent male kindergarten teachers, while in 2014 Kanvas's Oslo schools' gender ratio was between 40 and 50 percent male. The trained kindergarten teachers also earn roughly $75,000 a year. Of the one thousand Kanvas employees, including administrators, two hundred are men. "That is thanks to Pia. She made that revolution with the research."

The Uptown neighborhood in Chicago is four thousand miles and seven time zones west of Oslo. There are no forests in a child's walking distance from the preschool at the South-East Asia Center, a childcare center where a young man named Jeff Daitsman teaches. It's also not clear how wise it would be to take small children on an outing there. Once mostly home to displaced Dust Bowl farmers and poor whites from Appalachia, the neighborhood's population was turning steadily Latino by the end of the twentieth century, seasoned by a growing sector of Asian immigrants. Drug deals are as common as crabgrass. Shootings and robberies are nearly as normal as sunrise over Lake Michigan. The reception desk in the hotel where my taxi dropped me was protected by bulletproof glass; a sitting room next to the lobby doubled as a drug rehab center. It was the lodging closest to the South-East Asia Center, where I was to meet Daitsman.

Daitsman has built a wide reputation for his work with a culturally diverse group of kids in a gender-neutral "curriculum." No law, no public curricular code, governs the way he approaches the preschool activities. There are "units" on diverse subjects as in any other preschool: transportation, agriculture, and health among others. There is nap time, play time, and something he calls "circle group," in which all the four-year-olds he "teaches" sit in a circle and are invited to make up stories, or, as they are formally described, "dictations." Daitsman sits on a kid's chair with his legs crossed to bring himself down to their eye level. He starts by only asking the author to give the title to the story. Then, before anyone has heard the story and there's only a list of characters, he moves around the circle looking for volunteers to play all the roles.

One of the girls' stories is called "Sleeping Bed."

> *One princess go to her house. She go with the airplane and then she hit her and then she run away from the monster. Who was sleeping and then she fall down.*

This story, he explained, was a kind of homage to a story told by another child. "In the original story the princess is scared by the monsters. In this story she runs away from the monster. We see the monster as a bigger threat because it's a violent attack and then she runs away." Often the kids use "he" and "she" interchangeably. Why? Is it because they don't understand gender? He had no clear answer. "In general they tend to use 'she' more than 'he.' It might just be the language ... an easier sound to produce, 'she' than 'he.'"

A little later another girl has a story:

> *Branden wants to play with me. My mom lost me. I live with somebody. We go to party by myself. Branden hits. Mom loves Branden.*

In this story no boy wants to play Branden, so a girl takes his role.

But that's not what intrigues Daitsman about the Branden story. The author's bringing out a lot of scary things. "'Mom lost me. Branden hits.' I know Branden," Daitsman says. "He's not a child that usually hits. I imagine her mom did not actually lose her. She's exploring some frightening possibilities in the world through fiction. The way people use to do with the big bad wolf or a monster."

Often enough boys ask to play a princess or girls want to play the dad or a monster. In another story that day, two different boys ask to play the role of a grandma and a sister.

Daitsman doesn't ask why the kids choose nonconventional gender roles. He simply lets them choose what they want to do. The reasons, he thinks, very often have nothing to do with gender perception but instead are about whether a character in a story is more or less interesting, has more or less importance in the narrative. Sometimes, he suspects, it's just about the seating arrangements and who gets asked first. The boys tend to sit together on one side of the circle and the girls on another. The narratives are all very short, usually not more than a minute each.

Conventional wisdom suggests that girls don't invent stories about superheroes and boys don't make up fairy tales. Daitsman's experience over several years is that all the kids tell tales about whatever interests them—when they're left to their own. One story from some years back was written by a child named Mary.

As time went by Mary began to get interested in princess stories, but still the heroes and bad guys didn't go away.

Bad Guys Bad Guys

by Mary 11/15/07

Once upon a time it was bad guys. And a fight. And then a big giant came. And then a monster camed. I pay the paper. I pay the paper. I don't have paper in my home. I have paper in my home. Jeff that one is run ink. And then a dinosaur camed. The pencil's inside. Huh? And then Elmo camed. And then THE END.

A week later Mary wrote a princess story, but still the bad guys hadn't gone away.

Sleeping Beauty

by Mary 11/21/07

Once upon a time it was Sleeping Beauty. And then went to the castle. And then it saw a monster. And a holding flowers. And then it saw a big Superman. And then it saw a bad guy. And then a Superman camed. And then a monster camed. And then a dinosaur camed. And THE END.

The same day she wrote "Sleeping Beauty," Mary asked to play the role of Santa Claus in a story written by a boy named Joshua. Then Joshua asked to play a girl's role in another story Mary had written, but she refused, insisting that the girl role had to be played by a girl—though for her own part she was as eager to play male roles as female roles.

Daitsman's use of the kids' own stories follows a well-developed tradition in early childhood education, drawing not least on Bruno Bettelheim's famous 1976 book *The Uses of Enchantment: The Meaning and Importance of Fairy Tales*. Bettelheim took a neo-Freudian approach to analyzing the importance of fairy tales to small children, arguing that the classic Grimm Brothers tales remained compelling long after wild wolves and evil kings and monsters had disappeared from contemporary culture because these mythic figures enable children to address their fears of injury and abandonment symbolically. Likewise for the stories that the kids make up in Daitsman's classes. In fact, he finds that the kids nearly always become more excited and engaged in stories made up by other children than when he asks them to play parts from children's books. And more, when they're encouraged to take on whatever roles they like, gender strictures largely disappear. It's the character of the characters—or sometimes just seating order—that draws them into the stories.

Daitsman's comfort with permitting, if not encouraging, gender fluidity is deeply influenced by the work of Vivian Gussin Paley, whose *Boys and Girls: Superheroes in the Doll Corner* and *The Boy Who Would Be a Helicopter* have taken on almost biblical importance in preschool classes. Early on as a kindergarten teacher Paley began encouraging her students to make up their own "dictations." She recounts scores of them in her books. In *Helicopter* Paley recounts two children's revisions of a classic African tale, "Hot Hippo," about a hippopotamus who asks the god Ngai for permission to go into the water to cool off. The all-powerful Ngai refuses Hot Hippo's request because Ngai fears the hippo will gobble up all the fish. The hippo promises not to eat Ngai's fish and Ngai permits him to go into the water to cool off. But two students in Paley's class made up new endings. A little boy named Joseph constructed a violent end: "Jump in the water, Hot Hippo, and eat the fish! I hate the fish! Eat up all the animals!" Disturbed by Joseph's version, his classmate Samantha altered it. But instead of merely recounting the story as a witness, Samantha became the hippo, and when she plunged into the water, the old god Ngai dropped dead and Hippo replaced him as the new god. "Hippo is the god of the whole everyone and no bothering is allowed," Samantha concluded.

Mythmaking and re-mythmaking and more re-mythmaking are critical elements in Paley's pedagogical approach, following Bettelheim's notions that childhood fables, whether passed down or newly created, enable children to work through their fantasies, their fears, and their hopes. More importantly, she argues, it's not just the story-making but the process through which small children play at the roles inside the stories that enables them to imagine a whole range of realities and futures for themselves. It is indeed the reverse of teaching boys to play with balls and trucks and girls with dolls and make-believe kitchens. Both boys and girls, when left to their own devices, are likely to play all the pretend roles at some point or another, gradually drifting to whatever they find most compelling, all the while using open-ended play to fuel their explorations.

Sometimes Jeff Daitsman finds himself plunged unexpectedly into one of those exploratory stories among his very ethnically diverse students. One of the most striking instances happened when he was a teaching assistant in an upper-middle-class school in California.

"As we were seated at the snack table, Ellie turned to me and said, 'boys have penises and girls have vaginas.' This was a two-year-old. My mind started to spin. All [kinds of things about gender formation] passed through my mind in a fraction of a second. I barely missed a beat before responding, 'That's true.'

"Ellie then went on to say, 'you're a boy, so you have a penis.' Still unsure where this conversation was going, I responded, 'That's right. I do.' She then informed me that 'Jill, another teacher, is a girl (seated behind her) so she has a vagina.' Not sure that Jill had heard, I responded, 'That's right, she does.'

"Ellie asked, 'Where is Jill?' I gestured, she turned around, then looked back at my left hand and asked me, 'Why is your nail polish like that?'

"Suddenly the impetus behind the conversation coalesced in my mind. My nail polish chipping away after [I had] been working with my hands for a week had drawn Ellie's attention to my gender. It seemed she was reconciling the fact that most males don't wear nail polish with the fact that I'm a known male, and yet I was wearing nail polish, albeit only on one hand. In examining these things, she began by identifying some defining characteristics of males and females. Once that was resolved, she could then proceed with the discussion of the nail polish and why I had allowed it to become chipped."

On another more recent day back in Chicago, a little boy kept declaring to a little girl, "I'm not a boy, I'm a boy."

"I didn't understand [what he meant]," Daitsman told me. "Maybe it was just a Vietnamese tonal thing. She said, 'No, you're a boy.' Then it turned into him saying, 'I'm a girl.' She said, 'You're not a girl.'

"I said he can pretend to be a girl if he wants to be. I used the word pretend, things like that are more acceptable. I said he can pretend. Then she said, 'I want to pretend to be a boy.' Then we talked about things we pretend to be, and I said I was pretending to be a dog earlier today. Everybody was having a lot of fun, everybody laughing and the other children started talking about what they pretended to be."

I asked Daitsman what would have happened in his grandmother's era.

"I think that the pretend thing could easily have come in, but I'm not sure we would have had a Vietnamese child sitting next to a Hispanic child . . . the issue turned out to be primarily a pronunciation issue, but then it got transformed into something different. That conversation wouldn't have occurred without someone with a Hispanic accent and someone with a Vietnamese accent."

Gender, language, accents, facial types, ethnic stories: All these elements seem to float freely in Daitsman's kindergarten classes, along with heroes and monsters, anxieties, wishes, and games. Very little is fixed or rigid, and that of course distresses more traditional pedagogues and many parents who understand these tender years of childhood as forming the foundations of personal identity, where the girls are taught girl games and domestic modeling while boys are encouraged to explore rough-and-tumble independence. Few American preschools are as open and free-floating as Daitsman's classroom or the ones in California where he was trained. If the forefront of gender-free, or "gender-neutral," schooling is across the ocean and far to the north in Sweden and Norway, it is an expanding approach to busting stereotypes of what it means to be female and male.

~

After twenty years working in Norwegian kindergartens, having quit high school before taking his final exams, Øivind Hornslien decided to pick up a master's degree in business administration. The Kanvas kindergarten he manages has a staff of thirty-five—about the average size of most Scandinavian small businesses. Working with little children in a kindergarten did not, however, earn him particular respect in the business school where most of the other mid-career professionals were doctors, lawyers, and even soldiers. "Mostly when you meet someone," he said, "they ask what do you do for work. When I say I work in a kindergarten, it's like shut down. They have nothing to say. They have no interest in it, no expectation of a man working in a kindergarten."

He took a thoughtful pause. "For a male the role for being a boy or a man is exactly the same as it was twenty years ago. You should not step very far out of line, or choose untraditional work." For Hornslien, as for Pia Friis, who also started out without any formal education, Kanvas's success—it's now sought out by the national education ministry to train kindergarten teachers all over Norway—has been both a refuge and a radical mission for changing how men and women perceive and understand each other. Often the real "education" addresses the adults as much as it does their charges.

Friis offers an illustration.

"Let's say I ask you to write up a report for next week. Or I ask if you can fix something that's broken or I ask you to organize a special group. I was used to the women always saying, 'Yes,' but then they didn't do it. They'd say, 'Oh, I'm sorry I didn't have time to do it. I'll do it next week.' Then next week comes and I ask have you done it? 'No, I'm really sorry, I have so much to do.' It became very irritating." But when she asked male staff the same sort of request, they would answer, "No, Pia, I don't have time to do it, we have other jobs to do."

"I found that quite fair because they were fulfilling their priorities in their work and they knew what they had to do. So if I asked, 'Can you do it next week?' they might answer, 'Okay, maybe I can do it next week.'"

She might have concluded, as many administrators do, that the men were lazier or less responsible for the school as a whole. But she drew a different conclusion: The adult women were never trained to refuse a request from a superior, while men learn very early to set limits. "Instead of everyone doing the same job equally, the men said, 'I'm good at this; I prefer to work like that.' It was easier to organize the whole kindergarten based on the jobs that had to be done rather than everyone doing all the same things. It's also that the men dared to say no to their leader. The women didn't dare to say no. Many women at that time thought well, we can do everything. They could say yes, but they couldn't say no. They [felt they] should be brave and clever and fix everything."

I asked Friis if she was like that too.

"I think I was like that, but I'm not like that now."

Women's propensity to defer to authority and hierarchy is hardly a new insight, neither by feminists nor by workplace sociologists. But the aim of Kanvas, and indeed most Norwegian kindergartens, is to spot how the adult teachers and staff inculcate those unconsciously gendered behaviors and then replicate them in three-, four-, and five-year-old boys and girls. Or, as Friis added, children as young as two or three watch everything the adults are doing from when they arrive from home at seven thirty in the morning until they go home at five o'clock in the afternoon—the better part of their waking lives for their first six years—and it is there that their first role models appear.

It is equally in those earliest years that children "learn" who boys are and who girls are and how they should act toward each other. Another Kanvas teacher recalled how during the winter when the children got ready for their daily outing into the forest or playing in the snow the boys often seemed to have more trouble putting on their boots or buttoning up their coats. She would automatically ask the girls, who normally develop physical dexterity earlier than boys, to help the boys with their outdoor clothes. But she never asked the older boys to help the girls with their boots. "I realized," she said after watching an internal school video, "how even at three years old we were teaching or training boys to be served."

Like Jeff Daitsman in Chicago, the Kanvas teachers say there seems to be hardly any difference in what develops as the unconsciousness of gender, of how boys and girls see themselves or how they treat and view each other during their first three years. But then things begin to change. Hornslien recounted the story of the colors one child chose for his annual "birthday crown." In Norway small children are often awarded a "crown for a day" on their birthdays, and Kanvas kindergartens carry on that tradition.

"One boy from my school was always playing with the girls," he said. "He loved pink, he liked to wear a dress like Rapunzel. On his third birthday, we made a crown for him. It was pink and purple and he was walking all day with it on in the kindergarten. But his parents were a bit worried; they said they don't like this so much. Then on his fourth birthday he came to the kindergarten very unhappy. Most kids are very happy on their birthdays. The teacher said, 'Okay, let's go make the crown.' That's something they do together. The boy said, 'Okay.' Very flat. Totally lame.

"The teacher asked him, 'What kind of color do you want?' He wanted black or blue. He was not interested at all. She's known the boy since he was one year old. She said, 'We have pink. We have yellow. We have every color.'

"'No, black,' he answered, still flat. And he didn't want to be Rapunzel anymore. He wanted racing car stickers on the crown. He was not happy. This time he did not wear the crown they made at all during the day. He did not have a festive birthday. So, what had happened? Something had happened since the last year, or maybe just in the previous week." Once the sad birthday was over and the boy returned to playing with his usual friends, most of whom were girls, he returned to his normal good humor.

Usually, Hornslien added, the problems with such boys start with their fathers, who fear their sons are not sufficiently "boyish"—even at age three or four. The opposite, however, seldom provokes parental anxiety. "If a girl is behaving like a boy," Friis said, "if she is climbing trees, playing football, that's expected. 'Wow!' the adults or parents say, 'what an energetic girl you have. She's great!' But if you have a boy whose voice seems a little bit soft, who wants to play with the girls, he wants to read books and draw, they [fathers] get worried. They come to us and say, 'Can you get my boy to be a little tougher please? Can you get him some boys to play with, so he's not always with all these girls? He's too soft. I want him to be tougher.'"

"What do you say?" I asked Friis.

"I say you have to accept your child as your child is, to his or her own personality. You can't form your child to be different from who he or she is. You have to accept that. You can't press your ideas or the child will become very insecure and become a very sad child. We had one of those here; he was very sad because he didn't feel he was accepted by his parents. He always feels he has to be something else than who he is. But we try to accept the child for who he is."

Frequently skeptical journalists visiting Kanvas or its much smaller analogue kindergarten project in Sweden, called Egalia, ridicule these Scandinavian approaches as trying to erase gender from boys' and girls' lives. One old friend with whom I worked for many years in public radio all but lectured me once on how clearly different her infant son had been from her infant daughter, a difference visible during each child's first months of life. I recounted that anecdote to several Kanvas teachers. They agreed that often gender differences do become apparent very early—just as some other parents have told me that gender dysphoria—or discomfort with one's body—also can surface very early.

"The formation of gender often starts when they are born," Hornslien said, "pointing out how often visitors to a pink and blue coded maternity ward will automatically say, 'What a pretty cutie she is!' or 'What a sturdy little boy!' There are lots of studies about how parents talk to their children differently between boys and girls, how they have different voices, how they use different words. All this is forming boys and girls." One of the most frequently cited studies about gender assumption used a video of a six-month-old infant who was crying. One group of students was told the crying infant was a girl and was asked why the child was crying. Because she is sad, they said. The other group, told the infant was a boy, was also asked why the child was crying. Because he's angry, they insisted. "So," Friis said with a smile, "they interpret feelings depending on which sex they think the child is. Are the children born differently, or is it education and expectation that forms the boy and girl differently. What we do know is that the brain changes according to the experience each child gets and by six or seven years old their brains are different."

Friis, Birgitta, Ullmann, Hornslien, and all the Kanvas teachers I met categorically reject claims that they aim to limit any child's innate gender. They distinguish themselves from Sweden's Egalia kindergartens that have drawn criticism for seeming to push children toward each other's toys—mixing up trucks and dolls in the same baskets—as well as other gender-equality activists who have advocated purging the Swedish language of gendered pronouns and creating nongendered first names.

"We don't think like that about gender in kindergarten and which toys do we have, or how is the environment," Friis said. "Isn't that just a result of traditional thinking about boys and girls? There are different kinds of toys here. [They even have copies of *Cinderella* and *Snow White* that many Swedish schools have excluded.] But if you work consciously with the boys and the girls, you can encourage the boys to play in the kitchen area before they could be stopped by adults who say, 'Oh, you don't play with dolls or in the kitchen.' You can encourage a boy to play with dolls, you can be proactive but let them do as they want."

"But still," I asked, "don't you usually see certain fundamental differences between boys and girls?"

"It doesn't matter," Friis answered patiently. "Children are born differently. They have different personalities. We don't know how much is biology and how much is society. Our object is not to make boys and girls the same. We want to give boys and girls the same opportunities to do whatever they want or be whoever they are. When we work with the children, we think like a children's book whose title is 'Give the Children 100 Possibilities Instead of Two.'"

Note from across the sea: Sociologist Arlie Russell Hochschild at the University of California, Berkeley, has spent decades studying the working lives of families; she is particularly known for coining the term "second-shift" work—the domestic work that women in dual-income households do after they come home. Overwhelmingly, she and others have found, American women do most of the cooking, cleaning, and shopping in most households; the same holds true in most of Western Europe as well. The same paradigm seems to hold fast across the generations into today's young heterosexual households, though not in households run by same-sex parents (see Chapter 8). To figure out what's going on, a team at the University of British Columbia spent two years talking to several hundred parents and children, asking both about their beliefs concerning work inside and outside the home. Then they asked who in the home does the housework. What they found was that it mattered very little what fathers or mothers *said* about sharing housework—but it mattered enormously how the girls envisioned growing up based on what they actually *saw* their parents doing. Girls whose fathers cooked and cleaned were far readier to imagine themselves becoming doctors, lawyers, and scientists. Girls whose fathers left the housework to the mother saw themselves becoming nurses, teachers . . . or housewives. Seeing and acting, the researchers concluded, counts far more than talking.

CHAPTER 8

Bringing Up Baby

Some years ago my friend Lynn was visiting in France with her two preadolescent granddaughters, one in school in Pennsylvania and the other in North Carolina. Both were bright girls who seemed extremely curious about everything they had seen on their first trip abroad. We were finishing lunch and just about to order dessert when I asked Lynn if I could pose a "sensitive" question to the girls.

"Go ahead—they're not bashful," their grandmother answered.

"Okay," I began, "are there any kids in either of your schools who have two mommies or two daddies?" They looked across the table at me and then at each other, then they rolled their eyes and answered in unison, "Duh? Of course."

Lynn later told me that my question had struck even her as rather anachronistic. She reminded me that Family Week at Provincetown, Massachusetts, has been drawing thousands of same-sex parents and their children from all over the United States for some twenty years. Reservations for hotels and campgrounds book out months in advance. The U.S. Census Bureau estimated that in 2012 there were more than 900,000 same-sex families in the United States, of which 110,000 were raising children. Some of those families, though increasingly fewer, were the result of divorces followed by same-sex re-partnering. Contrary to much popular belief, most same-sex families live not in New England or the West Coast but in the American South. And notwithstanding the uproar posted on Twitter in 2014 when two shirtless black gay fathers posted pictures of themselves washing their daughters' hair, the Census Bureau reported that African Americans were 2.4 times as likely as whites to be same-sex parents. Same-sex parenting, as common as it has become in the United States (much rarer in most of Europe), remains a sensitive topic on many levels even among the majority who count many gay and lesbian people among their friends. Anxiety about adult sexual behavior remains a concern, but still more problematic for others is the sort of role models their children will have, how lesbians can provide masculine models for little boys, how two men can offer parallel models for little girls, and, still more, how same-sex parents can provide the different varieties of nurturing that conventional nuclear family models do.

These questions are real and understandable, but another broader issue is raised by the proliferation of same-sex parenting: the impact that legitimizing same-sex marriage and child rearing would have on heterosexual nuclear families. Indeed, the case that the U.S. Supreme Court took up regarding same-sex marriage grew directly from lower-court rulings in Michigan and Kentucky overturning both the right of same-sex parents to marry and their right to be acknowledged as the joint parents, biological or adoptive, of the children they are raising. The appeals that finally sent the marriage ban to the Supreme Court focused explicitly on the impact that same-sex marriage and parenting would have on conventional heterosexual families. In both cases the courts ruled that it was discriminatory for one state to refuse to recognize any legal marriage and adoption that another state had granted, whether the originating marriage had been between two men, two women, or a heterosexual couple. More to the point, the lower appeals court rulings stated clearly that same-sex marriages in no way threatened the stability or viability of conventional families.

Reassuring as that may be to social progressives, are we sure that expanding the legal standing of these new families and their children will have no effect on everyone else? The family-life author Dan Savage, who with his husband is raising a son in Seattle, argues to the contrary, often upsetting other gay and lesbian parents. Savage has argued repeatedly that same-sex parenting has already helped undermine domestic gender roles in the sort of families he, his husband, my friend Lynn, and I as well knew in our childhood. He concurs with conservatives that same-sex families, along with dual-income households, are having a cataclysmic effect on conventional gender roles. The division of labor that was once established by centuries of tradition is increasingly being negotiated by the middle-class men and women living in heterosexual households, just as same-sex mates have always had to do in their households.

As a simple example, household shopping in America has become almost equally divided between men and women (unlike my memories of my father sitting in the car reading his newspapers while my mother pushed her cart alone through the supermarket). Now in parks or on sidewalks, dads are almost as likely as moms are to carry infants in kangaroo packs or backpacks. Despite the fact that house cleaning still remains predominantly women's work, deep shifts in the division of domestic labor have taken place, and they cannot be attributed solely to same-sex parenting models; the fact that two incomes are necessary to maintain a middle-class lifestyle has also forced parents to reimagine domestic behavior and to invent solutions that their parents never had to face. Still, the solutions that same-sex parents have found and the wide media attention they have garnered appear to have played a vital role in providing new models for everyone.

The half dozen families I visited for this research were nearly all solidly middle class living in major urban centers though, I would learn, thousands of others have also begun to move into the countryside—even in my home state of Kentucky, where they rarely report hostility or discrimination. Liz and Elizabeth are both tough lawyers, Jean and Barb (see Chapter 1) are respectively a public health administrator and a doctor, Jeff is an insurance executive and his husband, Woody, is an emergency room doctor, while Victor, now a home husband, has run a chain of health clubs and his husband, Chris, is a corporate middle manager. Shirley Royster, the former junkie from a black town in Virginia, turned her life around when she met Catharine, the Boston glass sculptor. As much as I had expected to find profound differences from my own childhood background, the most startling realization came when I recounted the details of each family's life to my friend Lynn, the grandmother. Unlike her two granddaughters, she didn't roll her eyes at me but said simply, "Raising children is raising children. We all do the best we can, then look back on all the terrible mistakes we've made."

~

Liz, a Bostonian, and Elizabeth, daughter of a Kentucky family doctor, got married in 2009. Unlike most couples who marry, they placed babies far lower on their original agenda than building careers and comradeship. They certainly hadn't envisioned raising twins.

It was feeding hour when I arrived, and the two-year-old twins were at best tolerating each other. Liz had begun to explain how it all had come about when baby Mary Frances let out a yelp.

"Lillian! Did you take that froggy away from your sister?" Elizabeth scolded. "That's not very nice." Both babies were in their high chairs. Liz tried to comfort Mary Frances, who was squalling.

Talking to the two women was as disjointed, exasperating, and charmingly chaotic as I'd experienced in any kitchen during infant feeding time—except that these parents had to tend to two impatient babies in high chairs. Spoons, plastic cups, burping bibs, and squeegee toys scattered everywhere.

At some point—they couldn't be precise about when—the notion of pregnancy had arisen between them, something of a pleasant surprise to Elizabeth since Liz had been doubtful from the start of their relationship. They had elected to try artificial insemination. Liz got pregnant first, and, as often happens with artificial insemination, she found twins growing in her womb.

Much as I've always enjoyed older children, I have been mostly clueless about what to do with tiny infants, especially about feeding and diapering; but convention pressed me to ask whether they thought it had been good luck that they had produced girls. Both their facial expressions indicated they found the question strange, so I tried again: Did they think it's easier for women to have twin girls instead of twin boys?

Again they both obviously thought my question off-the-wall.

"In what way?" Liz asked.

Despite the absence of any solid psychological literature indicating any developmental difference between same-gender parents and heterosexual parents, opponents to same-gender parenting protest that girls raised without a father in the house can suffer identity disorders, just as they claim that boys raised without fathers suffer from the absence of male role models.

A continent away under the bright sun of flatland Los Angeles, Victor and Chris had just finished swaddling the shrubs in their front lawn with Halloween gauze to prepare for trick-or-treating with their two girls, Coco and Kiki, born a year apart. Victor, a man built like an Olympic wrestler, was raised in Virginia. Before the kids were born, he ran a major three-city health club chain based in New York. Chris, fair and slight, was reared in a tony suburb of Hartford, Connecticut, and directs management training sessions all over the United States. They'd announced their union on the Weddings page of the *New York Times*.

"I always knew I would have kids," Victor said as he stretched out on an overstuffed chair and ottoman, allowing Coco, his oldest, to crawl on top of him. "I knew I was gay really young, five. Even when Chris and I started dating, having kids was on my list of nonnegotiable items. I wouldn't date anyone who didn't want to have kids. So I asked him on our second or third date. If he had said no, we would probably have been friends but we wouldn't have been together now after ten years."

Victor picked up his smartphone and dialed Chris, who was away on a business trip in Chicago.

"Hey Snaps!" a pleasant voice on the phone said. Each of them calls the other Snaps for short. I directed my voice toward the phone and asked Chris if children had always been on his agenda.

"I thought it was kinda nice," Chris answered through the crackle, "but Victor was clearly the driving force behind it because there's a lot to do and if it were up to me, we'd probably still be talking about it. He's the one who says, 'you need to be here at this time for this meeting.'"

Victor and Chris found their kids through Growing Generations, the nation's leading surrogacy and egg donation service, which is only a short jog away from their modest house in the heart of the Miracle Mile. One of their daughters is fair and towheaded; the other is tawny and brunette. At the time, Coco was just starting school.

"When we were getting pregnant with Kiki, Coco was a little over a year old, and I was busy with her," Victor explained. "But now that we have two kids, we take equal responsibility for taking care of them. Because Chris has like a job-job, my job is to be a stay-at-home dad. I do more of the logistics—the stuff a stay-at-home parent does. I take Coco to school and dance class. When Chris can do that stuff, he does."

"Does he not miss work?" I asked.

"Yes and no. I don't miss having to go to an office and manage people and travel. Chris tells me I . . . sort of identified myself through my work, so finding a different identity is sometimes . . . challenging. You walk into a room and people ask what I'm doing . . . pause . . . oh, stay-at-home dad. I change the diapers. It's not the same sort of conversation starter that I had before," he said with a smile. "But I don't think there's anything better than walking Coco off to school every day and picking her up for dance class. There's nothing better!"

Chris, far away, waiting on the blustery platform of a Chicago L train, acknowledged a measure of jealousy. "I clearly think Coco has bonded maybe closer to Victor than me. I love being at her school, there are times I wish I could be more involved. But I do need to work, and I make work a high priority."

Each child came from a different egg donor that the two men chose from a vast computerized grid describing the mothers' characteristics sorted by work, by ethnicity, by age, by geography, by educational level, and artistic and intellectual interests. Both eggs, however, were fertilized with the sperm of both dads, and the fertile eggs were both implanted into and carried by the same surrogate mom, who still drops by and has gone on to be a surrogate mom for others. A passing glance leaves little doubt who each child's biological father is. "We are each the biological father of one of our children ... Chris is white and I'm black, and we wanted to raise our family biracially, so when we used my sperm, we used a white egg donor, and when we used Chris's sperm, we used an African American donor. It's pretty detectable." He rolled his eyes. "Other than that we just wanted to know that our egg donors were healthy."

As exotic as same-sex parenting may seem to the majority of heterosexual families, visit after visit seems to illustrate Lynn's observation that, theories aside, child rearing for attentive parents relies on pragmatic problem solving more than anything else. The same goes for raising twins, Elizabeth told me back in suburban Boston. "You just get with the program ... people ask us all the time, isn't it horribly difficult to have twins? Well, it's all we know."

"It's very hard, but I don't know how easy it is to have one child," Liz added as she shoveled chicken soup and mashed carrots into each child's mouth. "This is what I know, so I just do it. So guys with six-year-old girls, I suppose they just do it, and if they don't know, they ask somebody."

~

If twins are hard, surely "triplets" are harder. The first time I met Jeff and Woody and their tribe we were six at a breakfast diner. Jeff and Woody are both Midwesterners and high-income earners, which proved essential given how much they had to pay successive surrogate moms for their kids. Jeff runs a global travel agency; Woody is a pediatrician, but those details would come later. Jeff and Woody had been married for almost ten years that day. Their "triplets" were six years old, and they were hungry.

"Flapjacks! Flapjacks!" one of their two girls shouted when the waitress came over with a tray of water glasses and six gargantuan red and blue plastic menus. "O.J. everybody?" the waitress asked. She clearly knew the family. "I want an omelet," the more demure of the girls said, while their brother, Brian, was still making up his mind. Woody, who describes himself as the nurturing disciplinarian in the house, turned a stern eye to all three and the decibel level dropped sharply. The table talk bounced along as each of the kids told Jeff what had happened to them all week at school while he had been working in New York and L.A. Slyly he caught the waitress's eye and ordered a second pitcher of orange juice. It arrived and she was about to pour it. "No more for the kids," Woody instructed. "That's enough sugar for now."

Jeff calls the dawn of their two-dad family "the baby storm." Later, he recounted how it all came about: Woody's early declaration that their mateship could only work if they had children, Jeff's steady recognition that their commitment to each other was worth more than the fun scenes and beach parties where he'd always been a hot success, the eighty-hour workweeks he had gotten used to while launching his global travel company, the more-than-eighty-hour weeks Woody had spent as an intern and an attending doc, each of them at the same time wondering how they could squeeze in all the things parents have to do to *be* parents.

It was warm enough that spring morning to have the plate-glass windows open, a faint smell of lilacs wafting through as dogwood blossoms fell in their backyard. Woody sat on the couch looking out at the springtime; Jeff, across from him, kept getting up to check on one parenting project or another.

Although I had known Jeff for decades since the first time I'd visited his parents' house when I was in college, we had never had an "intimate" conversation; I had followed his career only through conversations with his older brothers or his parents whom I'd also come to know and like. But now I'd come to probe many of the personal details his family might not have known: not just diaper bags, but how the couple had found a biological carrier for their sperm, how much they'd had to spend to "make" their children, how these two hairy men felt talking to their daughters about vaginal hygiene, and what to say to their son, who, statistically at least, was unlikely to want the same kind of sex as his fathers like. Working as a journalist, I had learned to plow ahead with hard, pointed questions in search of terse answers, but that was not what I had come into their home to do. Instead I waited for them to break the silence.

"I can't imagine my life childless. I'd be bored," Woody said, standing by the open window and looking out at the garden. "I like this dynamic."

"We talk about this all the time," Jeff responded.

Not that the two men led boring lives in their pre-parenting lives. With Jeff's access to free tickets from his travel business, they would pop off to Rome or London for the weekend or spend weekend nights in dance clubs. They understood that all that would end with children. They talked about those pending sacrifices repeatedly, but, Jeff added, "We didn't realize we'd have quite the baby storm we had."

The "triplets" are Jeff and Woody's biological children, but creating new children was not their original idea. Adoption had been their first choice. Oddly, even as dormitories of orphans around the world grow more and more crowded, the barriers to adoption in the developed world have also risen higher and higher. Some nations, like Russia, officially bar American adoptions. In France, where the waiting list is long, procedural controls are dense and can take more than a year to fulfill, while most South American countries have entered into treaty agreements that all but block adoptions except to Americans. Nor is adoption inexpensive. Americans typically pay thirty to forty thousand dollars per child to cover agency fees, health checks, and travel costs. For gay males, money, and a lot of it, is a requisite. Same-sex male couples who don't have either high salaries or family support are essentially out of the game.

"And," Woody explained, "[gay people] can't adopt internationally. There is not one country that accepts gays for adoption." They'd thought they had made a firm agreement with a young woman who'd been impregnated by her drug dealer husband. They had even housed her in a long-term hotel in Los Angeles, where they were then living. "Two days before she was about to deliver," Woody continued, "the husband wouldn't sign off on his parental rights and said, 'If you try to do this, we're going to sue you.' So the woman flew back to Wisconsin and the baby went into foster care."

"Then we went for surrogacy," Jeff picked up.

Like Victor and Chris, Jeff and Woody turned to Growing Generations to find their eggs and a surrogate mother. "You can't use the surrogate's eggs," Woody, the pediatrician, emphasized. "She has parental rights. You'd have to go through psychiatrists and that's fraught with difficulties—maternal psychological attachments. You want to iron out as much as you can up front." They followed all the advice and correct procedures. They each had healthy sperm. But after five expensive attempts, the ova "didn't fertilize or didn't take." Each fertilization effort ran tens of thousands. Each egg donor had to be paid. The surrogate had to be paid, as well as the fertility doctors, the lawyers, and other consultants.

"And you fund it all," Jeff, the businessman, pointed out "because it's your show. So now we're five years into this. The adoption problems, the threats of suits, multiple surrogates. The emotional stress. The miscarriages."

It was then that the two men had to confront what for many might seem like a troubling moral dilemma. While they had built genuine friendship with a surrogate mom in California, the costs just kept mounting, none covered by health insurance. They tried a second surrogate and that didn't work either. "We asked the doctor, 'What's going on? What's not working?' He said, 'Nothing's not working. Each time you come in it's a fifty-fifty chance.'"

"So," Woody said, "we reasoned that if we get two surrogates at once, we're going to have double our chances?"

"Right," Jeff picked up. "So we got one surrogate from California, then we found one from Texas. Surely one will get pregnant," he said, stretching and remembering. "So we decided to do two at once." He stopped and looked directly to me to make sure I was understanding. "They both got pregnant! We'd used separate agencies, we created a whole parallel system. We tried the first time, and this particular surrogate had a late-first-term miscarriage. Then on a second attempt with her, she started bleeding. So you know what's coming? She's going to miscarry again and we're going to be another six to nine months trying to reset. We had another separate system cued up, so we said let's go. We'd paid the money. And *she* started bleeding but she didn't miscarry and the first baby was born. Brian.

"Then came the twins [from the first surrogate]." Jeff added.

"They were premature by three months," Woody continued. "They were born at under a thousand grams each. And sick. We had a brand new baby at home, Brian. He was born in October. He'd been at home for two months before they were born in December, and then [they spent] three months in the hospital. So we'd just got him sleeping through the night when the girls got home—and neonatal graduates are notorious for taking forty-five minutes each to get to sleep. They're like hummingbirds. You got to feed them day and night. We had a night nurse for one night and I did the other night to get them to grow because they were so tiny. They could have heart, eye, lung, brain problems."

Woody, who'd been speaking faster and faster, stopped to catch his breath. Jeff extended his foot to caress Woody's shoeless toe. "They had NONE of it. Their eyes are good. Their hearts are good. Their brains are good. They're tough little kids." Woody looked as though he might begin to cry.

~

Chris and Victor were luckier with their surrogate, who has become a friend, but they had a different concern. As a biracial couple they had hoped to find a biracial egg donor.

But they never found that perfect donor and concluded finally that it didn't really matter. "We don't love one child differently because of biological relations." Victor says. "That would be like thinking that someone who adopted wouldn't love that kid as much as a regular biological kid. You love them because you have a type of love for a child that you're caring for that's indescribable."

Not the least part of that attachment revolved around lineage and heritage, even though it wasn't exactly expressed in those terms. For two men approaching middle age, raising children had as much or perhaps more to do with grandparents' longing. Frequently the great fear articulated by same-sex parents, especially when they are men, is how their own parents—the grandparents—will react. Or, as Chris put it, "one of the first things parents think about when their kids come out is to say, 'Oh my goodness, I'm not going to have any grandkids out of them.'" It is a clichéd scene reenacted over and over in memoirs, stories, and films depicting the weeping mother when her son at last declares himself gay. It is not an unreasonable fear; it is a primordial fear even within contemporary families uninfected with religious bigotry. The family story—the legacy of memories and sentiments, tender or bitter, through which the great majority of humans have established their sense of place in the world—is seen to be somehow erased by a son's or daughter's sexual self-declaration. And then life goes on.

Victor had no problems coming out to his father, a military man, but it was harder for his schoolteacher mother. "It wasn't a big deal to him. He said he thought I probably was [gay]. My mother was a lot more emotional. She got over it very quickly. I think she actually likes Chris more than she likes me." He chuckled.

"She thinks I'm more generous with my time," Chris said from Chicago.

"Yeah, she'll often call him and talk to him. She loves him. I think at the core she is standard Southern mom, but people live their lives based on experience. What her perceptions of gay people were in 1991 when I came out . . . and what her experiences of gay people have been [since then] are two different things. She's an intelligent person who knows that everything she hears isn't true. More than anything my mother loves me and Chris and the kids. Our parents are in love with our kids. I don't know anyone whose parents aren't 100 percent over the moon that they have these beautiful grandkids."

~

Six years had passed since Jeff and Woody's three kids, Carol, Julie, and Brian, were born when I last visited them. They had grown into vigorous, self-sufficient little people who seemed genuinely to enjoy each other's individualities. Still, as with the vitriolic Twitter attacks on the video image of two black dads washing their daughters' hair, deep suspicion and anxiety remain when people in conventional families actually see same-sex parents nursing, feeding, and cleaning their children. The barrage of media attention devoted to pedophilia and child abuse has sensitized the public to see with new eyes how adults treat their children. We are particularly not used to seeing thirty-five-year-old men being intimate with small girls. Bathing and diaper changing lead the list on ever-proliferating websites concerned with dads tending their daughters. Secretions from the vaginal area in infant girls. Whether to wipe their bums forward or backward to avoid infections. To touch or not to touch. I once asked my friend Diane, a heterosexual mom, if she thought gay men, or dads in general, were worse in that department. She wrinkled her eyebrows. "Nobody knows that stuff," she said; "we all had to learn it." After a bit more of a pause, she went a little farther, adding that her gay male friends seemed much more relaxed about talking about sex and body parts than most of her straight friends did. Nor are we familiar with fathers showing thirteen-year-old boys how to clean their foreskins. Those duties, like cooking and cleaning, were and still mostly are left to mothers—much as my mother, not my father, was left to instruct me about "washing my private parts." Those kinds of questions burbled into my consciousness as I talked with Victor and Chris and Jeff and Woody while their children crawled into their dads' laps. The notion, much less the images, of adult men taking on these roles is at first unsettling. Victor and Chris had always hoped to raise girls, while for Jeff and Woody, their kids' gender never seemed to have made much difference.

"That's presupposing that girls need something that's tangentially different from what other kids need," Woody the pediatrician told me.

"I don't think they do. It'll be different when they menstruate or when they get secondary sexual characteristics. At that point they may shy up and maybe not be as comfortable talking. So my plan is just to maintain an open dialogue about their bodies. It's like how chores get—guys taking out the trash and girls doing the dishes. I think the same kinds of things happen with intimate conversations, a sort of assumed gender delegation [arises]. So girls get shy about talking about those kinds of things with dads and boys get shy about things around their moms because they get delegated out within the family unit. In our case we just have to pursue those kinds of conversations so they're comfortable talking about it. We maintain those kinds of open conversations. I don't think gender matters as much as the openness and the intimacy within that relationship."

Woody, an only son, in fact grew up surrounded by girls and women. His father and mother also only had sisters—"all women in every direction." Their kids' gender differences started showing up early. "They perceive nail polish to be a girl thing. We're still explaining that. To them girls have long hair, they wear jewelry. They have pierced ears. They get to wear makeup when they're older. They have these ideas in their heads."

I asked him where they get these ideas.

"Observation. TV. Then they see a guy and say, 'Wait, that guy has girl's hair, and I say no that guy has long hair; it's a male with long hair just like a girl with long hair. They're just now teasing apart the imagery . . ."

Just in the previous year their daughters had been going through their princess-dress phase.

"It's huge. Our girls have three or four princess dresses each. They know that Cinderella, she wears blue and she has a friend and he lives in a castle. It's like him with fighters [planes]," he said, pointing to Brian, off by himself on the other side of the room. "This is an E-95; he knows all these facts about all these little Lego creatures. They just pick it up from their friends; it's like osmosis when they're at school."

"We've never told our kids one thing!" Jeff interjected. "We don't direct them one way or another. I don't care what toys they play with. Sometimes they all play make-believe with one kind of toy, and another time they play with other toys. We went to the mall the other day and the girls traditionally like stuffed animals. Then Friday, Brian really wanted a stuffed penguin. It's right there by his pillow. That's unusual. They develop these things."

"And what have your kids taught you?" I asked.

"My main thing," Jeff said quickly, "is you see that little kids are PEOPLE, and they have characteristics and value traits that seem to appear very quickly. They're very distinct who they are."

"What I've learned most," Woody said, "is that despite all this nature/nurture business, they come prewired with a lot of stuff. For example, when Brian was two, I was headed out the back door and it was icy. And he said, 'Be careful, Slip! Slip!' From the first day he was an anxious kid who worries and really thinks about things. He's always been that way, but he is also rough-and-tumble and loves to catch balls. Carol is messy but she's quick to help around the house, while Julie is obsessively neat and insists on having her hair put up in a bun at bath time."

Jeff shrugged: "We can only do so much, we can say, 'No, No, you have to be nice. You have to be polite.' You can teach them . . . but they're three separate little humans."

Woody added that while he never expected their kids to be "cookie cutters of each other," he did believe they would have greater similarities than they do. "They're brought up like . . . like a batch of cookies. We had to mass-produce everything because it was three kids at once . . . diaper, diaper, diaper . . . bottle, bottle, bottle. We have to do it all at once . . ." His voice softened. "And they're all so different."

CHAPTER 9
Parents and Storks

"I'm not the mom–I'm just the stork," Kelly Enders-Tharp told me when I contacted her to ask about her experience as a surrogate mom. I'd been introduced to her through Growing Generations, the California surrogacy agency, but they had told me little about her except that she was open to talking.

"Wow! Sounds great," she wrote in an initial e-mail. "I'd love to speak to you and find others as well." She closed her note with a phrase she often uses: "My uterus is an ally." A very active ally. Enders-Tharp has been pregnant six times—three times with children of her own and three times as a surrogate for gay men, producing two sets of twins (two girls, then a girl and a boy) and a single boy for the men. She stays in touch with all three families, she said, and continues to meet them as often as possible.

Enders-Tharp's three surrogate children are among what appear to be several thousand—possibly tens of thousands—born each year. The numbers, collected only once, in 2007, by the Centers for Disease Control and Prevention, are very hard to establish in part because IVF (in vitro fertilization) numbers are mixed with traditional direct fertilization of surrogate mothers. Furthermore, for the year 2007 the CDC reported 142,435 "gestational cycles" (or pregnancies) that led to 43,412 live births and 57,569 infants. This discrepancy was a result of the disproportionate number of twins and triplets that arrive through artificially assisted reproduction. How many of those surrogate births were by surrogate moms specifically dedicated to helping gay men have children remains unknowable, but what is certainly clear is that the national legalization of same-sex marriage is leading to an increase in the number of surrogate fertilizations. That new medical reality, which is as yet only legal in a handful of states, signals a revolution in gender roles that may turn out to be as important as the birth control pill was in separating sex from reproduction.

There is also little reliable demographic data on who surrogate mothers are aside from what the surrogate agencies themselves provide. Enders-Tharp certainly does not fit the imagined profile of the surrogate mom often described in most public debate about surrogacy. She is not poor—or rich—or desperate. Trim and athletic, she said she enjoys being pregnant. She has enjoyed it so much that she maintains a blog called *Just the Stork* where she posts photos of all the kids she's birthed as they're growing up, along with advice and exchanges with other surrogate and would-be surrogate moms.

"I always think it's interesting when people have a view of surrogates as poor and uneducated," she said. "It's one of the reasons I started blogging about my surrogacy, hoping that people would see that I was the opposite of what they thought, with my master's degree, great job, my own business, and a 3,400-square-foot house." She takes offense at claims that she and other surrogates only "do it" for the money. She has in fact become something of an activist for Growing Generations and counts twenty-six other surrogates in the network as her long-distance friends.

Stuart Bell, the co-owner of Growing Generations, came to the company from Tennessee, first as a client searching for a surrogate. At the time he was a television producer in Nashville, where surrogacy is neither explicitly legal nor illegal but is prone to generate lawsuits between the surrogate and the biological parents. Stuart knew very little about surrogates at the time, but he did know that Growing Generations had built an international reputation for its work. The surrogate for his first child has no biological connection to his son, but she remains close to Bell and his male partner. After their second child he left his life in television and joined the company.

Surrogates' motivations for bearing strangers' children vary, he told me. Money—about thirty thousand dollars for each impregnation—is an important motivator though, he insists, it's not generally the women's primary motivation. "The reality is that they chose to be surrogates because they see it as empowering. These are not poor women. They are teachers. They are nurses. We've had surrogates who are lawyers. These are not women who are being handcuffed." Most, he said, live in middle-size suburbs. "A typical surrogate [for us] is twenty-five to thirty-five; she's probably lived in the same place all her life, works earning twenty to fifty thousand dollars, and believes this is something she's called on to do."

"Called on?" I said, rather incredulous.

"Surrogacy is considered a very Christian thing to do. In the church you have people who are told to give ten percent to those in need and then you have secular philanthropy. That doesn't exist in most other countries, but it's not unusual for us as Americans. They're simply saying, 'I'm going to help someone who can't do this themselves.' It's no different than somebody who donates an organ or gives blood. We are called to help other people."

The notion of undertaking surrogacy as a Christian mission was surely the most shocking element of all the details I'd heard about the practice. Surely it doesn't reflect the sort of Christianity that is dominant in most southern states, where conservative evangelists continue to mount virulent campaigns against same-sex marriage, not to mention same-sex parenting. And yet remember, it is also in the most conservative Southern states that same-sex parenting is most common.

Enders-Tharp says she is typical of the surrogate moms she has come to know at Growing Generations. She first became interested in surrogacy in high school near a Marine combat base east of Los Angeles. She was, she said, fascinated by the procedure that enabled childless couples to have children. In college during the first years of the century she developed close friendships with several gay men right about the time that gay parenting first captured mass-media attention.

"When I took my first step to be a surrogate, I knew I wanted to help a gay couple. I hopped on Google and entered 'Surrogacy for gay men,' and Growing Generations, the agency I ended up doing my surrogacies through, popped up. I thought, at the time, that there must not be very many women applying to be surrogates and of those, how many were open to helping gay men?" She calls her surrogacy for gay men "Uterine Activism." I feel strongly and passionately about equality and figure that if I don't have tons of money to donate to the cause, I at least have a uterus and blog that can send a powerful message." She even posed midway through her second surrogacy displaying her pregnant belly during a campaign to reverse a former California law banning gay marriage. "Even when my uterus is retired," she told a gay magazine, "I will continue to 'fight the fight' because no one has the right to tell my friends, the fathers of my surro-babies or—many years from now—my own children that they can't marry whoever they love and have children."

Sixty percent of Growing Generations' parents are gay men, while the rest are heterosexual couples in which the female is unable to bear a child. A growing percentage of couples seeking surrogates come from China and Western Europe—especially France, which strictly outlaws surrogacy.

~

Officially, the first child born of a "surrogate mother" came into the world in New Jersey on March 27, 1986. Identified as Baby M, her arrival immediately precipitated a lawsuit when the surrogate mother, Mary Beth Whitehead, whose own egg had been used, renounced her surrogacy contract with the biological parents, William and Elizabeth Stern. Lawsuits over the procedure have largely disappeared due both to legislation that has been passed in most of the world and because a large body of contract law has developed for couples using surrogacy to bring children into their lives. While surrogacy motherhood is technically legal in many U.S. states, the procedure is regulated by scores of differing rules; and it is outlawed altogether in still more states. New York, regarded as generally very liberal, explicitly bans surrogacy, while North Dakota outlaws payments for surrogacy. California and Texas offer the most accessible surrogacy options combined with medical expertise and experience.

Aside from legal issues, the word *surrogacy* itself is hotly contested. Proponents like Kelly Enders-Tharp and Stuart Bell regard surrogacy simply as a medical procedure that benefits both heterosexual and homosexual couples who cannot bear children themselves but need another woman to carry a fertilized ovule to term. *Rent-a-womb*, however, is the term preferred by its opponents, who see the procedure alternatively as a betrayal of nature or as the exploitation of women. Outside America, surrogacy is illegal everywhere except for Britain and Belgium, and even there surrogates are forbidden to take money for carrying a fetus. Surrogacy had been legal in Panama and India, but those nations outlawed it in 2013.

Opposition to surrogacy comes from both the right and the left and, in the first instance, focuses on the physiological risk all women face when they become pregnant. Roughly 650 women die in the United States each year as a direct result of becoming pregnant; worldwide the World Health Organization estimates that eight hundred women die every day from pregnancy or miscarriage complications. Aside from the risks of pregnancy and the additional problems surrounding IVF, the most fervent opponents of surrogacy are religious conservatives, including Catholics, Muslims, and orthodox Jews, who view the procedure as an assault on nature and on the centrality of marriage in the creation of families. Opponents to surrogacy from the left and secular groups for the most part regard the procedure as an abuse of poor women: The women are presumed to be pressured either through payment or societal influence into becoming "baby-making machines." Or as Kathleen Sloan, a 2012 board member of the National Organization for Women (NOW), once put it, "Surrogacy is a stark manifestation of the commodification of women and their bodies" based upon a "contract between the parties to surrogacy [that] would not exist if the parties were equal. The woman must give her entire body and all its life-sustaining systems to gestate a child. Within this framework, the contract is always biased in favor of the financially secure intended parents. The freedom of the surrogate is an illusion; the arbitration of rights hides gender, social, and class issues that make surrogacy contracts possible." Sloan further argued that upwards of half of all American surrogate mothers were military wives—a figure sharply rejected by surrogacy proponents given that, among states with large military bases, only California and Texas permit contractual surrogacy.

Yet even within conservative circles, attitudes toward surrogacy are far from clear. Former *National Review* online columnist Carol Platt Liebau characterized herself as a devout, conservative Episcopalian, a "pro-lifer" who regards every child as a sacred child of God, but she expressed her own doubt about a number of pro-life positions; notably she asked whether banning abortion for women who have been raped is not a sort of fixed-term slavery. Further, though she expressed sympathy for Kathleen Sloan's concern about the potential for merchandizing women's bodies, she also acknowledged feeling sympathy for married couples—several of them have become her friends—who have been unable to have children on their own. "Indeed," she wrote, "a dear friend (and yes, it *is* a friend; I was blessed to be able to bear healthy twins for them at the ripe old age of 40!) and her husband were parties to a surrogacy agreement because of a medical condition that had always rendered her medically incapable of carrying their child. No one was 'exploited' or 'commodified' in any way—and having watched the child who resulted grow up, it is absolutely impossible for me to believe that any part of that decision was a mistake."

Vigorous debates about surrogacy of course proliferate on the Web. One of the most articulate exchanges registered by two pseudo-anonymous women addressed the psychological ties that many believe are established between a woman and the child growing within her womb. "Naturally a woman will start to develop an attachment to that child," the opponent wrote. "Another issue is the fact that the child is being separated from the loving lady who carried it the nine months before their birth. That can't be good for the baby who will grow up to find out their mother never conceived them. Other issues concerning the surrogate mother's access to the child can come into play. And if they are denied access/parental rights because it is not their child then that can destroy a woman's mental state. The woman bearing the child will also experience negative physical effects and the pregnancy will not be easily forgotten when her body will not return to the shape it was before the pregnancy." A more extreme writer in the Web debate characterized surrogate parenting as akin to child abuse, arguing that "any women who does not bond with a child that is inside her for nine months or longer is mentally ill."

For the most part, however, modern secular opposition to medico-technical reproduction comes from a different direction. During one drawn-out conversation I had with a long-time friend, a mother of two, whose social views are generally progressive, the problem came down to the question of rights. "Look," she told me, "of course I accept that we all as human beings have a right to a decent home, a competent education, and good medical care when we need it. I also agree that any two people who want to become married should have the same right to that as any other sort of couple. BUT," and here she paused as she always used to when she was a heavy smoker, "I do not believe that anyone has *a right* to have a child." Again and again in France, and to a lesser degree in America, I have found a large proportion of old friends who after a few glasses of wine express their deep misgivings about turning child rearing into a judicially or constitutionally guaranteed right.

Other opponents have argued that couples unable to have their own biological children should better pursue adoption, but as Jeff and Woody discovered, adoption can be as difficult and nearly as costly as surrogacy. "In an ideal world all of us parents who cannot conceive or carry a child to full term would be approved for adoption and take care of one of those children," one woman responded in the Internet debate about surrogacy, "but sadly not everyone is approved and it can take years before you are told you are not approved. Alternatively even if you are approved you can go before the matching panel, be told you are due to be matched but more than one set of parents can be lined up as possible parents . . . yet again you can fall at the final hurdle when the other couple are chosen over you. There is only so much heartache a person can take." While certain American states do allow gay individuals and couples to adopt, gay people are still almost universally excluded from international adoptions.

Surely the "right" to have and rear a child is problematical—as Mary Warnock argued in her compact but carefully reasoned book, *Making Babies*, published in 2002. Warnock, who had served many years on a British council considering the ethical issues surrounding assisted reproduction, first took on the language of the rights debate. For no small number of people, biological reproduction under any method is impossible, be it because of injury, organ malformation, genetic heritage, or other complications. The same is true for the right to conception, be it by in vitro fertilization or direct injection of a specific sperm into a woman's ovum if for various biological reasons she still remains unable to conceive. When an act, a wish, or an intention is plainly impossible, it cannot be a guaranteed right any more than a blind person can insist on the right to become an airline pilot. Therefore the language of rights must be refined, which takes Warnock to the more reasonable—and more difficult—issues surrounding the right to *try to have a child*. Until recently, in most societies, no such right was granted to unmarried individuals, and even now doctors rarely agree to assist single adults—male or female—in making babies, though surrogacy agencies do not always insist that two males be "married" to use their services nor do sperm banks always demand that female clients be married so long as either individual can pay the charges. Warnock goes farther, however, arguing that no medical professional should be compelled by law to help either an adult or a couple to conceive a child. Doctors and other reproductive specialists should be free to decline their services if they believe the prospective parents to be unfit or inappropriate parents—if, for example, they are longtime drug users, suffer dangerously high blood pressure, possess incompatible Rh factors, already suffer what is likely to become a terminal illness, or are likely to put their own survival at risk via pregnancy—objections that most people would accept and that also apply to ordinary heterosexual people contemplating parenthood.

Yet opening the rights debate to personal medical judgment raises other problems. It was only in 1967, for example, that the U.S. Supreme Court struck down a Virginia anti-miscegenation law that prosecutors had used to sentence Richard and Mildred Loving to prison for having married each other in another jurisdiction and then bearing a child. That law, dating back to the so-called Racial Integrity Act of 1924, aimed to prohibit any cross-racial breeding. The court's ruling also struck down a similar law in Alabama. Nonetheless, as a Columbia Business School study showed as late as 2007, cross-racial dating and marriage has continued to be far rarer south of the Mason-Dixon Line than in the north, reflecting both individuals' preferences and social stigma. What was once true of racial discrimination, now technically illegal, can also apply to other ethnic and mental-physiological judgments that are not based on biology or medical science. The temporary or long-term legal status of one parent in a trans-national couple can present special issues. The number of older children in a family cast against their economic security can also affect a doctor's decision—and even a dramatic difference in the physical size between a very large male and a small female is not an unknown rationale used by some medical practitioners to reject a couple's request for reproductive assistance.

And there remains the matter of money. As of 2014, IVF typically cost between twelve thousand and fifteen thousand dollars and had a one in three probable success rate—for women under age thirty-two. As a woman's age increases and the quality of her eggs declines, the IVF success rate also declines to a lower-than-five-percent success rate for women in their mid-forties; at the same time the possibility of costly or dangerous complications rises. Conventional insemination within the uterus incurs fewer risks, and is usually cheaper, but success rates there also decline with age. The cost of male parenting by surrogacy in the United States is vastly higher, generally around $150,000 per child from IVF fertilization of a surrogate through delivery. In countries with broad national health care services, as in Western Europe and Britain, the rights issue has already taken on an additional dimension: Should couples with fertility problems have reproductive intervention covered by those tax-based health care systems? For Mary Warnock, the answer here is clearly yes. Just as devout Catholics cite Saint Augustine's argument that procreation is a divine and God-given obligation for properly married adults, Warnock draws a secular, quasi-existential parallel. Human beings seeking to have children do so because of an insatiable curiosity that she finds innate to most if not all adults: "What will the random mixture of genes produce? What will be familiar, what unfamiliar?" With or without divine inspiration, she finds it an integral element to the endless quest: Who am I and what am I and what will my offspring reveal about my/our place in that unfolding story? The ancient truism that I only understood who I was through the rearing of my children, she argues, is no less true for two married mothers or two married fathers than it is for a woman and her husband. If a society has accepted both forms of human union, why should it not offer procreative assistance to both, she asks?

Finally there arrives the most entrenched objection to same-sex parenting, an objection Warnock largely dismisses as a deep-seated fear of science and/or a sentimental attachment for what passes as "natural." The well-known Green activist José Bové, who has led France's and Europe's opposition to genetically modified agriculture, declared in the spring of 2014 his absolute opposition to *any* manipulation of "natural" biological propagation including all "technological interventionist" varieties of child making, which, except in the case of lesbians previously married to men, would constitute a blanket ban on homosexual people having children. Bové's opposition to assisted reproductive technology (ART), like his campaign against genetically modified crops, has a number of sources (including, some say, a rebellion against his own parents, who were pioneers in the development of genetically engineered plants), and is a generalized and not altogether irrational fear of how such genetic manipulation might lead to unintended mutations that in botany could produce super-weeds, or in humans and animals might result in unintended forms of physiological and psychological aberrations. Nothing captured that anxiety more starkly than the opening lines of Aldous Huxley's science fiction masterwork, *Brave New World*, describing a future human reproduction complex, where the director leads a group of eager young students on a tour of a squat, gray, non-descript building on a side street of central London. Above the door a sign reads: CENTRAL LONDON HATCHERY. The director, who is unnamed, takes them first into a heavily insulated room marked FERTILIZING ROOM where racks upon racks of test tubes hang containing the week's collection of human eggs, each one bearing its own number. They are kept at exactly 98.6 degrees Fahrenheit, the normal temperature of human blood. "These," he explains with a wave of his hand, "are the incubators."

Next, he takes the students, notebooks in hand, through a second insulated door; they have entered the sperm room. The test tubes here are kept two degrees cooler than in the ova room. Male gametes, we understand, are far more fragile than the hot sturdy ova. "One egg," the director pronounces, "one embryo, one adult-normality."

Huxley's dystopic vision bears little resemblance to Growing Generation's surrogacy operation in Los Angeles, though comparisons are not unreasonable with the Cryos International Sperm Bank operating in Denmark, Orlando, and New York or the Fairfax Cryobank headquartered in Fairfax, Virginia, with branches in Minnesota, Pennsylvania, and Texas. These and other sperm banks in the United States and Europe offer thousands upon thousands of frozen sperm donations, each one categorized by race, hair color, and eye color. Similarly human ovum or egg banks exist in some thirty-one U.S. states. Egg donors are screened by age, physical and psychological health, drug and smoking history, and numerous other markers including skin, eye, and hair color. Some include presumed intellectual references based on profession. For people who view the creation of a child as a union of two souls, following the teachings of Saint Augustine, open access to these methods constitutes a blatant, sacrilegious insult to Christian teaching. Equally, for many romantic secularists who regard making a baby as a quasi-mystical celebration of love between two people, these sorts of institutions cast a stark techno-severe shadow on the act of bringing new beings into t he world.

The fear of runaway science is the Huxleyan nightmare. The second fear, infused as much as anything by the progressive industrial degradation of the planet, is that "we are alienating ourselves from what ought to be our dwelling, from the place where we want to be at home." But then, what does "home" mean? Inside that sense of "home" is a panic at abandoning the vital truths we have inherited from our ancestors. If we continue to dismantle our sense of "home" as we have always understood it, how is it possible that healthy children can grow up in such a homeless home?

~

By the early years of the current century, data began to trickle in about the well-being of the children of same-sex parents. A variety of conservative reports, including one from University of Texas sociologist Mark Regnerus, claimed that such children suffer everything from heightened birth disorders to unstable gender identity in adolescence. And indeed there is plentiful psychological research detailing childhood developmental deficits in broken families where a gay or lesbian parent had been present; in nearly all those cases, however, the homosexual parent had ceased to be a full-time member of the household. But there was a more serious flaw in Regnerus's research. As with a number of other anti-same-sex parenting claims, several different kinds of family formations were blended into a single category and compared with traditional mom-and-pop families. Single parents who had been divorced following a "coming out" of the other, mostly absent parent were lumped together with heterosexual single parents of both genders, and those were blended with same-sex parents, all of which were collectively contrasted with "traditional married two-parent heterosexual households." Other critics have cited Freud's early belief that early gender identity begins to be formed as the child develops a distinct sense of self in contrast to his or her opposite-sex parent. Girls understand themselves as girls when they see themselves as different from their fathers; boys understand their masculinity in their difference from their mothers. Unfortunately for these critics, Freud's views shifted frequently across his lifetime on exactly these issues of gender identity formation until, late in his life, he wrote that he saw no particular influence, positive or negative, on children raised by two mothers or two fathers.

Freud, however, concerned himself mostly with case analysis of particular individuals and especially individuals who had come to see him because of their existing psychological distress. Nothing in Freud's work addresses large groups of population or even pretends to speak to general psychological or social modalities. Since the opening of the 1990s, however, several dozen psychologists and sociologists have addressed the consequences of same-sex parenting on a broader scale, and their findings are remarkably consistent. Two major meta-studies, one conducted in Britain and Europe and a second a few years later in the United States, have shed considerable light on the question. The first, published in 2007, is an exhaustive examination of the literature on childhood development and parental gender. Authors Charlotte Patterson and Paul Hastings surveyed the ever-expanding varieties of family structure in the Western world, and they reported one outstanding difference in family structure and childhood well-being: "Children growing up in economically impoverished families are at greater risk of encountering problems in development. These range from poor nutrition and housing to inadequate access to health care to coercive parenting and family instability. Family economic circumstances are related to children's health, behavior, and educational opportunities, and those whose families have fewer economic resources are likely to suffer on all these counts." They went on to say that in social settings where racial and gender discrimination is strong, same-gender and other minority parents could suffer financial disadvantages with negative developmental consequences for the children. Households with two parents, whatever their gender, are more likely to be economically stable than is any single-parent household and are therefore likely to make better homes for the children.

Mindful of the tendentious quality of debate around same-sex-parented households, they examined all the available comparative data. Again they found no significant differences. "More than two decades of research on children's self-esteem, academic achievement, behavior and emotional development has revealed that, for the most part, children with lesbian or gay parents develop in much the same ways that other children do." The one difference that seemed to be consistent was that lesbian parents were less likely to smack or spank their children than heterosexual parents, and they engaged in more imaginative play with their children. "On measures of self-concept, peer relations, conduct and gender development, however, no significant differences emerged between children with lesbian and heterosexual parents."

In a still more extensive meta-survey of the literature on parental gender and childhood development published in 2010 in the *Journal of Marriage and Family*, Judith Stacey and Timothy Biblarz concluded that "the entrenched conviction that children need both a mother and a father inflames culture wars over single motherhood, divorce, gay marriage, and gay parenting. Research to date, however, does not support this claim. Contrary to popular belief, studies have not shown that 'compared to all other family forms, families headed by married, biological parents are best for children.'"

None of which, however, should be construed to mean that children raised by same-sex parents will be indistinguishable from kids raised by a mother and a father—especially when it comes to how they understand gender values. It is still decades too soon to draw conclusions on how the children of same-sex parents will vote, what faiths they will or won't adopt, or even how they will regard proper domestic gender roles for themselves and the society. In Scandinavian countries that have had gender-equality laws on the books for several decades, traditionally male professions are still male-dominated while women still carry most of the burden of household work. Fundamental change, as Norway's Kanvas schoolteachers point out, does not come quickly.

Advocates for both same-sex parenting and its dependence on surrogate motherhood sometimes cite the sociological literature, but for the most part their approach is far more personal and pragmatic; or, as Kelly Enders-Tharp put it, "I really believe that in the future, when I look back on all my accomplishments, [surrogacy] will easily be one of the best things I ever did. I was able to help give a wonderful gift so that two people could experience what I know so well: the incredible love and joy that can only be experienced by having kids."

CHAPTER 10

Rebuild the Hearth and Humanize the Firm?

Nowhere have the complexities and contradictions between home and work struck more deeply into today's gender upheavals than in the doctor's office. Nearly 50 percent of American medical students are young women, while in Europe women hold a slight majority in medical schools. Nearly all of them are heavily subsidized in their studies by taxpayers, and yet most stop working full-time before they are thirty, the age when the demand to make babies and to treat patients approaches a peak. The result: There are only about half as many women doctors practicing their craft as there are men, and in general the specialties that give them more "home time" are more poorly paid than men's specialties.

Women's enrollment in American law schools as well has boomed over the last half century from a mere 10 percent to roughly half by 2013—yet only about one fifth of women attorneys in law firms become partners.

Medicine and law remain the dream careers across the Western world for people who value both money and community prestige, but both professions face built-in contradictions in the gender field: Personality types tend to be ambitious, aggressive, and self-initiating and are often drawn toward similar mates. Today's Marcus Welby can no longer look forward to having a submissive wife or girlfriend who will stay home to mind the kids and tend the roses. And indeed the lower down the career track young couples go, the greater is the likelihood that the female in the couple will become the primary breadwinner. In four out of ten American households with children, it is the mom who earns most—a near four-fold increase over the last half century, according to the U.S. Census Bureau. And women increasingly say they prefer to work full-time.

Who, then, manages the home? The answer for many was captured in a 2012 essay that Carol Hymowitz wrote for Bloomberg News that went viral, "Behind Every Great Woman." The focus of Hymowitz's piece was the growing proportion of men who have given up their careers to become full-time house husbands. Or as the boss of FemaleBreadWinners .com Suzanne Morris declares, house husbands have become "full-time accessories" for successful professional women. Every good woman needs a man behind her if she is to realize her full career potential. It's not quite the role articulated by Pope Benedict XVI or by *Manif Pour Tous* leader Béatrice Bourge, or for that matter presidential candidate Mike Huckebee and his fellow red-state governors. But full-time house husbands are proliferating just as tiny fissures have begun to open in the Fortune 500 boardrooms. Data from the U.S. Census Bureau reveal a near doubling of house husbands and stay-at-home dads (not exactly the same thing) over recent decades—from just over 2 percent of family dads in 1976 to 3.5 percent in 2009. As exciting as those percentages may be for people who concentrate on growth rates, they indicate just how scant are the households where men actually assume the daily domestic duties.

Researchers at Boston College reported in 2013 that 85 percent of new fathers now do take "maternity time" off for a first child, but only for a few weeks; very few depend on their spouses to buy the baby formula. Karen Sibert, an anesthesiologist in West Hollywood, California (hardly a skid-row terrain), raised a modest firestorm of outrage when she counseled bright young women to think twice before taking up a profession as tense and demanding as medicine. Parenthood and patient care may not be morally compatible, she scolded, especially in light of how much the public pays to train top-grade doctors. Worse yet, she argued, women overall in America are simply *less productive* than their male cohorts: They are in the office four and a half fewer hours per week than men, a gap that is very likely associated with their domestic duties. Sibert had resurrected the hardly new, and generally politically incorrect, life-work wrangle. Her message was loud and clear: No, young lady, you can't have it all.

Denounced as she was by many feminist voices, Sibert may well have performed a favor for all kinds of dual-income parents, be they moms and dads, two moms or two dads, or still more complex family configurations. Lisa Belkin, who has long written about managing work, independence, and domestic duties, confronted Sibert straight on. "I think that [Sibert's] argument gets it backwards. The problem is not that workers—mostly women at this point—are demanding too much, but rather that professions are archaically structured. Also, that the push for change still comes mostly from women. The answer is neither to shut up, nor to buck up. The answer is to recalibrate the hours and expectations of professions so that they can be done by the 'new worker'—not a man with a wife at home (which is the assumption of the old structures) but rather a mother or father with a working partner and responsibilities at home."

Belkin's formulation may sound easy, but the unstated assumptions underlying the conventional roles most of us have been raised with still permeate our daily habits. Performance in the kitchen in places like West Hollywood or Santa Barbara, where Belkin lives, is hip, chic. Planning the shopping week after week and taking the children to doctor visits and treating the colic and cleaning the bathroom bowl and then explaining why Mommy can't read a bedtime story *tonight* just as she didn't last night because everyone in the office is working late to close a deal is less charming: Few boys and men are reared with these expectations, even if the teachers in the Oslo kindergartens see and confront them daily with their three-year-olds. Still harder, as study after study by work-life sociologists has shown, is rethinking the nature of either the industrial or the professional workplace, be it in patient care, filing court dockets, or designing software. "Recalibrating the hours and expectations" of the workplace and the workforce in an ever more competitive global context constitutes nothing less than a full-force assault on the fundamental organization of the current economy and not just shifting men's and women's roles within it.

"Just because things have always been done a certain way does not mean that is the way things should be done," Belkin retorts, which is very likely true. It is also true that for decades business school productivity analysts have consistently urged everyone from factory managers to law partners to press their colleagues and employees to take brief afternoon naps: Those few workplaces that have done so consistently see drops in worker errors, better physical motor performance, improved memory, and overall increases in quality productivity. But except in Japan, few large businesses have instituted the practice. Not least, and despite evidence to the contrary, ambitious, competitive professionals are leery of being seen as softer than their mates, an anxiety that women who are new to "leaning in" often feel more intensely than men. "I'm still surprised that people are put off by napping," sleep specialist Terry Cralle told *Entrepreneur* magazine in 2014. "We've got great research supporting the fact that naps can help corporations and employees, yet we still feel reluctant to make it an acceptable part of a healthy lifestyle and a healthy workday." The blockage to napping, she says, is often middle and senior managers who equate naps with slacking—an attitude that is not only outmoded but profoundly wrong-headed. "Some large companies have workout areas or gyms on-site and yet we're turning a blind eye to sleep and it's a biological necessity," she says. No company had been more aggressive in encouraging rest breaks than Google—not known as a slacker's retreat—where tech workers inhabit personal pods that permit them to recline their chairs in relative privacy.

Yet despite both productivity and medical evidence to the contrary, doctors and health care professionals have been among the slowest to change work habits, which Lisa Belkin argues is not only abusive to the workers but also a disservice to patients. More flexible work programs, she believes, would very likely be better for patients who arrive at the end of the workday when the physician's mental acuity is measurably lower. But Belkin and her allies argue for a still more profound rethinking of how we work throughout our lifetimes, encouraging all workers to reinvent the relation between work life and domestic life. Reduced productivity—or fewer hours worked per week—should not be only the privilege of the preretirement years, nor should stay-at-home dads lose promotion status because they cook and nurse the kids. "Intolerance toward women who are comfortable scaling back their ambition for a period of time in order to achieve balance in their lives does such a disservice for women everywhere. Taken to its extreme, Sibert's position would bring us back to a time when medical school students were predominately men, and women with an interest in medicine went into nursing." The solution to fighting gender discrimination, Belkin and her allies maintain, is not to train women to behave more like men but to rethink jointly how both men and women understand and accomplish quality work. "All professions have people like Dr. Sibert," she wrote, "who feel that women can only be successful on men's terms. I sincerely hope that my seventeen-year-old daughter finds better role models in whatever career she chooses."

Lisa Belkin's hope for her adolescent daughter reflects more than a simple feminist fantasy. Notions of rebuilding the contemporary family reflect core rethinking of men's roles in the family. The Boston College Center for Work and Family spent four years specifically studying how male attitudes and behavior have changed over the last generation. Among their most obvious findings is the dramatic decline of the traditional dad-as-breadwinner model from 45 percent of families to barely 31 percent in 2013. Nearly every family today has two breadwinners. Still, the effects of dual incomes in the household are not equal. The Pew Research Center's Social and Demographic Trends project, which regularly monitors family life and attitudes, reports that while more and more women want to work full-time, they still spend nearly twice as many hours per week on childcare and housework as men. Not surprisingly, women with children find it more painful to balance their work and family obligations.

More startling is the shift in how new fathers see their responsibilities to their children. Slightly more than 70 percent of the almost two thousand dads surveyed said they saw their duties as "both caring for my child and earning enough money to meet his/her financial needs." Hardly 5 percent saw earning money as their primary obligation. Included in care was close emotional support for the child, or, as one father expressed it, "I think [being a father] means a lot of things. It means love. It means demonstrating your love for someone and a commitment to them at all costs. So supporting them, being there, and I think not only as a father, but as a guide, as a mentor."

The demand for more and better-quality "personal time" to respond to the needs of family and spouse, aging parents, or simply other social and community responsibilities is hardly new. But somehow asking for more emotional presence in the family is nearly as radical as calling for women's parity in the boardroom. Current trends in the workplace in fact are moving in exactly the opposite direction in the most high-pressure professions—including law, accounting, certain medical specialties, advertising, and corporate management consulting, where the eighty- and ninety-hour workweek remains the sole golden route to success. It's an issue I raised with an old friend, Linda Hunt, who had risen to the highest levels of two of Los Angeles's most glamorous public relations and advertising firms.

"Loyalty to the client is everything," she said. "They're paying you a lot and they want a lot and they don't want it tomorrow because you're home with a sick kid." In her case "they" included one of California's two largest banks, a national accounting firm, and a national tobacco and fast-food conglomerate. "Yeah, of course people were talking about work-life balance thirty years ago, but it was all bullshit then and it's all bullshit now: They've bought you and they own you, and in exchange you make a lot of money, a lot." Hunt left her high-stakes and very successful career when the consequences started showing up on her electrocardiograms, but she says nothing much has changed in the lives of the younger colleagues she trained in the 1980s and '90s.

The arrival of the high-speed Internet in the early years of the century was greeted with glowing promise that dual-income parents would be able to mix home and work life—picking up the children from school and depositing them on the soccer pitch, then finishing that deadline report at home. A few years later ultra-high-speed smartphones promised even more flexibility: Stay in touch with the London and Singapore offices *while* you're waving to your ten-year-old on the pitch. But rather than leading to a new and more flexible balance between home and work, the Internet and all the magic toys that accompany it appear to have led to even more reported stress in family relations—up 74 percent over the pre-Internet, pre-dual-income-households era, researchers on work-family spillover reported in the journal *Family Relations*. Clients whose businesses operated on a global clock facing global market competition expected even more after-hours service once the information technology turned continuous access into a global norm. The highest level of stress showed up in employees between ages thirty and forty-four, widely understood to be the period most important for childcare and job performance evaluation, according to the CDC's 2010 National Health Interview Survey. Stress-related disability claims have also continued to rise, especially in dual-income households both at the middle and upper managerial realms, estimated at an annual cost of more than $200 billion. The American Institute of Stress, a Texas non-profit research group focused on health and stress, estimates that three quarters of physician visits in America have become directly stress-related, ranging from neuroskeletal pain and distortion to binge eating and drinking to cardiovascular problems.

What's true in New York or Los Angeles is equally true in Singapore, which has seen an increasing toll of physical and psychological responses to ever-mounting workloads. A very successful twenty-nine-year-old banker who called himself Andy went to his doctor reporting recurrent nightmares, mostly related to work. Andy acknowledged spending fourteen hours a day planted before the bouncing financial digits on his computer screen, then dragging himself home to an admittedly comfortable apartment. To compensate he began snacking throughout the day. Before long he had added twenty-five pounds to his slight frame and, his doctor warned him, risked becoming obese. A psychiatrist at Singapore's Gleneagles Medical Centre told the *Straits Times* that such cases of intense stress and its physical consequences—especially insomnia and intensifying depression as well as suicidal thoughts—have grown sharply in recent years. A generation ago, most depression was reported among the elderly. Other psychiatrists reported upwards of 90 percent of their young and mid-career patients complain of unsustainable stress leading to collapse or burnout. "Everyone is putting in long hours," another twenty-eight-year-old said, adding, "It looks bad if you leave early."

Family relations sociologist Jeremy Reynolds at the University of Georgia combed through national work-life survey data to examine how in fact middle- and upper-dual-income couples are managing the intensification of daily stress, especially in the world like my friend Linda Hunt inhabited in Los Angeles. Women, it turns out, appear to react very differently from their husbands. "I find that work-life conflict makes women want to decrease the number of hours they work whether the conflict originates at home or at work. Men only want to decrease their hours when work-life conflict originates at work, and some men facing frequent conflict actually want to increase their hours," he reported. He also found that having children had little or no effect on wanting to decrease working hours, though earning sharply more money did. Other survey data on employer's outlooks have repeatedly shown that nothing counts more on promotion evaluations than the worker's stated and demonstrated readiness to place dedication to the organization above all other concerns—including child rearing and other domestic duties to family, friends, and parents. Or, as Hunt recalled about a conversation with a senior executive at a Big Seven accounting firm, "He really did want to hire more women onto the team, but every time he did, he said, they'd get pregnant and quit." If men frequently addressed their anxieties about work-life stress by embracing the organization more tightly, women, already regarded with suspicion, appeared to reinforce those organizational suspicions by demanding to work fewer hours. "And by cutting productivity and profits," Hunt added when I mentioned the research.

"But might not the core problem rest with rising demands for employees to work more and more hours?" I asked. "Why should you and four other account execs have had ten power clients each and been forced to work ninety hours a week? Why not simply double the number of account execs?"

"That would cost the firm twice as much money," she laughed.

"Possibly, but possibly not," I answered. "Wouldn't ten specialists billing fifty hours a week bring in five hundred billable hours while five specialists could only bill four hundred fifty hours? That would be a ten-percent increase with maybe better performance due to lower stress levels."

When she quit laughing on the other end of the line at my naïveté, she explained "the rule of thirds" that dominates nearly all service consultancies and, to a lesser degree, many middle-level workplaces. "The first third [of your billable fee] goes to your salary. The second third covers overhead. And the third pays top management, long-term debt, dividends if there are any, and long-term capital investment. That's not just LA; that's the whole world—Pasadena or Singapore."

All that is what's really under attack by inviting the other half of the gender equation into the office suites and giving the guys real time to change the diapers and toss the soccer ball. "It's not just about glass ceilings," Hunt concluded. "It's about how we think about and organize work and what kind of profits make sense." How major global corporations' ever fiercer insistence on primary dedication to the firm already confronts the growing insistence by dads for primary dedication to their children, and how those plainly contradictory forces are resolved, will almost certainly set the outlines of domestic conflict for the next generation.

If competition for clients in the global marketplace appears to be more and more corrosive to family life, there are exceptions, many of them in the high-tech arena. One of the most surprising, OwnLocal, is a media advertising company based in Austin, Texas, with clients as far away as Chicago, Los Angeles, and Australia. OwnLocal creates outsourced, online ads for newspapers and other media sites, mostly traditional newspapers that have seen both their circulation and ad revenue plummet in recent years. Among other strategies, each new employee at OwnLocal is fitted with a pedometer that monitors heart rate, blood pressure, and calorie consumption per day in the company's own on-site gym. It doesn't do much for childcare support, but it does illustrate the growing emphasis in start-ups for personal health among their employees. Among the most creative companies addressing work-life issues is Discovery Communications, the multifaceted media company in Silver Spring, Maryland, that started up thirty years ago as the science-focused Discovery Channel. Online critiques of Discovery give it high marks for providing an on-site pharmacy and full childcare facilities and for encouraging employees to develop flexible hours to meet their family needs—although many Discovery employees regularly complain of a less-than-stable management structure in which job and wage promotions are rare. Few companies have won as much employee praise as Geico Insurance in Chevy Chase, Maryland, especially for its ancillary athletic programs and encouragement of all employees to create non-work-related social clubs of their own interests. Yet at the same time many of Geico's employees complain that the company mantra emphasizing low-cost premiums leaves them working long overtime hours with little time for either a private life or participation in the company-promoted cultural forums. Yelp, the San Francisco headquartered multinational online service that evaluates local businesses—everything from restaurants to car repair garages—again wins employee praise for a raft of social activities. But like most other companies that boast of rich human resource services, the underlying objective, according to many employees, is not so much about offering flexible hours to aid families raising children as it is creating team identity. One employee in its Arizona branch characterized the company atmosphere as like living in a college fraternity house. Rare in any of these cases is an active project to acknowledge the new stresses that women face in taking on ambitious careers; nor, despite a certain New Age marketing style emblematic of today's human resources sector, do these companies forthrightly confront the prejudices men face when they are the ones to take days off to deal with sick kids.

The answers are not easy. Contrary to the Baby Boomer promises of reinventing the world of work "on a human scale," middle-class professionals now complain more than ever of being caught in the vise between unbearable hours and globally enforced stagnant wages. Neither do the complaints come purely from liberal social scientists. In a major study conducted by the Rockefeller Foundation and Time Inc. in 2009—one year after the great financial meltdown—government and business employees overwhelmingly stated they needed more flexible hours to deal with family and medical leave. Two thirds of conservative respondents, as well as nearly 90 percent of liberals, said employers should be required to provide paid flexible leave to address family requirements—and despite relentless conservative demands for lower taxes and less government intervention, half of self-described conservatives and three quarters of "moderates" said that "the government" should pay for those benefits. Even three quarters of Christian evangelicals took the same view. The work-life conflict has only intensified in recent decades as heavy industry has moved into the developing world, not least in China, where global marketing of so-called "Communist" China has generated longer and longer working hours for both men and women. Until very recently Chinese leaders have preached that the time is not yet ripe for the individualist luxuries of the West and that workers should follow a revised form of Confucian discipline: "Get rich first, enjoy life later." Both the intensifying wealth gap in Europe and the United States and the repeated billionaire corruption scandals in China and other East Asian nations, marked by declining labor union protections, have led to sporadic outbreaks of middle-class rage. A flurry of books focusing on workplace rage by jobsite sociologists began to appear in the 1990s, most famously by Mark Ames in *Going Postal*, where he characterized the modern workplace as increasingly stressful and dehumanizing despite the new move by employers to organize soccer teams and offer after-hours cooking classes. As women increasingly take over the breadwinner's role in the modern household, that level of rage, often played out on the commuter highway, shows no sign of decreasing. Indeed, as one serious study by Michigan sociologist Nancy Herman found, women who have had to fight their way into the workplace and up the job ladder are now more likely than ever to erupt either on the highway or in the workplace.

PART IV

Fluidities

CHAPTER 11

Transitions

Gender confusion. Gender dysphoria. Gender displacement. What today's multisexual activists now call gender liberation arguably began with Elizabeth Cady Stanton, Susan B. Anthony, and Margaret Sanger well over a century ago before it found its contemporary embodiment with Betty Friedan, Gloria Steinem, and the theorist Judith Butler. The twenty-first century has already produced yet a new generation of college trans-identity activists and their older pop models, bisexual Lady Gaga and the now transsexual publicity hound Caitlyn Jenner. The chaotic gender puzzle that conservatives long warned us about since they sentenced Margaret Sanger to jail for promoting birth control has reached new heights that were unimaginable just a generation ago. None other than the CIA, whose essential trade, like that of most espionage outfits, is identity replacement, now openly embraces and recruits transmen and trans-women, the most famous recent example being a Middle East expert whom the agency presented to the *New York Times* in 2015 under the cover name Jenny. It was no accident that the CIA chose the *Times* to promote its support of transsexuality: The newspaper long known as "the gray lady" of American journalism had itself already become a national leader in promoting transsexual rights and identities, not only through repeated editorials but as well by opening an entire online section devoted to personal transsexual coming-out stories. It is hard to become more establishment than being embraced by the CIA and the *Times*.

America, however, is far from alone. There is hardly a major newspaper or television news company anywhere in Europe or Asia that does not run regular reports on its trans population. Shanghai's official Museum of Contemporary Art featured a major show of the pop-kitsch and heavily trans painters Pierre et Gilles in 2013. Thailand has long been recognized as the world's busiest surgical ward for highly advanced transsexual surgery. Yet the pinnacle of trans notoriety most clearly arrived after Conchita Wurst, née Tom Neuwirth, a little-known sometime transvestite performer who delighted in provoking Austria's neo-Nazi Freedom Party, won the 2014 Eurovision song contest.

When the Austrian public television channel ORF nominated Conchita, a self-described drag queen who wears a beard but performs in women's wigs and clothing, as Austria's official entry into Eurovision 2014, outrage erupted. More than thirty thousand hate messages piled up within days on ORF's Facebook page. The vitriol went viral across Eastern Europe. Then when she took the Eurovision trophy, Russian president Vladimir Putin called the prizewinner an "abomination" and an insult to nature. Within a week a new anti-trans movement sprouted in Russia and its adherents started shaving off their beards—an option not available to the disgusted radical Muslims and orthodox Jews.

For the Russians, for much of Eastern Europe, and undoubtedly for thousands of silent Americans who dared not speak their thoughts, everything about Conchita Wurst (including the not-too-subtle play on words Tom Neuwirth had chosen for his nom de guerre) spelled out the worst of our era's gender confusion. Had Neuwirth undergone surgery to remove his "wurst" he might have been less troubling. Gender reassignment surgery has gradually won acceptance even in deeply conservative zones, but that was not Conchita's intent: Her message, both visual and verbal, is that all of us exist in a fluctuating spectrum of masculinity and femininity; the fixed-gender categories enshrined in the Jewish Torah, the Christian Bible, and the Qur'an are not only antiquated but probably never bore much resemblance to reality.

Transsexuality is a troublesome reality for almost everyone who has not lived inside it, myself included. "It gives me the creeps," one longtime and very progressive straight friend admitted to me. "These people ridicule women; they hate women. They reinforce all the worst stereotypes," a normally mild-mannered feminist friend exclaimed. Among middle-aged radical feminists, near hatred bubbles up not infrequently over the matter of transsexuality, as in Janice Raymond's book *The Transsexual*

Empire. "All transsexuals rape women's bodies by reducing the real female form to an artifact, appropriating this body for themselves," wrote Raymond, constituting a patriarchal suppression and violation of both the female body and women's spirit. An angry argument broke out between two thoroughly masculine gay men when I asked for their thoughts about Conchita. "Ugh! It's disgusting," one of them spat out. "No, not at all," said his husband. "Remember what she said in Copenhagen? 'I just want people to be free to be who they want to be.'"

Queens. Transvestites. Transsexuals. Drag artists. Gender queers. The apogee of it all surfaced in 1979 with the creation of a San Francisco troupe who called themselves the Sisters of Perpetual Indulgence. Made up mostly but not exclusively of gay men, many with beards, they dressed as nuns, they mocked conservative politicians, and they undertook charitable missions for the sick and the homeless. Their primary mission, however, was the same as Conchita Wurst's: to question the body and soul of all gender categories. They were mostly transvestites—men who dressed as women—not transsexuals; they had not undergone hormone treatment or surgery to change themselves into women. Their technique, in the language of the time, was to engage in "gender fuck" demonstrations and parades. Their most prominent leader called herself Sister Boom Boom, or more completely, Sister Rose of the Bloody Stains of the Sacred Robes of Jesus. Boom Boom ran for mayor of San Francisco. Born Jack Fertig, the son of a Jewish father and Christian mother in Chicago, she eventually converted to Islam. Chapters of the Sisters sprang up all over the world, including one in Paris that drew the support and sympathy of an otherwise conservative Dominican monk (who only wore robes in his monastery) whom I came to know. The "gender fuck" movement withered—at least in the mainstream media—as gay men and lesbians sought political respectability in suits, ties, and heels and gender scholars took on serious theory-making in the social science departments of major universities.

But what had been an amusing, and for some embarrassing, San Francisco performance act remained very real for an estimated seven hundred thousand Americans who either feel uncomfortable in the physical gender of their birth or actually have changed their apparent visible gender. While "transvestite" remained an act in clubs, transsexual and transgender became common entries in medical, psychological, and social work studies. Conchita Wurst as a "working drag queen" may not have qualified for any of those categories, but her stunning performance took the notion of gender uncertainty onto an undeniably global stage far from San Francisco, Paris, and Amsterdam.

~

A straight road runs tight between the Colorado River west of Moab, Utah, and a line of sand-burnished red, black, and ochre cliffs hanging high above. When I caught up at last with Candace and her two boys, they were just finishing a ten-day desert trek during their spring school break back in Salt Lake City. The boys—Will, fifteen, and Luke, eleven—were used to sleeping in tents on the cold desert floor since they were old enough to carry backpacks. They helped their father tote tripods and other camera paraphernalia in what had become a lifelong quest to document the trail of petroglyphs scratched into the ferrous and sandstone walls long before the soldier-explorer John C. Frémont attached his name to the river, after which the surviving natives had the name extended to them. The petroglyphs leave little doubt that the "Frémont Indians" were irrepressible storytellers. Their markings recount their journeys, the animals they encountered—and not least the part-human, part-fantasy creatures they appear to have encountered in their vision quests. Among those fantastical creatures are not a few whose gender seems far from clear or at least mixed, reflecting the two-spirit individuals in the Mojave, Navajo, and Lakota peoples.

Candace's story isn't easy to tell even though she seemed completely comfortable telling it. As I sat next to her in her mini-SUV, her sons bantering in the backseat, my mind wobbled. I could not decide whether to be submerged in the sublime red-rock landscape or to look intensely at Candace, at her very female exterior and the heavy, very male skeletal frame supporting it—or simply to focus my attention on what she was saying about the mystery of the petroglyphs, several of which she later pointed out also seemed to portray transsexual creatures. What images and thoughts, I wondered, were speeding through the prepubescent minds of Will and Luke, who appeared as much at ease as any two sons with their mother, or their father, of which Candace is both? Even the language fails in the space of proximity—hardly a novel insight, as Shakespeare taught us in a half dozen of his plays, notably in *The Taming of the Shrew* and *Much Ado About Nothing*.

My role was to listen. Candace first fell upon the Moab petroglyphs when as Scott, her birth name, he began venturing into the desert with a group of wilderness explorers. Later, those exploratory treks led him to form a non-profit called Wilderness Watch that gradually turned into a young white man's own version of a Native American "vision quest," the rite of passage through which each individual, or at least each male individual, went out alone into the night to discover the strength of his inner soul. "This is actually the twenty-year mark of that trip that started me down this road. Where we were camping last night—that was the place I lost myself. That was the place I found myself. That was the place I got back to myself. When I transitioned [from male to female], that was a time I tried to push my old self out, and allow this new person to come into existence, that inner struggle. It was really hard. Luke would have been three or four, Will was probably seven or eight." She recalled her experiencing her first inkling of a "second spirit," or at least a discomfort with her masculinity, when her mother bought the then three-year-old Scott "big boy" underwear—and he would turn up his nose and take it off, replacing the shorts with the old diapers. "I knew even at that age," she said, "that it wasn't right."

These days pronouns—he or she, his or hers—are less and less a problem for Candace and the two boys. Luke easily learned to use female pronouns in speaking about his father, who, for a while, used the androgynous name Shannon. Candace has carried full breasts for most of Luke's life. Will, who knew him longer as a man, seemed to avoid gendered pronouns altogether around the transwoman who is their biological father. Both sons are high performers in school. As a young adult Scott was a residential building contractor during the boom years of the early 1990s. He was a sturdy, muscular man. He had been a high school wrestler. He played soccer. He'd been sexually active with a number of women before he married and tried to settle into Salt Lake City as a young man in the Mormon church, on his way to what that religion calls the priesthood of the Latter-day Saints (LDS), a member of the all-male quorum through which the power of God is given to man.

We snaked alongside the river, searching for the petroglyph markings on the rock walls to the right, a hard, painful light bouncing off the river through the windshield. Young men, and a few women, were grasping onto handholds or dangling from ropes attached to the pitons they'd pounded into narrow crevices. Will sat in the backseat, also watching for the pictographs. "I had all these amazing things," Candace continued. "I had the life that I think a lot of people want. I had a beautiful family. I had a job running a business. I had a non-profit organization and I liked going into elementary schools. We'd go out and adopt certain parts of wilderness. We'd do cleanups, teach the kids about Native American rock art. And yet there was this black hole that was still just devouring me inside."

Nearly all the transgender people I have encountered speak of parallel torments and frustrations, most often beginning at or well before puberty. A sense of incompleteness, displacement, or otherness had seemed to gnaw at them from some uncertain direction while a few had violently resisted their assumed biological gender from near infancy. For many that "dark hole" began to lighten as they secretly began to dress in the clothes that seemed to make them feel more at home with themselves or as they began to use external hormones that led to a definitive "transition." For thirty-year-old Candace the critical drive to change grew more intense after Luke, his second child, was born.

Scott had always wanted kids and a family: "Those were things I knew I wanted. It was just a matter of trying to find a way to keep pushing things out . . . to not let 'this thing' take control of my life." Children might have driven the voracious black hole away, but they didn't. Scott's commitment to the environment, heading into the desert to clean up the trash left by others, might have displaced it, but that didn't work either. Finally, two things converged while Luke was still an infant: deepening and recurring thoughts of suicide and confrontation with the visceral fear he experienced climbing the sheer face of a desert rock. "Climbing is where I really found myself," Candace told me after the sons had gone off for a wander on their own. "I really learned a lot more about myself than [I knew] when I started down that path."

For me rock climbing or even high balconies equal vertigo. My knees grow cold just watching rock climbers. Candace laughed and her earrings jangled. "I really am afraid of heights," she allowed. "It scared the hell out of me. For some reason I just wanted to push past that. You get up above where your last piece of protection is. You're fairly high. You are risking a potential fall. You learn how you operate under pressure. I learned I have a lot more courage than I *ever* imagined. I was able to pull myself through some really terrifying moments. And be very proud of that. That was the metaphor for what I was facing in myself."

In a later conversation we delved deeper into the linkage between Scott's fear of heights and Candace's success as a doctoral scholar and public speaker on transgender issues. As he came to understand the structure of his multiple internal fears—be they the fear of falling, the fear of losing his family, the fear of rejection by his friends—the one fear that united them all was his fear of taking responsibility for his own life. It no longer mattered how or why he as a Mormon male and husband remained an unfinished person: His only choice was to act, to take the leap into an uncertainty where he would discover who and what he could become. That leap was not instant.

Not long after second son Will was born and Scott had left the Latter-day Saints, he found a doctor in Colorado who began prescribing the female-hormone estrogen doses that would slowly produce large breasts and lead eventually to the removal of his penis and testicles. When the breasts began to grow round and full and when finally Shannon/Candace returned from Colorado with a constructed vagina, that was more than Scott's wife could handle—and more than Candace expected of her. "To be honest, she did not want to see me transition. She also did not want to see me hurt myself, which was becoming more and more possible. I think, in the end, we both loved and cared for each other a great deal and wanted to try to find a way it could work. But transition was not something that was going to work for her."

"Were you surprised?" I asked. "No, if you want people to give you that kind of space, you also have to give other people the space to claim what is right for them. That only seemed fair."

Candace's exploration of her emerging life did not stop there. She had, more or less, developed the physical form of a woman. Yet her memories, her language, her education and training, the jibes and jokes made with contractor colleagues and secretaries, even the touch of the razor to the chin or knowing how to urinate properly, had been male. These intimate and often unconscious banalities of waking up and walking through the day count far more in the formation of personal gender than the growth of breasts or the pinning on of earrings. To have the form of a woman, to have female hormones coursing through the body, does not equal *being* female. Nor do long-buried or suppressed feelings brought to the surface by the surgeon's knife constitute *being* a woman. These and other arguments permeate the exclusively "women born of women" sectors of radical feminism that have, for example, set the ground rules for the Michigan Womyn's Music Festival, the so-called Women's Woodstock, which since 1982 has drawn thousands of women every August to a small town in lower Michigan a few miles inland from Lake Michigan. It is a mass gathering of women who want to play, make music, dance, sing, and talk anywhere. Lesbians have long been welcomed to the festival as integral participants in the mostly heterosexual feminist program and membership.

Transwomen, people born with a Y-chromosome but who through surgery or hormonal treatment present themselves and live as women, are, however, strictly excluded. They are seen as threats to the psychological peace and security of those people who from infancy were raised in what the festival's leaders say are the patriarchal sufferings that no person raised as a male can ever understand.

~

Mark said grace as we sat down to mashed potatoes and roasted hen, each of us holding the hands of our neighbors and adding a personal amen. A two-foot-tall plaster Jesus watched over us from the sideboard in the adjacent den. Mark, fifteen, trim and athletic, faced two more years in high school before heading off, he hoped, to the Air Force Academy in Colorado Springs, following in the path of his older brother and his dad, Rick, a career pilot who flew helicopter rescue missions during the first Iraq war, called Operation Desert Storm, in 1990. On this night, as the table talk revolved around Mark's latest basketball victories and how much longer the ski season would last, Rick and his wife, Sherry, were clearly strained, almost tense, their voices shaky. Rick's earrings, which complemented the turquoise brooch hanging just above his cleavage, seemed to bobble with independent nervous energy. This night was to be the first time that Sherry and Rick, who at home preferred to be called Robin, would recount the story of how they had met, fallen in love, and raised three children and were now coming to terms with Rick's transition to Robin. That transition was far from finished. Fairly quickly after the small talk about snow and my experience writing two books about apples, we decided to delay the serious talk until after dinner when Mark would go off to tend to his homework.

Adjourned to their L-shaped leather couch, Rick tried to find a starting point in his Vermont childhood when his Baptist parents converted to Mormonism. His eyes were watery, his voice still uncertain. Sherry took over.

"Do you mind if I give you just a smidgeon of my life at that point because that will tell you why we bonded so strongly?" she asked without waiting for an answer.

"I was managing a beauty school. I ran the night school. Okay? And Robin came in to have me do his hair. Pretty quickly he told me he wanted to take hairdressing classes."

Not many Air Force men came to the salon or took her classes. During the day Sherry held down two other jobs while completing a degree at Weber State University. She spoke calmly and carefully. "I had recently returned home from my two-year Mormon mission in France. In Biarritz. While I was in France I had a fiancé, or I thought I had. My fiancé was from South America, but while I was on my mission, my mother started an affair with him. He and *his* mother, and his brother, moved in with my mother. *My* brother and *my* sister were also living there in the house. So we had this little 'family unit' that had moved into my house while I was gone."

There is no piece of America where "family units" are as highly prized as in Mormon Utah. Utah claims one of the country's lowest divorce rates. Family camps and personal church missions are nearly universal, and outside Salt Lake City nearly 80 percent of the population are regular practicing members of the Church of Jesus Christ of Latter-day Saints. Everyone in Sherry's new "family unit" was LDS.

"So when I came home, I found my ex-fiancé sleeping in my home with my mother, plus my brother was living there. My mother begged me to please move into the house with them because she wanted the neighbors to see that she wasn't really having an affair with my ex-fiancé. She wanted to save her reputation. My life was in a lot of pain. I was twenty-five. I was the only person in the house who had a job—actually three jobs and I was going to school and supporting everybody."

Dumbfounded, I asked Sherry if she still talks to her mother.

"Yeah," she answered flatly. "I was a very strong person. Very strong or stupid. I was working those three jobs and going to school and trying to make sure that my family didn't lose the house, because my brother and my sister would lose a home too. I was trying to support all of them. I was hurting a lot. I was pretty much at the end of my rope where I couldn't see how I could get up and go on. And he—" she turned to Rick/Robin—"was the first person I could tell. I had tears. He was this amazing person. We'd become such great friends. We were the same age. He was someone I could trust to tell where my life was and the hell I was living in. And I trusted him.

"He said, 'You don't have to love your family that much. You deserve to have a life yourself.'"

Rick proved to be a good student in Sherry's hairdressing class. For a long time they did each other's hair. Hers is blonde in a bouffant twist. Rick's, when it's not put up, is as long as a braided blacksnake's tail. Now they go to the same salon where, Sherry insists, no one notices the breasts that are steadily rising on Rick's chest or the loss of his chin whiskers. Ready to start his own story, Rick breaks in.

"I wouldn't mind saying a piece, and there's a reason I want to say a piece. I did it by myself. And that's not smart. I started taking medication ... without a doctor's supervision ..."

"Off the Internet," Sherry adds. Rick somehow had attached estrogen patches on his ribs.

"You were not aware of it?" I asked Sherry.

"Yes, I was, and I was not happy with it. I was very worried."

"Worried for my health," Rick answered, tugging lightly at the corner of his blouse.

"There's no way to measure it and know if it was safe," Sherry pointed out.

"And your breasts began to grow?"

"Not so much ... until ... I kind of got permission to see someone and talk to him about it."

That initial dilemma over estrogen and breast building took place a little more than two years before our chicken dinner. Finding a doctor in Utah proved challenging. Rick first found the name of a well-known California transsexual specialist, who referred him to other doctors at the University of Utah School of Medicine, but no one on the university faculty had any interest in taking Rick's case; instead they handed him a list of private doctors in Salt Lake City but they offered no particular recommendation. He found it a chilly response from a university medical school. One of the private doctors on the list was Rixt Luikenaar, a Dutch doctor who had begun developing a specialty in transsexual issues.

"She showed the compassion, that you shouldn't be judged, or be discriminated against, no matter whether people think it's right or wrong. You serve people's souls, and that's what she does."

Tears welled in both Rick's and Sherry's eyes.

Sherry had more to say: "We've never been a judgmental family or a prejudiced family. We've taught our kids to be very open-minded and nonjudgmental. When this all came about, that's why it was so easy on our kids, because we already, they were already, very open-minded and nonjudgmental. We have three kids. Our oldest doesn't know. He's twenty-three and lives in Phoenix. He's been in Phoenix for almost three years. He's in the Air Force. Mark's fifteen, and we have a twenty-year-old daughter, Elizabeth.

"How did the younger kids react?" I asked.

"We sat here on this couch," Sherry said. "I asked them if they knew what 'transgender' meant, and they went, 'Yeah?'" As though it were the latest software app.

"I cried because I was expecting the worst," Rick said softly. "And Elizabeth said, 'Robin, does that mean we can swap clothes and shoes now?'"

"He had a pair of boots she liked," Sherry explained. Robin finished her wife's sentence: "I already gave them to her."

"I said to Mark, 'This doesn't mean that you're going to grow up like me,' and Mark said, 'Dad, I would be honored to be like you.' He's a good kid."

A long silence settled over the three of us on the couch as the plaster Jesus looked on. At last the voice attached to the long snake-tail hair and jiggling earrings spoke up as Robin. "I like Rick. He's a good man. He's done a lot of good. But at the same time you balance the selfishness of it."

Rick/Robin turned to Sherry. "It's not really who you bargained for, is it?"

"It took a long time to figure it out," Sherry took over. "I don't think he even knew himself what it meant. He wanted me to tweak his eyebrows and this and that. But why? We couldn't figure it out . . . until when he retired from the Air Force and started wearing patches, I said, 'Why do you want to grow boobs?' I didn't get it. Even when he started going to Dr. Luikenaar. I still didn't know what it meant. I just knew he wanted to grow boobs. And that's all I knew. I don't think until two years ago, when she started adjusting the other hormones and stuff . . . and when they finally gave it a label, 'transgender,' that was when we finally got it. I'd never heard of it before."

~

The story of Sadie and her daughter began when Sadie's mother was on her death bed during the end stages of an irreversible cancer. Sadie was pregnant with her third child. "We were in the hospital with her," Sadie told me, "and she so wanted to see the baby before she died. The midwife said, 'Why don't you get an ultrasound?' She really wanted to know. It was a long ultrasound, and I was on my back in the eighth month. We found Silas. He was a boy. Then my mom said, 'I really want you to have a girl.' She wanted me to have the same kind of mother-daughter relationship that we'd had. I said, 'Well, Mom, I'm going to have one more, so why don't you order me up one?' I think of that every now and then when

I have my daughter . . . who I thought was a boy at the start and then very quickly came to realize that she was someone very special and very different than the brothers."

Sadie's first clue about her fourth child's "difference" came when "Morgan" flatly refused to wear hand-me-down underwear printed with trucks from her older brothers. Morgan was eighteen months old when the underwear episode erupted, but that was not the only thing Sadie noticed that set him apart from the three older brothers. "Morgan did everything way earlier than anybody else. She would get her own snacks for school. All my boys were catered to—she just took charge of herself."

The first violent showdown between Morgan and Sadie came during a shopping trip to Target in search of new underwear. Sadie had assumed that her youngest son just didn't like wearing hand-me-downs; so she took him to buy new shorts, also with trucks and tractors and rockets printed on them in bright colors. Perched in a stroller in front of the boy shorts, Morgan started crying and then began screaming. So Sadie moved a few feet farther and said, "What kind of underwear do you want? You choose it. And she picked princess." Pink and yellow bikini-type underwear with pictures of princesses on the front.

Mother and son went home and Morgan was content. A little later when Morgan entered nursery school the clothing issue broke out again. "That year she wore pajamas all year long to school. Then that Christmas her grandmother sent her a robe, a green robe with a little monkey on it, and that became the coat she wore." Often the robe and pajamas weren't warm enough in winter and the school would send Morgan home or out to play with spare outer clothes they had on hand. The children could choose the clothes they wanted to borrow. Morgan picked a pink-striped long-sleeve shirt, which on a small child almost seemed like a dress. On another occasion Morgan chose a light lavender hoodie to wear home and asked if she could keep it. "Every day, she was kind of stealing clothes from the clothes bin. And they were all girls' type clothes, mostly pink and purple."

"Why pink and purple?" I asked.

"Because that was what she'd see looking at TV, or cartoons. It's amazing how many things are gendered. I had kind of noticed, I'd shopped at specialty toy stores and geared my shopping toward toy blocks. Little hideout tents. I'd get scarves. And costumes for dress-up before I even knew I had a transgender kid."

By the end of our initial conversation, it was time to go collect Morgan a few blocks away at the grade school where she was pulling down top grades. Nine years old, her hair was long and silky, falling midway down her back. She and another curly-haired girl were playing on swings and a push-me-round; the other girl, who also had been born a boy, was there with her mother. To anyone who didn't know, they were both cute, energetic young girls. A third trans child had already gone home. Soon all three parents would decide whether to have their pediatricians administer puberty-blocking hormones to their kids until they reached age sixteen. The hormones, generally considered to have minimal side effects, essentially delay pituitary activity in the brain that comes to girls between ten and twelve years old and to boys after age twelve; these so-called puberty blockers inhibit the body from expressing conventional secondary sex characteristics—Adam's apples and genital growth in boys and breast development and menstrual expression in girls. Once the hormones are stopped, their effects are fully reversible.

Morgan was then on the cusp of that first decision. Legally those decisions rest with the parents. Morgan, on the other hand, was a precocious child who was eager to talk and engage directly in all the choices that lay before her. In her school she had become a prolific writer and autobiographer. She asked me if I'd like to read one of her pieces. I asked her instead if she might like to read it aloud as we sat at the pink Formica counter in the kitchen while Sadie was washing supper dishes. The story recounted the first time she had confronted her parents with how she saw her sex.

> I hopped into bed and pulled up my covers. My mom . . . walked into my room and hugged me.
>
> "Mom, I'm a girl now," I explained after *years* of trying to show them by wearing princess dresses and using girly stuff.
>
> "OK," my mom said nervously, like she was about to throw up. "When your dad gets home, tell him that you're a girl now." My mom walks out of my room and there I was in the dark, waiting for any sounds outside.
>
> I walked silently out of my room and went down the stairs. Each step sends a little sound through the wall. I finally step on the smooth wood of the house. I looked out the window and saw my dad's car. I ran to the door.

The story Morgan had written years earlier in preschool didn't scan quite so smoothly for her parents, Sadie told me after Morgan had gone to bed. "She'd say, 'I'm a boy.' She'd pee standing up, but she was in the bathroom trying to put on my makeup. You can say, 'My sweet boy, my sweet boy, boys have a penis and girls have a vagina.' That's what we teach! That's how we categorize them. So they're little concrete thinkers at that age, and they don't know that there's another possibility unless you tell them. I'd ask every now and then, and she'd say, 'I'm a boy.'"

When Morgan was five, Sadie went to a transgender conference for parents of transgender kids. It proved to be a turning point for her as she listened to hours of testimony by one parent after another. "These moms were supportive and all that but these moms didn't understand who their kids were, but there it was and it hit me like a ton of bricks. I cried and cried. It was just streaming, streaming, streaming. I couldn't wait to get home and ask Morgan really what she was, whether she was a boy or whether she was a girl. I got home. She was in her room. It was in April, dogwood season. I said, 'Morgan, I had lunch with some people today who were really interesting. There are people whose bodies don't match their inside mind and spirit. They just don't match up. I just have to ask you a really important question. It won't matter what you say, I'll still love you, but I have to ask you, are you a boy or a girl?'

"She looked up and said, 'I'm a girl.'

"I couldn't just leave it like that. I looked down and said, 'There's a difference between wanting to be a girl, you like their toys, you like their clothes better, you like pretty things, and then actually feeling like you're a girl. And she looked up with a little more annoyance in her face and she said, 'I'm a girl.' I said, 'okay,' and I grabbed her up and said, 'I'm so sorry I didn't understand before.' She grabbed my face, gently, and said, 'That's okay Mom.' And we just hugged."

~

Dr. Rixt Luikenaar had traveled from The Netherlands in 1994 from the medical school at the University of Groningen to spend a season with Robert Jarvik, the famed inventor of the artificial heart, at the University of Utah. Before she returned to The Netherlands she'd already started dating an ex-Mormon she calls "this American dude," who returned with her to Groningen for her training in obstetrics and gynecology. Groningen was not only known for ob-gyn; it was also well established for addressing "gender variance" issues, including the care of people going through gender transition. Holland is a world center in managing transsexual transition. Luikenaar and the "wild dude"—actual name William—who became the father of her children bounced all around the world together, from Curaçao to New Zealand to West Virginia, while William fashioned himself into what he identifies as a "primativist" sculptor. On their eventual return to Salt Lake City, where William had family, she began an obstetrics practice at the university medical school, steadily growing closer to Utah's [LGBT] Pride Center to build her patient base, and that, little by little, drew her to more and more people who wanted to undergo a transsexual gender shift.

"There was such a need for it," she told me during a break between patients in her office. "I remember a patient in 2004 [when she was still at the university] who wanted a hysterectomy in order to become a man. I tried to see if the university would take [her] as a charity case to do the surgery. I thought that since sometimes they will do free surgeries for refugees that come from other countries because they're poor and that since this was a person in need psychologically to change his body ... I tried to get it approved. It was cut off immediately by the faculty of the ob-gyn as being ridiculous."

That was her first sign of the university's hostility to addressing transsexuality. Still, she continued seeing transsexual patients until, in 2011, she ran into trouble with one of her colleagues, whom she only describes as a senior-level Mormon and former Army doctor. "I told him I wanted to take on this LGBT population and transgender patients. He was very angry about it and he didn't want to talk to me after that. He didn't support me in it but I did it anyway. So for about a year, while I was at the university I did a clinic once or twice a month for a whole day, so they wouldn't have to sit with other patients in the waiting room. But I knew I wanted to be away from the university."

Unlike Brigham Young University, which is a wholly owned property of the Mormon Church, the University of Utah is a tax-supported public school. She said she found supportive colleagues there but "never a whole department, generally only one or two people. The chairs of the departments are usually Mormons. The whole administration is Mormon. The department chair of ob-gyn is Mormon. I did research for him in the nineties. When I kept coming back to him, wanting to help transgender patients, he wouldn't have it."

Next she was invited to join a private clinic in Salt Lake City with two midwives and two other doctors. They at first were excited to have a younger, female doctor bring her own caseload into the practice. "I started working with that group on March 1, 2013. I brought my patients there.

My clinic was doing really well. After one month there, one of my partners, who was LDS, said he was going to leave [the practice] because of my transgender patients. He couldn't deal with it. His wife couldn't deal with it. His patients were making comments when they were sitting with my transgender people in the same waiting room. He had patients who were really important people here in Utah. I don't know what changed his mind to first say it was okay and then not. Maybe it was his wife . . ." She laughed and shook her long, bright red hair. "Now that I have my own clinic, he's been telling my [ob-gyn] patients that I do transgender health and maybe these patients would consider switching to him . . . because the care I provide can't be right. Because I do transgender health. He's talking to my pregnant LDS patients. He made a point of talking to my patients encouraging them to switch."

Most of Rixt Luikenaar's obstetrics patients stood by her, she said, while her forthright commitment to transsexual people steadily drew attention across the Western Rockies region—bringing patients from Wyoming, Nevada, and Arizona. Two females on their way to becoming transmen had come into the waiting room while we were speaking. They invited me to sit in on the consultation. Each of them had slight facial hair, one a goatee and the other a mustache, but it wasn't clear on first sight in which gender direction each was moving.

"Me, I stay in my pit," said Max, the shorter of the two, who had been taking hormones for several months and had grown a black goatee. Luikenaar asked each of them about their moods and feelings. "The pit—it's my room. I stay in my room. I don't leave it. It's in the basement. They—my parents—say they support me. They say they love me. But they don't even try. They don't try to use the correct pronouns."

Max is thirty-two. He explained that he had always seen himself as "a man. I always have. Since I was knee-high to a grasshopper. But my mother, she doesn't want to see it. Because she grew up in the LDS religion. So as far as that religion goes, it's just a challenge you have to overcome. If you have the feelings, then you have to overcome it. I believe it's part of any Christian religion. You have these gay feelings. You have these transgender feelings. You have to overcome them or else you're going to hell."

Max's friend, Simon, interrupted to explain the Mormon notion of hell and how it differs from the usual Christian version where the damned burn in endless flames. The LDS hell comes in two forms. The first, lesser hell is a psycho-spiritual state of pain, guilt, and anguish, a so-called "spirit prison" where bad or wicked people go after death until "final judgment" or when they are resurrected through prayer by living Mormons—or, if they had never been Mormons, by posthumous baptism (which is how everyone from Cleopatra to Shakespeare has been converted to the LDS). The second and much graver hell is understood as an "outer darkness" into which a very few are cast in perpetuity.

Homosexual acts or acting on transsexual feelings and undergoing a gender conversion, they both explained, would cast them into the outer darkness. Not surprisingly both Simon and Max had left the LDS church. Max had gone so far as to have his name permanently erased from LDS records. Both had been taking testosterone injections to accentuate their masculine features under Luikenaar's supervision for several months, affecting their menstrual periods, which in itself frequently produces mood swings.

"How are your moods?" she asked Max.

"They get better when I'm not at my parents' house. When I'm at my parents', they're more down. It's like a win-lose, lose-lose situation. You know, I feel better when I'm on my meds, than being stuck there where it's constantly thrown in my face, 'Well you're not a man, you were born a girl.' And hearing that evil name that I was given when I was born." He and Simon both laugh. "Don't laugh. It's hard when it's in your face twenty-four seven. And so it puts me back down. It puts my mood back down."

"So what do you do?"

"Go hang out with Simon."

"What do you do at home?"

"Play video games. Look for jobs . . ."

Max and Simon met when they were both working as security guards—jobs they said they couldn't continue once their hormonal transitions began, largely, they said, because of the hostility they met from other guards. Max had returned to his parents' home once his money ran out.

"Have you noted it's harder to find a job when you're in transition as a transman?" Dr. Luikenaar asked him.

"I really don't want to say yes," Max answered, "but the coincidences are just too much. A couple years ago I was applying for jobs, and I could get interviews but now that I'm avoiding that gender question, now I'm getting more and more rejection letters, when it's basically the same jobs I was applying for a couple of years ago. So, the coincidences are staring you right in the face. You don't want to scream discrimination . . . when all these companies are claiming to be EOEs [Equal Opportunity Employers]. But if these companies are equal opportunity employers, why are we still filling out these questionnaires? About gender. About age. About race. Why does it matter? Why do these questions matter?"

Simon added: "They don't ask religion. But gender they ask. Race they ask. Age they ask. If they're equal EOEs, why does it matter?"

Simon's family story was little different from Max's. He and his father had descended into a bitter dinner-table conversation the previous summer. "One of the last statements he made to me was, 'You can dress up a pig as much as you want, but it's still a pig.' And I answered, 'I'm done.'" He had not spoken to either parent since then and was living on small disability payments due to other health problems.

Having no job, Max had no health insurance and because he was unemployed he found he didn't qualify for coverage under the Affordable Care Act. He was still waiting to hear if he could get minimal care through Medicaid, though in Utah Medicaid is mostly restricted to the aged, the blind, pregnant women, children, and certain approved caregivers, and almost no American health insurance program covers treatment for men or women transitioning to another sex. Luikenaar often provides care to poor patients free or for minimal charges, and she advised Max that certain Internet sites offer discounted analysis of blood draws.

Neither Max nor Simon have addressed the matter of changing their sexual organs through surgery, nor, at the time I interviewed them, could either of them imagine how to pay the fifty to seventy-five thousand dollars it normally costs.

~

There is little about the trans world that is not contested, neither the psycho-physical reality of transitioning from one body profile to anther nor the language and pronoun choice any given person may insist upon nor the terminology people find agreeable at any given moment. One single 2014 post on Tumblr.com opened a debate over use of the prefix *trans* or *trans** as the correct descriptor. The use of "trans" alone, many felt, was more restrictive than "trans*" in what both specialists and activists have come to understand as a rapidly expanding spectrum of life possibilities. After some 350 heated exchanges quickly surfaced, the site attached a "triggering warning" advising that the whole discussion risked provoking profound distress and hostile denunciation among the Trans*users who signed in.

Since 2007 Stephanie Brill and Joel Baum have coordinated an annual summertime conference called Gender Spectrum in Berkeley, California, for families and kids facing gender questions. Brill, a midwife and family counselor to same-sex parents, has long worked with parents of gender-variant children at UCSF Benioff Children's Hospital Oakland, while Baum grew up Jewish in Salt Lake City and worked for many years as a grade school teacher. Neither identifies as gender variant but through their work with kids as counselor and teacher, they both came to see gender uncertainty as a rapidly expanding concern among American families. From a handful that gathered in 2007, Gender Spectrum's summer conference has grown to more than twelve hundred participants in 2016. Both Brill and Baum keep busy schedules counseling parent groups and schools across the United States on everything from adjusting restrooms for trans kids to formulating new guidelines for athletic teams to confronting violence and harassment directed at transgender students.

Baum cited a recent experience he had in a racially and economically mixed middle school in a West Coast city. "A child was transitioning from female to male. The child was assigned female at birth but had been living as a boy most of his life—except at school, where he continued to be seen as a girl. He was in the seventh grade. He was having sleep problems and health problems. He was already in puberty. We worked with the family and did a training in the school, all in preparation for the kid 'coming out' as a boy in school. I was in the class where this kid was, and he chose to stay there while we were doing the training."

Addressing the boy's classmates, Baum began, "We talk about democracy and diversity, and by the way, there's another thing: All you who know Jennifer is actually transgender; Jennifer would prefer to be called Joseph and be treated like all the other boys and go by 'he.' First two or three kids said, 'That's so cool,' and another one said, 'Hey, you want to play ball after school?' Next came restrooms. The training was on Wednesday. By Friday, it was all a nonissue. There were a couple of calls from parents asking why there was a girl in the boys' locker room, but that was it."

During the school training one male teacher spoke up about a pair of leather sandals he'd bought in Panama. "I like wearing them," the teacher said. "They're really comfortable, but I have to think twice about where I wear them. People say to me, 'Oh, you're wearing *those*. They're pretty girly.'"

Looking back on his own youth thirty years earlier, Baum, a straight married parent, grew both wistful and worried. "You remember thirty years ago and 'free to be you and me?'" he asked me. "We've become lots more rigid and reified [about gender] in the last ten years. Now it's all very rigid what you're supposed to be as a boy or a girl. Making fun of how people dress, particularly men, is still a big go-to punch line." Baum's concern, however, was more complex. Even the "trans" dialogue distresses him. "So much of this now focuses on 'trans issues' when what we really need to be talking about is gender diversity for everyone. What it means for you to be a guy or a girl or something else. A lot of times people think it's just a question of switching the boxes." The media obsession with trans issues, rather than opening up a world in which each and all of us might explore our own masculine and feminine fluidities, had instead generated just another category of being. Categories by definition are the enemies of fluidity and internal exploration. By focusing on the search for a singular biological key that would "explain" transgender being, the movement seemed to be blocking both children and adults from examining their internal impulses as they vary from hour to hour, day to day, and across a lifetime—in short how to move within the spectrum of genders that we all confront.

Switching the gender boxes particularly annoyed Utah rock climber Candace, some of whose friends wondered if after surgery she would feel more at ease having sex with men, a question that at first seemed shocking to her. "I was never interested in having sex with guys. I was always drawn to feminine things," she said. Candace has lived with a biological woman for several years, a woman who identifies herself as a lesbian. "I got together with her when I was homeless. I went through the process of losing cars, my job, my home, sleeping at one or another friend's place. She was one of those friends." Candace's mother was also supportive after the transition: She kept looking for men her new "daughter" might like, but it took her longer to accept Candace as a lesbian than it had to accept her sex transition.

Language, most of us are told in our earliest school years, is what distinguishes people from all other animals. Dogs, cats, foxes, and chimps can exchange vocal signals with each other, but they are not capable of language. And even though they appear to possess memory, as any dog owner who returns home after a long time away knows, they cannot tell stories. Our gift of language frees us to explore and to learn not only about the worlds beyond our skin but still more about the potential worlds within ourselves that we might find and develop. Candace took more than two decades to identify and grow into her inner world and make it public. Morgan found herself even before she could speak. At the same time the specificity and concreteness of language can just as easily cover up fluid uncertainties within. To my knowledge, Miss Vernace, the strange tall woman in my childhood who plowed the fields on her tractor and went to the men's barbershop, never spoke about her internal complexities, though she also never tried to hide them.

When Vladimir Putin, the current hero of the ultra-rightist movements in both the United States and Europe, spat out his denunciation of Conchita Wurst as "an abomination," he may have just been playing an opportunistic game to win favor with his Slavic base across Eastern Europe. Or he may have genuinely believed that Conchita, Sister Boom Boom, Candace, and the half dozen transgender Mormons I met in Utah pose a genuine threat to human progress and civilization. Those who fear gender fluidity and uncertainty are not, however, restricted to rightist authoritarian circles. Although it has been fashionable since the 1990s to lump lesbians, gays, bisexuals, and transgender people under the same LGBT umbrella, the alliance has nearly always been an uneasy one—for those gays who increasingly insist on their uber-masculinity, for feminist lesbians suspicious of a false femininity, or for bisexuals who cringe at the thought of altering their bodies.

My own reactions underwent upheaval a quarter century ago during several visits to Naples, which at the time was reputed to possess the most joyously perverse set of sexualities in Europe. Two Neapolitan friends, Claudio and Marcello, agreed to be my guides to these perversities, centered in *quartieri spagnoli* (the Spanish Quarters), where the so-called *femminielli* worked the streets at night and often took care of professional families' children by day. The femminielli were famous, a distinguished gentleman on the train to Naples advised me, for their beautiful legs, their sumptuous breasts, and their large penises. Among street workers, as one wag told me, they offered a full-service menu of sexual options. The real femminielli had begun to age when I was in Naples, increasingly displaced by bigger, tougher Brazilian so-called she-males. Yet for older Neapolitans, the femminielli held a special place in the city's cultural history stretching back to the ancient Greeks, who had ruled southern Italy two millennia earlier.

One spring I went to visit Domenico Scafolio, a noted elderly anthropologist at the University of Salerno. Professor Scafolio, who was neither homosexual nor transsexual, had spent his life studying the myths of Pulcinella, the double-sexed creature who might be called the pagan patron saint of Mediterranean fertility. Pulcinella was capable of fertilizing himself and giving birth via the hump on his back. Around Professor Scafolio's office in a once-grand seventeenth-century palace was his collection of phalluses. Some were on his desk. Some were mounted on the walls. Others were propped up on sideboards. One double-ended phallus had seven heads emblematic of Pulcinella's seven lives. The largest of them all, made of wood and painted red and blue, was suspended from the ceiling by thin wires. For contemporary Neapolitans, the femminiello, he instructed me, was nothing more than the ancient figure of Pulcinella incarnate, recalling the tribal dream of male parthenogenesis in which the first human is a male who himself gives birth to the first child. It's an idea rather central to the book of Genesis in Eve's emergence from Adam's rib. A young man I'd met a day or two earlier regularly went with femminielli, because, he said, to be in their presence is an *ingrippo*, to be gripped by a magnificent obsession that opens the door to the mysterious.

Exoticism in image and collective perception have long been celebrated in the life and myth of the Neapolitan people, one of many cultures that abhors rigid categories. Although the followers of Vladimir Putin may not know it, femminielli-like people, and dual-sexed gods, have existed throughout time and across the earth, from the Hijra of South Asia to the Oyamakui and kami spirits in Shinto belief to the burrnesha virgins of Albania, to the Mwari god of Zimbabwe and a panoply of mixed-gender spirits in Ghana, to Malyari and Bathala in the pre-Christian Philippines to the two-spirit berdache of tribal North America, to the machi double-gender warriors of pre-Colombian Chile and many of the pre-Colombian peoples across South America. Castration has equally been used from imperial China to Vietnam to Byzantium, frequently to convert a surplus of males into symbolic females, who, once the procedure was complete and the victim had survived, were usually thought to possess special and sacred powers, just as femminielli were thought to hold in nineteenth- and twentieth-century Naples. Very often their betwixt/between qualities afforded them not only special vision but special status in the world—and condemnation by Spanish conquistadores and their Jesuit allies.

Like trans or trans* people, all these beings bore some sort of linguistic identifier, a label that suggests their special status. In the older traditions, the label very frequently simply suggested a broad possibility of being. In our era of medicalized identities, the language of difference has become more specialized even to the extent that when American Medicare authorities decided in 2014 that they would pay for transgender reassignment surgery, the definitions, labels, and rules of identity had become as fixed and rigid as an aerospace engineer's workup for an intergalactic missile.

In our last conversation in Salt Lake City, not far from the famed Mormon Tabernacle, Candace had her hair tied up in a sort of messy bun as we were speaking about labels. She admitted that while most of the old gnawing within had gone away, not all of it had. She had come to find the term "trans" itself problematic now that she was finishing her doctoral degree on the subject and regularly lectured in college classrooms and to community groups.

"We put those labels on certain people," she said, "when in fact they're just being who they are. For me it was just discomfort with my body, dysmorphia. The problem is using a person's genitalia to identify them in a way that doesn't feel right to that person. 'Trans'—transition, transgender, transsexual—is just a manifestation of people trying to put others back in a box. We are 'trans' only to the extent that we are becoming more and more—not less of anything—in transition to discovering that there are so many more gender possibilities than most people acknowledge."

CHAPTER 12

That Can't Be Sex

Everybody, including nuns, has a first-time story. Frottage. Oral. Self. Cracked cherries. Stained or sticky sheets. Massage of a) nipples, b) clitoris, c) sphincter, d) glans by a) fingers, b) vegetables, c) tongues, d) toys, e) sex organs. And likely a dozen more erotic activities involving genitalia that in one girl's mind or one boy's imagination might or might not qualify as "sex." Yet as our notions of gender—gender roles, gender identity, gender behavior—grow ever more fluid and as the Internet dissolves any restriction on what can be written or discussed, our notions of what constitutes *real* sex have become less and less clear. Doubtless in part that is yet another consequence of Margaret Sanger's lifelong crusade to separate sex from reproduction. As soon as sex no longer threatened to create babies, the terms of what constituted sex were turned upside down, left to the torpor of the erotic imagination. Oddly, even though one or another activity may end in orgasm, not all activities these days seem to qualify as sex, at least not among all people.

The first time I ever heard men—hip, sexually experienced, supposedly counter-cultural men—talking about lesbians in a dope-infused bull session at the University of Michigan, one of the guys declared forcefully that "they" (lesbians) obviously didn't have real sex because "they didn't have the right equipment." Decades later real debates emerged in the gay and lesbian press about whether surgical transsexual people could still have *real* sex—since the surgery had presumably sliced off genuine sex organs. Later yet in the current decade, fully reconstructed transwomen are regularly denied access to certain radical feminist gatherings because, according to certain feminist arguments, they had not suffered the emotional and physical degradation that *real* girls with *real* female sex organs had suffered. Much as the fluidity of outward gender performance and perception has evolved, our understanding of how sex relates to gender remains confusing and very often contradictory. Indeed there just may be less agreement about what constitutes *real sex* now than ever before.

To take only one example, the U.S. Centers for Disease Control reported in a 2005 study that 54.3 percent of girls between fifteen and nineteen and 55.2 percent of boys of the same age had engaged in "oral sex." Other research, however, indicates that anywhere from a third to a half of those teens do not regard what they have done as "sex." They only accepted that the acts constituted sex because the CDC defined oral-genital contact as "oral sex." A generation earlier, fewer than a quarter of those surveyed acknowledged having engaged in "oral sex." For readers of this text these distinctions might seem silly, even daft. But for most of human history and for a very large sector of people living today these distinctions are real and are very much tied up in our changing notions of gender.

Bizarre as it may seem to our ever more a-historical Western culture, "sex" as understood by the American founding fathers bears faint resemblance to how we understand sex today. We shall return a bit later to those earlier conceptions of sex and how sex across time has distinguished itself from gender. But first another both popular and shocking book published at the apogee of the second-wave feminist movement offers still deep insight into what sex means to both men and women in our own era. Nancy Friday's *My Secret Garden* stopped many a dinner table conversation when it appeared in 1973. Friday was already a well-established author, but her first publisher, the house that had previously brought out Norman Mailer, D. H. Lawrence, and Jean Genet no less, seemed struck by apoplexy when she presented her manuscript recounting the stories of dozens and dozens of women's sex fantasies. The male editors apparently had never read such accounts rendered not in blue fiction but drawn from real, live respectable women. One of the most explicit fantasies Friday recorded came from "Patricia," a respectable British lady who was spending a year in Rome separated from her husband (to whom she was devoted); both had elected to take an "exploratory" sexual sabbatical from each other in order to renew their mutual attachment and to enrich their sexual repertoire. Patricia is at the time playing with "Antonio," an attractive but traditional Roman who is giving her exquisite oral sex during which she slips into a still more exquisite fantasy: She sees herself seated at a posh restaurant with several friends when, from beneath the starched linen tablecloth, one of the table guests whom she's been watching all evening—sometimes he's Latin, sometimes black—begins to gently part her thighs and apply his warm, wet tongue.

A tongue applied to a tender quivering clitoris is not, as a rule in America, an approved topic for dinner-table discourse, but she is gripped by her fantasy however blind her table mates are to it. What's more, she seems to have attended to all the necessary details required of such a fantasy. The bearer of the tongue perhaps slipped beneath the table cloth to retrieve a dropped fork or napkin . . . or he may seem to have gone to the men's room while in fact he crept into the basement and reemerged through a trap door beneath the dining table to press apart her willing thighs. If the fantasy is powerful enough, she says, the details always work out.

> It's funny how little time during a fantasy it takes to sort out the mechanical details . . . I want him, this fantasy man, as much as I want the man who is actually between my legs. There is always the most amazing amount of detail in the fantasy at this point: me, casually arranging the tablecloth over my lap so that no one can see he has raised my skirt, or see his head tight up against me, or his tongue.

Patricia doesn't dare explain to Antonio that the intensity of her actual orgasm was heightened by her table-linen fantasy, that her fantasy escalated still farther as she thought about the risk of the other guests finding out what was going on beneath the linen, and that thanks to his expert "tonguing" she feared that she would scream when she came into orgasm, alerting the entire restaurant. Her actual orgasm brought on by Antonio's licking technique was indeed a "noisy" event, she told author Nancy Friday, but Antonio would never know about the fantasy film she had invented to accompany it. He would be left to believe that her excitement was due solely to his expertise. In a post-script to that confession, Friday acknowledges that some men "will say that Patricia's fantasy is no example of how sex can be enriched by sexual fantasy, for the simple reason that when a man goes down on a woman, *it is not real or complete sex at all* [emphasis added]; that of course a woman has to fantasize in that position: She isn't getting the full benefit of him. If she were—if he were giving her a good old-fashioned man-into-woman fuck—she'd have no need to fantasize at all."

QED, oral eroticism for many of Friday's subjects—even when it led to screaming orgasm—wasn't really regarded as sex because . . . because it didn't engage full reproductive capacity. Indeed at various moments of the eighteenth and nineteenth centuries much of post-Enlightenment Europe regarded nonreproductive sexual contact, and even coitus interruptus, as a sort of fraud. For many Christian theologians, the sex act within holy matrimony was nearly as sacred as Holy Communion: It was the act by which God creates human life. Any act or movement or technology that interrupted that sacred act of creation amounted to a fraud against nature far worse than one black-market speculator might commit against another businessman.

Across the decades I've had not infrequent conversations with women who have enjoyed very active sexual lives and who enjoyed reflecting on what constituted sex in their lives. One of them whom I met during my college years and whom I'll call Laura became a lifelong sex counselor for Planned Parenthood. Years later Laura confessed how aggravated she had been with me the first time we met. I was camping out during a stopover in Ann Arbor, Michigan, at her boyfriend's apartment. All that evening she was waiting for me to get lost so she could hop into bed with him. As I was staying over and never left, her frustration and blocked desire grew more and more intense until around midnight, exasperated, she threw on her winter coat and trudged out alone into the icy night. Sex hunger that involved no actual sex laid the foundation for our lifelong friendship, which has frequently included the most explicit dialogues about sexuality and sexual activity. In one of those conversations we dwelt on the importance of shame. "Follow the shame," she advised me; "that will tell you how girls think about what they're doing and whether they think it's really sex."

"Shame?" I asked, genuinely startled. "Sure," she answered. "Shame about getting caught, shame about your parents finding out, shame about possibly getting pregnant." Shame, in fact, was the tool employed by the Manhattan judge who sentenced Planned Parenthood founder Margaret Sanger to the workhouse for promoting contraception. Women, the judge declared, do not have "the right to copulate with a feeling of security that there will be no resulting conception."

Despite the easy readiness to link sex shame to confused clichés about the Victorian era, shame in one form or another has ever been linked to sex and sexuality. Shame since the time of the Greeks has been the glue that binds our personal and collective sexual archive. Shame defines the limits between confession and suppression. Shame distinguishes the sexually successful body from the dismissed and failed body. Shame describes the wall between brute power and sublime submission. Shame delineates the boundary between private possession and public expulsion. Shame draws the line between the taste of delight and eternal damnation.

For Laura's and my generation, longed-for ecstasy was bound to the nightmare and ruin that could come with untimely pregnancy just as later it was shrouded by the terror of AIDS. Laura's girlhood sense of shame was so intense that when her father, a medical specialist, took a new position in a new city, she silently believed that her family had somehow discovered that she had begun "making out" with a boy in her high school and therefore they had swiftly decamped to a new city. So it was that in the new city she passed the rest of her adolescence as a pristine and seldom-kissed virgin.

The shame that infused sex for those of us raised in the postwar years was not, however, simply about repression, silence, or censorship. As Michel Foucault and later sex historians have amply demonstrated, no subject was more central to nineteenth-century Victorians or to twentieth-century Methodists than sex. Wide-screen movie houses of the 1950s and '60s were filled with sexual fog. *Fantastic Voyage* (hourglass Raquel Welch), *Barbarella* (slinky Jane Fonda), and *Cool Hand Luke* (sweaty Paul Newman) exuded wanton sexuality even if Hollywood codes of the time forbade explicit images of vaginal and penile turf. Evangelical preachers railed about sex Sunday after Sunday. Priests scolded endlessly about secret sins while anxious schoolboys traded frightful stories about hairy palms and premature blindness. High school health teachers instructed cheerleaders about how not to rupture the sacred tissue that certified their virginity. Even in my country grade school every eighth-grade girl received a diagrammed brochure explaining her pending menstrual periods and how she should avoid getting pregnant (and at the same time leaving her no doubt about which acts could lead her to get pregnant). Shame was not imposed for knowing about sex, for thinking about sex, or for sharing naughty stories about sex. Sex shame concerned not thinking *correctly* about sex, which included taking sex out of its proper corral (the legitimate, codified family) and opening the zippers to an incorrect list of players.

But how to think correctly about sex when blatant sexual allure has become a nearly universal industrial and political marketing force—be it for selling hats, lipstick, or bully-butch politicians. Michel Foucault and his followers have traced in great detail how "incorrect" sex migrated through the past five hundred years from being a sign of spiritual failure—sin—to emerging as a "medical" phenomenon complete with its own perverse catalogue of "diseases" (nymphomania, degenerative self-abuse, hysterical obsession, homosexual inversion, physiological addiction). As medical historian Thomas Lacqueur has written in closer detail, the medicalization of the sexual body fell close upon the "discovery" in the late eighteenth century that men and women do not possess the same sexual organs—unlike the assurances advanced by most doctors until then that males and females alike carried testes and that the male pelvis was "designed" to prevent the penis from being reversed and driven inward into the man's body by a hysterical or overly active female, thereby converting his penis into a receptive vagina. Likewise what modern doctors call ovaries had until the eighteenth century been described in standard anatomical drawings as undescended (and therefore weaker) testes, since for most of Western history females were designated as lesser versions of males, whose vaginal fluids were described as "thinner semen" that could only be activated and agitated by the thicker and more forceful male semen, thereby resulting in reproduction.

All this medicalization of the human body, Foucault presciently explained, led the West to develop an altogether new notion: "sexuality." If concupiscence penetrated the near totality of Shakespeare three hundred years earlier—*Macbeth*, *The Comedy of Errors*, *The Merchant of Venice*—the Elizabethans' notion of sex was little different from our own since the myriad "sex acts" that the Elizabethans performed upon one another were no different than the sex acts documented by the periodic surveys conducted by the Centers for Disease Control. Ordinary as the term has become in daily newspapers and on nightly television, the concept of "sexuality" speaks not merely of the choices of acts any individual might avoid or pursue, but of the systematic organization of values and sanctions our current world uses to categorize and explain those acts. In the early days of psychoanalysis—or the "scientific" analysis of the psyche—the "non-normal" sex acts and non-normal gender displays were gradually removed from moral or pastoral judgment. The acts remained the same, but among the educated and governing class (farmers and industrial workers were largely untouched by medical intervention before the twentieth century) "abnormal" gender roles and sex acts began to be steadily translated into the language of medicine and illness. Abnormal people of social importance could be treated, sometimes even cured. Those whose abnormal psychology or sexuality was judged incurable—very often "hysterical" women and "inverted" men—were removed to "medical" asylums where they could be watched and their case histories written up for the flood of textbooks used in the newly proliferating departments of psychology at universities like Johns Hopkins, Yale, and Chicago. When American behavioral psychology began to displace European psychoanalysis—also very often associated with Jews—the science of experimentation subjected those seen as abnormal into still more categories of healthy or unhealthy sexuality.

The traces and effects of the new science of sexuality were everywhere. I remember one day when I was at the age of hairy-palm anxiety discovering one of my father's college psychology textbooks high in our family bookcase. My parents had gone into town to the grocery and I knew they would not be away for long. The book was thick and heavy. I could barely make out the title on its spine, discolored by decades of tobacco smoke: *Abnormal Psychology*. Reaching high as I stood on a footstool, I pulled it out and held it like a recovered bottle of old cognac. The pages inside had begun to yellow. I sat down and started to turn the fragile pages, many of them punctuated with Latin terminology. The chapter titles and subtitles were frightening. Dementia praecox. Schizophrenia. Manic-depression. Hysteria. Inversion. Onanism. Neurasthenia. Then came the case studies. Fascinating. Again and again they recounted "abnormal" sexual experience in adolescence, including the dire consequences of self-stimulation by girls and boys alike and the dangers to children trapped in oral fixation. I had hardly gone past the chapter headings when my parents' car began crawling up the driveway and I had to place the forbidden treasure back on the high shelf. By and by, my parents' grocery trips to town promised irresistible windows into the panorama of "scientific" sexuality, leading me of course to wonder into which healthy or unhealthy niche I fit.

Another thirty years would pass before Foucault, Butler, and expanding armies of gender and sexual dissidents would slowly overturn the fraying scientism that had defined sexual abnormality, before doctors and counselors could openly speak about children's nascent sexual impulses, about the normality of little boys' erections and the pleasure little girls could find in rubbing their vaginal zones. Nor even now have all those interdictions disappeared. In contemporary French schools fear of improper or premature sexual awakening has led to new laws that strictly forbid teachers to pick up young children and cuddle them when they take a bad fall for fear of being prosecuted for child abuse. Lobbying against and within the medical and psycho-medical estate has removed most "minority" forms of sex from diagnostic manuals, but confusion remains. As recently as the turn of the current century, transsexuality and cross-gender presentation were judged to be mental illnesses and were sometimes punishable acts across Europe and much of America. During that brief window most of those previously diagnosable medical abnormalities were marched into the light of day. Now they have taken their place as protected and codified gender-sexual categories that nearly everyone but fundamentalists says should have their status recognized and protected by law. It is no longer only in Brazil that trans people of one stripe or another have come to dominate the fashion model sector and are even seen by macho football fans as sexually exciting.

The stories of my longtime friend Laura and her daughter Liora have presented another illustrative window on how the "sexuality system" works, how it has evolved, and how internalized notions of pleasure and shame have developed. Unlike Laura, for whom sexual expression was an automatic danger presented at best as an obligation to marry and reproduce, Liora remembers her first instructions about sex as having to do with pleasure. "My mom sat me down when I was seven and explained how babies were made, that a man would put his penis inside me and that's how you could have a baby. I remember I thought it was really icky and disgusting, but my mom explained that no, it's a real pleasure—not having the baby but having the man's penis inside you. It wasn't a warning about something bad. It was about a pleasure I would find when I grew up."

Shame, as Liora remembers it, played no role in family sex instruction. Neither were lesbian and male homosexual expression cast as shameful acts. Both her parents were psychological and sexual counselors; both had numerous homosexual clients. They lived in California, not in Utah. Nor were oral sex play or masturbation—alone or with a partner—presented as shameful or abnormal. Sex play—as defined both by Laura and Liora—covers almost all the acts in the CDC survey short of heterosexual intercourse. (For people who don't identify themselves as heterosexual, the terms and consequences are not the same and carry their own medical, and therefore potentially shameful, warnings.) All that is not to say that shame is ever altogether absent. Instead its form and understanding have steadily become internalized.

The hallmark of "no shame, no blame" depends on two things for women, Laura said: "A, both people need to be on the same page; and B, both agree that what's going to happen is primarily just to have a good time and not meant to draw both parties closer." A problem, of course, is how to define "a good time" and for whom. Laura recounted the story of one adolescent girl who had felt she was both having a "good time" with her boyfriend and enjoying regular "make-out" sessions with him, usually in his car. She also felt they were steadily growing closer. For most of her friends "making out" was not "really sexual." Like "hooking up" or "playing around" or "doing a thing," "making out" with or without clothes was pleasurable, even erotically arousing, but not the same as "going all the way," as her mother's generation could have said. "Then one evening the boyfriend invited her to come over to his house when his parents were away. He took her into the family room where there was a large couch and began the making-out game. At first the lights were out and she felt comfortable. Migrating from the car to the family house also seemed to her reassuring. After some minutes he told her he wanted to turn the lights on so he could see her better. What she hadn't noticed was the large plate-glass window just in front of the couch. What she didn't know was that he had invited all his buddies to hide outside in the bushes. Not long after the lights switched on, the guys started whistling and clapping.

"I felt my innards collapsing with shame for her," Laura told me. "The girl was just an object for his fun."

Object. Subject.

In Laura's adolescence during the early 1960s, sex shame was still formulated in terms of formal family or community judgment. It was measured by how others might judge the act and objectify the shamed individual. A generation later the system of shame in relation to sex had become more personal just as the sense of personal freedom had grown larger. The game of play and exploitation between the girl and her boyfriend and the chorus of his buddies is easy enough to read and is plainly despicable. He felt larger. She shrank. But they were "doing" the same things they had been "doing" on previous evenings in his car. They had not "made sex" (performed conventional intercourse) in his car or on his family couch, but the dynamics of sexuality—of the role each was playing and the meaning of those roles—had been radically changed. The girl's shame in Laura's view was at least as profound as Laura had felt thirty years earlier when her parents had quickly decamped to a new city. But what would the consequence have been if both the girl and the boy had knowingly collaborated in mounting that exhibitionist show? Would it have mattered if they had simply thought of it as a game? Would the nature of the sex game have been different had they both experienced their performance as an erotic turn-on?

When I raised the question of sexuality and sex shame to Liora, who is also a professional sex counselor, she hesitated about offering definitions. Shame in her world has become a much more internal and private matter than it was in her mother's time, just as the acts that her mother interpreted as sex and that her grandmother would never even have spoken about had become as common as an April shower. Liora's adolescent clients felt fully free to make out anywhere: on the bus, in a park, waiting in line to board an airplane. It isn't even all that rare to see girls sitting on boyfriends' laps and caressing while waiting in the airport departure lounge. The only difference she could cite between her generation and girls fifteen years younger was the explosion of hard and soft porn available on anyone's smartphone as they sit silently on the bus. As an example, she asked me about a term I'd never heard that has now gone global: *twerking.* Compared to twerking, the 1987 film *Dirty Dancing* is a Victorian quadrille. Twerking, she counseled, is nothing more than a rhythmic online manual for girls who want to train themselves in the muscular movements of screwing but without engaging in full intercourse.

The number one twerking instructor, as of summer 2014, calls herself Tweetie, a hairstyled racially indistinct young woman dressed in a black gold lamé top, leopard-skin tights, and high-laced soft boots.

"First," she instructs, "you need to place your hands on your hips. You need to know which direction your hips are going in. So . . . feet apart. Good," as she spreads her soft-booted feet wide in a perfect A-form. "Bend your knees. Then you want to make sure your feet are turned out and your knees are over your toes. Place your hands on your hip bones. For your hips to go forward, you want to take your thumbs and press on your butt bone [otherwise known as your pelvis]. If you want your hips to go forward, press your thumbs. Press. Press. Press. Press.

"Now, if you want your hips to go back, take your fingers and pull back. You got to pull back on your own hip bone. Make sure you got a nice good squat . . . so the only thing you move . . . is your hip section."

Thrust and retract. Thrust and retract. Thrust and retract. Tweetie goes on to other positions straight out of basic sex manuals. Squatting still farther and pressing her knees back, her hips and sphincter rise up to meet . . . whoever or whatever is thrusting toward her.

Twerking, marketed on the Internet as a gymnastic workout, in fact has a complicated history, drawing first on black hip-hop and New Orleans bounce scenes, and much more deeply in West African Mapouka, a collective dance among women that predates the arrival of French colonists and is about as far from West Coast disco clubs as anyone can imagine. Alarmed white parents and school directors, knowing little of those roots, have attempted to ban twerking, or much of anything that resembles it, denouncing it as a crude and debased form of sexual incitement. The version made most famous in the United States by Miley Cyrus, her anatomy scantily clothed in sequins and her ultra-pink tongue extended like a serpent's (easily available on YouTube), might well fit that category, but for the women of Ivory Coast doing Mapouka, it is a collective dance of joyous celebration not disconnected from the way in which girls and young women are taught to walk with the sort of hip, shoulder, and neck control that allows them to move over rough terrain, carrying pots and baskets on their heads. Mapouka girls and women, too, dance in a manner that Western pastors and schoolmarms might well regard as a shocking physical display; but, unlike the daughters of Western schoolmarms, they are not engaged in sexual flaunting. For them the body and its capacities are ever-present expressions of their inner lives and their inner joys and sadnesses.

In Liora's counseling experience, the white adolescent California twerkers rarely expressed much shame either, even if it's hard to believe that they weren't testing the limits of their adult chaperones. To the extent that they did feel shame it came, as in much Internet imagery, from failing to master the moves and gestures that are unmistakably about both anal and vaginal sex, which, the CDC studies indicate, most girls have not begun.

In the midst of tunneling through the literature on the difference between sex and sexuality and whether activities of tongues, fingers, and sundry inanimate toys qualify as "sex," I was sipping a beer with my friend Christophe on an especially pleasant summer afternoon on an especially pleasant Paris street corner. A musician with a high-end electric guitar played delightfully and sensually, collecting coins from the happy people in the cafés. Couples of all ages were touching, even caressing each other tastefully. Christophe, who also grew up on a farm before becoming a Parisian architect, remained silent for a minute or two, listening. "It's crazy. Of course it's all sex."

"Yes, to you," I answered, "but really, not everybody agrees. What do you think makes something sex?"

"It's simple. If you're aroused, that's sex."

"Well, are you so sure of that?" I asked. In France not much more than a century ago, coitus interruptus, or Catholic birth control, was regarded as a sort of fraud against sex and society's need of procreative sexuality. France and all of Europe as well as the United States wanted babies. The more babies our great-grandparents made, the more they enriched the society they lived in. If what we call "arousal" is a prelude to making babies, it was in some sense a sort of patriotic dance. If, however, the arousal was not intended to lead to procreation but just to produce pleasure, it was taken collectively as a form of physical fraud. No less important an authority than the U.S. Supreme Court ruled in 2014 that companies whose owners oppose birth control on religious grounds do not have to provide health insurance that covers it. Even today they see sexual arousal that can't lead to reproduction as a fraudulent betrayal of nature. Moreover, sex counselors report that adolescent girls are again choosing anal penetration over vaginal intercourse because they don't believe that's really sex—that it's just having fun.

Christophe had no more patience for such "simple nonsense" and insisted we change the subject. Yet the subject persists. Courts in Britain and the United States continue to condemn transsexual men or transsexual women for perpetrating fraud when they hide their "birth sex" and initiate sexually arousing movements with partners who don't know "what they don't have." Judges no longer refer to the demographic necessity to breed, but they do rule that people who were born with vaginas and pretend to be men (or vice versa) are acting fraudulently and can be sentenced to prison for that fraud. By that juridical reasoning seventeen-year-olds who insist that masturbation or oral sex "aren't real sex" find themselves trapped by society's conventional codes. If there is resistance—and there is massive resistance—to that sort of judicial of reasoning, it only means that in the West we remain far from certain that we know what sex really is. Take a step farther and look at how gender display and ubiquitous play with sexuality evolves almost daily, and remember that the best neuroscience now tells us that our brains, the organs that guide us through taste, appetite, and action, are in continual evolution, and we are left with little doubt that "the sexuality system" and where we place sex within that system are far from clear.

Since Michel Foucault's death thirty years ago, and since more and more women have entered into direct philosophical debate on the nature of sexuality, a new sort of resistance has emerged over the norms of "scientized" sexuality, raising new strategies for the reinvention of sexuality. What could only be found on porn sites a decade ago has, like Tweetie's twerking class, emerged as a home learning exercise. Indiana University's Center for Sexual Health Education has for several years offered instructions on how to use your mouth and tongue safely and effectively on your mate's several erogenous zones, not altogether unlike the videos twenty years ago for stretching exercises and deep knee bends. Network American TV broadcasts offer instruction to transgender people on how to walk the walk and step the step in their new and evolving gender profiles. One of the most interesting thinkers on the subject of understanding your gender/sexual body as an evolving laboratory of discovery is Beatriz Preciado, who migrates regularly from New York to Paris to Barcelona. Preciado's studies have taken her through pharmacology, sex history, and architecture. Architecture, finally, is what she sees as the critical dimension, but she starts with the arrival of the birth control pill in the 1950s.

"In the 1950s," she said in a now famous *Paris Review* interview, "if you took the first pill consistently, you would stop because you wouldn't produce monthly bleedings any longer; your period would stop. The first pill was equally efficient in terms of preventing pregnancy, but the Food and Drug Administration entered into a type of epistemological crisis. Women wouldn't be women anymore if they were not being marked by the difference of bleeding every month." The woman who could not, or did not, ovulate had lost the visible, touchable hallmark of what it meant historically to be female. Even if her potential fertility remained intact her bodily sense of womanliness was erased both for herself and for her mate even as she experienced expanded erotic freedom. The more sophisticated religious opponents of chemical birth control understood the pharmaceutical "breakthrough" not only as an encouragement to sexual libertinism but more profoundly as an assault on something sacred in her body's nature. Had chemical contraception had evolved to restore menstrual marking, it would almost certainly have been abandoned, a realization that the marketing departments of the pharmaceutical industry quickly understood even if the men in lab coats didn't. Very quickly new formulas came on the market and female bleeding returned. Other secondary side effects also diminished as more refined molecular biology advanced—even to the point that scientists learned to manage women's hormonal production sufficiently well to enhance cosmetic effects on the skin, or to make the womanliness of a woman's face yet more "womanly."

"When my gynecologist said I needed to go on birth control pills at age fourteen," Virginia Sole-Smith wrote in an essay for *Elle* magazine, "my feminist mother rejoiced. I'd been missing several days of school every month since my period had started two years earlier, bringing with it vomiting, mind-numbing cramps, and the kind of heavy bleeding that ruins white jeans and fragile middle-school egos." Taking the pill has effectively replaced menstruation as the basic marker separating girlhood from womanhood throughout the modern world, and while its stated justification is for preventing pregnancy, the pill's off-label functions long ago equaled or exceeded birth control. A 2011 research report from the Guttmacher Institute found that 58 percent of American woman take the pill for reasons beyond contraception, including 14 percent for controlling facial acne, while 80 percent of sexually active women report having used the pill during their lives. The pill is of course not the only form of contraceptive available to or used by women. It is, for example, less effective than implants or IUDs, which remain vociferously opposed by conservative Catholic bishops. Nonetheless the pill stands physiologically and metaphorically as the symbolic blade that has cut sex apart from reproduction. As pharmaceutical laboratories have altered contraceptives' molecular structures to reduce unpleasant side effects, they have concentrated more and more on what can only be seen as a form of gender enhancement: beauty, personal independence, and physical mobility. Or, as Beatriz Preciado has written, the pill redefined heterosexual sex and that, oddly enough, opened the gates to what may well have been the most fundamental reimagining of all the acts listed in the CDC's catalogue of current "sex acts." Once sex became reliably dissociated from pregnancy, it also became free both of its traditional moral sanctions and its biological function.

None of the foregoing is to say that sex has become free of risk, stigma, or shame. Erotic freedom has carried with it viral and bacterial proliferation, including resurgences of syphilis, gonorrhea, human papilloma virus (HPV), and, of course, HIV, which when it first surfaced stimulated global panic and widespread "safe-sex" campaigns. Initially AIDS was identified among gay men in the United States and France; very quickly, however, Brazil and sub-Saharan Africa developed massive epidemics that within a very few years spread almost equally between men and women. The sex acts themselves remained relatively hidden and shameful in Brazil, Nigeria, and South Africa, but other stigmas arose in Europe and America: the clean versus the dirty—those who were infected and those who were not. For men to have become infected overwhelmingly indicated that they had been having penetrative sex with other men, since vaginal intercourse presents males with relatively little risk. On top of that came a new biomedically defined condemnation of being an "unclean" person. In a scholarly article examining the resurgence of risky sex, cultural criminologist Brian Frederick addresses the effect of many well-intentioned safe-sex campaigns. "Safe sex ads that prey on gay men's feelings of guilt or that try to frighten them into a more health-conscious way of living can often stigmatize them, regardless of their HIV serostatus. One ad, in particular, features the image of an HIV virus particle with a gift tag attached that reads, 'To: Adam, From: Eric.' At the bottom of the ad is a simple message: 'Nobody wants to get HIV.'" Public health officials briefly succeeded in closing down many brothels and sex clubs that were initially blamed for spreading the epidemic, but by the opening of the current century new sex houses returned, very often in private or "underground" venues, and they were soon followed by thousands of Internet "hook-up" sites for both men and women that were beyond any sort of public health surveillance. Among them were so-called party 'n' play clubs featuring methamphetamine use.

As my old friend the sex counselor Laura had advised, the consistently reliable approach to tracking sexual mores is to "follow the shame." Just as families and churches in the 1950s and '60s sought to separate the good girls from the bad girls and inculcate a sense of stigma in each, biocleanliness resurrected the old theme. "To circumvent the substantial harms of being revealed as an HIV-seropositive drug user," Brian Frederick found, "many of these individuals retreat into hiding, where they often become engrossed in a subculture comprised of others who are similar to them and who separate themselves from the non-drug-using, HIV-seronegative 'others.'" Add to that a growing enthusiasm for bisexuality and a new term, "sexually curious" (meaning curious about all options for erotic stimulation), and the groundwork was set for a new and even more explosive epidemic of sexually transmitted diseases (STDs). Indeed, because many of the younger players insist that non-penis vaginal intercourse isn't actually sex, and therefore might seem less risky, the potential parameters appeared even grimmer.

What constitutes a plague for one sector, however, often opens opportunities for other sectors, especially in a microbial universe that unifies sex and gender. The global pharmaceutical industry, dominated by American, Swiss, and French firms, lost no time in producing a basket of products to meet a growing demand from men and women who had moved well beyond pregnancy anxiety to fear of infection from so-called "non-normative" sex. When in 2012 the U.S. Food and Drug Administration approved the use of Truvada, a powerful drug manufactured by the Silicon Valley firm Gilead Sciences, as effective protection against HIV infection, sexual adventurers were ecstatic—and so were many public health professionals. Condoms had never been popular among men or women for oral sex. For anal and for vaginal sex, they were often regarded as not especially comfortable for the recipients. Truvada, which had become a critical element in treatment of people already infected with HIV, promised both freedom and safety—at least from HIV if not from other STDs—and it seemed that the stigma and shame of being "dirty" would diminish as well.

Shame and the struggle to avoid it had not disappeared; they had simply migrated to the info-molecular age. Alongside Truvada and other protective antiviral drugs and inoculations, pharmaceutical science has worked equally intensely on improving the sexual experience itself, all the while further complicating the conventional gender-sex equation. Viagra and its more powerful cousin Cialis were designed to reinforce the symbol of masculinity whose roots long precede Greek and Egyptian iconography. The man who is incapable of maintaining an enduring erection is almost universally taken as an "unmanned" male regardless of his haberdashery. Cheaper compounds sold over the counter or in sex bars have also proliferated. Add to these pharmaceutical liberators one more chemical that is easily available on the Internet underground or by prescription: testosterone.

Beatriz Preciado recounts her own experiences using testosterone creams in her book *Testo Junkie*. As estrogen is the definitive hormonal indicator of feminine "sex," so testosterone marks masculinity—except of course that we all contain varying balances of each substance. How any particular person's gender is perceived by others depends in great measure on that balance—as my visits with the transgender Mormons in Utah made clear. Beards, breasts, pectorals, hips, and vocal range are all chemically variable in all of us. Preciado, a high-order intellectual who consistently rejects convoluted academic jargon, spent a year addressing her own already androgynous body as a living gender laboratory, applying various intensities of testosterone creams. As of this writing she remains visibly female, the gender to which she was "assigned" at birth, although she consistently says she will almost certainly one day undergo sexual reassignment surgery. "What look like natural organs are, in reality, the result of complex cultural interpretation processes, a concentrated scientific metaphor," she said in another interview. "Thus, we are convinced that a penis is a virile organ and, as such, associated to erection, penetration ... But, why an anus could not be a virile organ? This is why I am interested in bodies where the certainty of assigned sexuality seems to be blurred, and which challenge the binary logic of sexual representation: fetuses, children or senile bodies, disabled bodies, anorexic or extremely obese bodies, fakir and contortionist bodies, animal bodies ... " As much as these variations on the human form may fall in the minority, the studies by the CDC and by European public health agencies of how individuals make sex with each other leave little doubt that erotic expression aimed specifically at reproduction is—and may always have been—a minority human activity. Anyone who has ever visited an exercise club, taken regular dance classes, or even tried to follow Tweetie's twerking routines at home learns quickly that the body is a profoundly plastic apparatus whose elements are in constant dialogue with the brain. The body may respond to the brain's commands, but equally our brains "learn" from the pain and pleasure signals telegraphed back from abused or toughened muscles.

While global chemical laboratories almost yearly produce newer and less risky erotic stimulants, Beatriz Preciado raises doubts about how long or even whether conventional male-female intercourse will remain the dominant form of human reproduction. Penetrative heterosexual coitus, she argues, is but the current dominant form of reproduction based on a bodily "architecture" and presentation that is rooted in patriarchal supremacy, which itself owes its power to ancient and less and less observed religious authority. "Compared to civilizations where fucking was part of a general art of corporal pleasures, our ways of fucking, derived to a good extent from religious mythologies and political restrictions, are rough and repetitive. That is why fucking per se—not the fantasizing about fucking—is nearly always so boring [compared to] almost any other possibility of articulation—penis-anus, vulva-vulva, hand-vulva-anus, object-mouth-clitoris, penis-object, etc.—[and] is considered a deviation, pathology, a nonsense phrase ... Eventually, everything is reduced to a penis, a vagina, and a domestic place. Just because our ways of fucking are not determined naturally, but are part of a cultural language, these can be, and in fact are being, modified."

Beyond all these acts that more or less directly involve traditional sexual organs, there remain a panoply of other sorts of erotic arousal. Stefan, who grew up in Dusseldorf, recounted one of the most intense experiences he had ever had with Michael, an American with whom he had been living in Amsterdam for several years. "We had sex ... we had I think you could say good sex," he began. "We penetrated each other, but you know after some years it was not, I can say, truly passionate." You mean "solidarity sex" like most married couples have? I asked. "Yes," he answered, "I never thought of it that way, but that could be correct." There was a pause as Stefan gathered his thoughts. "Then, not very long ago, well before dawn when the pigeons started to sing, I kind of awoke to find two very warm fingers pressing upon my forehead. I don't think Michael was even awake, but his fingers remained there warming my skin. It was an autumn night, the first chilly one we had had. As his fingers rested against my head, I began to be aroused ... No, not aroused, but *very* aroused, very, excuse me, *hard*, like I had not been in many years. My breath became short and I began to twist myself. So, okay, I won't say more. Michael's breath became short as well and then we both sighed, exhausted, and fell into a deep sleep that not even the crying pigeons could disrupt." Another quieter pause. "Was that sex?" he asked rhetorically. "Most of the people I know would shrug and say of course it was not. But it was more intense, more bonding I can say, than any wet sex we had ever had."

Even if older conventional reproductive labels and categories continue to divide sex, gender, and eroticism into distinct camps, sex, as stylish women's magazines have been telling us since the opening of the current century, happens in almost every square centimeter of the animal body, from the interior cavity within the ankle to the soft glottal skin beneath the voice box to the extended lower lobes of either ear. A lightly licked toe or a softly caressed sacrum, as most porno viewers also know, may prove for one or another of us as ecstatic as a chemically reliable penis. Or as Beatriz Preciado predicts, "On the one hand, pornography, as a masturbatory virtual prosthesis, will reach universal proportions. As such, it can be said that over the course of the twenty-first century, pornography will become a part of popular culture. In this way, 'Jenna Jameson shag' or 'double penetration' will be as widespread hits as Disney's *Pocahontas* or the Big Mac were in the twentieth century."

From one perspective, that day will mark the ultimate degradation of a sacred intimacy. But for Preciado and many others, it may mark the moment when sexual acts and personal identity, however they are defined, have at last left behind the dual stigmas of shame and degradation, when being sexual is neither more nor less normal than any other animal activity.

CHAPTER 13

Is the Clitoris a Sex Organ?

Rarely has the occasion arisen to talk with women about the clitoris—theirs or anyone else's. Breasts were as common as sunrise in the marble ateliers of ancient Greece and Rome, as they were for Leonardo and Michelangelo at the height of the Italian Renaissance. Testicles were tenderly crafted and marginally pendulous while penises were generally small and retracted save for creatures that were half-man, half-beast, but neither clitorises nor labia nor any of the other rather magical curtains and protuberances of the human vulva gained attention from the classical masters of the plastic arts. Indeed even today visitors to the Louvre, the Metropolitan Museum of Art, or the National Gallery will be hard-pressed to find much sculptural evidence that female primates possess any sexual organs. That territory of the sculpted female anatomy is nearly always as smooth as polished ivory. The wings of desire are clearly missing.

The erasure of these key elements of female erotic expression first emerged for me in a conversation I had in the woods of Vermont with a young pre-med student who was earning extra cash that summer working as a furniture builder's assistant. She was as puzzled as I about how the world of fine art, for centuries controlled by males and until the eighteenth century mostly by priests and bishops, had focused almost solely on the mammaries. Hardly ever were the generative genitals revealed. (Neo-Freudian explications about male anxiety and sexual representation weren't on the agenda.)

"Let me tell you, some guys' penises, yeah, they're really sensitive, really responsive, but they're nothing like a healthy clit," she told me as she was pushing an oak plank into a circular table saw. "The clit, it's like . . . nuclear. Wow!" If I was not devoid of experience, she left no doubt that hers was vastly greater. Or, as she added, "Why do you think we scream when it's good?"

The technical explanation is simple. A clitoris normally has about eight thousand sensory receptors—compared to half as many in an ordinary penis—and its sole function is to provide ecstatic pleasure to its bearer. That simple neuro-reality sets the stage for an enormous array of gender roles and rules, not least the general invisibility of women's erotic apparatus except in the gardens of lesbian porn. Among the great ironies suffusing the sexual objectification of women's bodies is the near total absence of female sexual organs from the framing of what feminists call "the male gaze." Men idolize and exaggerate breasts, hips, lips, even ankles in most configurations of female eroticism, but they rarely present or discuss actual female genital zones.

One of the few recent sites where the complexities of female sexuality and gender surfaced was in Brussels in the deep winter of 2015, when six African women artists came together to mount a provocative show under the rubric *Body Talk: Feminism, Sexuality and the Body.* Belgium, recall, was the great colonial power that forced much of central Africa into effective slavery for the extraction of raw rubber, and that echo of slavery was not missing from the work of the six artists any more than was the all-too-contemporary reality of clitoral mutilation as an element of gender-role enforcement. The Congo, the former heart of the Belgian colonial empire, not freed until 1960, was also one of the sources of black male and female slaves who were paraded around nineteenth-century Europe in cages as traveling human zoos for the amusement of white, mostly male, voyeurs.

Among the most famous, at the beginning of the nineteenth century, was a twenty-year-old woman from South Africa whose actual married name was Sawtche Baartman (renamed Saartjie, Dutch for Sarah) before she was sold to a Dutch Afrikaner, who married her and with whom she bore three children. When a British military surgeon and entrepreneur, Alexander Dunlop, came across her, he was struck by her very large hips and protruding labia, not an infrequent characteristic of the South African Khoi people. Dunlop managed to convince her to take a ship to Britain, where she was put on display under the name Hottentot Venus and reaped handsome receipts from well-heeled and elegantly coiffed white gentlemen who saw her as nothing more than one of the "bridge animals" between the hairy apes and the human ancestors in the pre-Darwinian notions of evolution that had begun to surface. But Saartjie Baartman and others in the human zoos were not merely carnival amusements. They served to illustrate the emerging theories of eugenics that aimed to codify the presumed superiority of white Nordics over all the world's colored peoples. Caricatures of black males aimed to portray a lesser species akin to apes and monkeys, but they were also oddly taken as less dangerous and, against all evidence, seen as possessing inferior sexual apparatus while the outsized black female sexual organs, like those of Hottentot Venus, appeared fierce, ferocious, indeed rather like "man-eating" mouths. The realities of ethnic differences in the form and size of humans' sexual equipment were not at issue. What was at issue was a primordial fear reflected in the folktales of human population around the world: While the male may possess greater muscular strength in his arms, his shoulders, his thighs, the female possesses a form and physiology that is at once attractive and dangerous—and that primordial female persisted most clearly on the African continent, already understood as the birthplace of human beings.

Algerian sculptor Zoulikha Bouabdellah was one of the six African artists in Brussels who addressed the web of fear and attraction that still persists in the gender dance, a dynamic she expressed in an homage to Louise Bourgeois's famous terrifying steel spiders. Bouabdellah's spider was much smaller than those cast by Bourgeois. It was composed of sleek black arches that also reflect an array of the sacred arches present in all the world's major religions—arches that at once beckon believers to enter their faith while excluding the infidels and the unfaithful, all united in the form of a fragile but toxic spider whose web can capture its far greater adversaries and enable the spider to devour them alive. "Why does the spider interest me?" she asked rhetorically in a seminar at the Brussels opening. "Because it symbolizes feminine sex. Fragility. Cleverness. It's a small creature but it captures bigger ones in its web." The mouth and the web, she explained, have always been at the heart of gender fear and gender violence in its most visceral form. "Violence against women exists everywhere. It's not important whether it's done by a woman or a man," she continued, reflecting on the imposition of female genital cutting so common now in Africa: "It's imposed by men."

Millions of women have had their genital tissue mutilated in Africa and the Middle East, and the procedures are unlikely to stop any time soon. But contrary to the usual Western portrayal of genital mutilation, it has been far from an exclusively African procedure. Both British and American doctors regularly undertook "genital cutting," or more politely "clitoral circumcision," well into the twentieth century as a treatment for "overexcited" girls who "touched themselves" too often. So-called "outsized" clitorises were but a part of the hysteria diagnosis provoked by a hungry, uncontrolled, "floating uterus." Frequently the almost universally male surgeons considered the body parts associated with the uterus, notably the clitoris, to be overly large and too close in appearance to a penis. Modern medicine no longer refers overtly to clitoral circumcision as a purification rite as many tribal cultures in Africa and the Middle East do. Western surgeons describe sexual cutting procedures as clarification of an identity that biology has left confused and uncertain. While the notion of surgical *clarification* may sound very different from tribal *purification*, the psychological and cultural parallels between the two terms may not be so remote.

Generally "purification rites" have been imposed on girls and later on child-bearing women to cleanse them of some sort of original or primal sin that females were so often judged to suffer from birth. Jews, Christians, Muslims, Hindus, Baha'i, Shinto Kalash, and indigenous North Americans, among others, have imposed physical purification rites on their peoples, but most strictly on their female members. Both conservative and orthodox Jewish temples require construction of a *mikvah*, or cleansing pool of rainwater, in which members of the temple, and especially women, must immerse themselves after they have already washed themselves scrupulously. Indeed even today orthodox Jews must not even touch the hand of a post-menstrual woman who has not been purified in the mikvah. These purification pools trace their origin to the story in Genesis when Adam, banished from Eden, went to cleanse himself in the stream flowing from Eden after he had tasted of Eve's corrupt apple of knowledge. It was the wily Eve, of course, who had corrupted Adam's purity. No major religion has nearly approached the woman-hating and woman-fearing reproach of Catholicism's founding fathers, who viewed the mystery of monthly menstruation and the agony of childbirth as a divine curse to be imposed through all eternity on those beings who carry XX chromosomes. Usually the purification procedures and rites have been carried out by women on other girls and women. Zoulikha Bouabdellah attributes the persistence of sex-related violence by women against women to ignorance and poverty, but the enforcement of those rituals seemed to her and her fellow women artists to tap into a deeper anxiety held by all too many men, educated or tribal.

"That fear [was] created not by women but by men themselves," she went on. "In Africa they talk of excision [clitoral cutting]. In England they burned the witches because they feared they were too intelligent. In China they bound the feet of girls. In each society there is that violence against women. Women are the unknown and men fear the unknown." That fear of the unknown in societies run by men—most societies—and of the female as ultimately unknowable is as ancient as hieroglyphics and as modern as Lacanian psychoanalysis. Bioethnographers have traced that fear of the feminine to the mystery of the persistently bleeding female. How could it be possible that these people can bleed month after month after month and not die while for men the sight of blood, which they mostly associated with battle and violence, nearly always signaled impending death?

"It is only natural," writes Nigerian theologian Rosemary Edet, "that women's blood should awaken fear, especially in men. However, although menstrual and childbirth bleeding can readily be distinguished from blood in murder or an accident, many [African] societies regard it as the most impure of impurities." That impurity, reflected in purification rites still practiced in Nigeria, Somalia, and West Africa particularly, derives from the association between sex and violence linked to mythic male fear of feminine mystery. Several Mediterranean cultures have portrayed the so-called *vagina dentata*—a symbol of the castrating woman who can literally bite off the testicles of both adults and male infants, recounted in the Book of Tobit used by orthodox Jewish and Catholic believers. In the Tobit folklore the fearsome young woman who places any and potentially all males in danger of emasculation is purified through exorcism. In that way, primordial fears around the world have linked the blood of menstruation and of childbirth to the inherent potential violence of sex. In each case menstrual blood is taken as more powerful, more dangerous even than the merely mortal blood that pulses out of the wounded male breast. So it is as well that for a male to "have sex with" or to penetrate a bleeding, menstruating female threatens not only his sex organs and generative capacity but also his spiritual fate. There, too, comes the association of ritual bathing, cutting, or even stitching up girls' and women's labial tissues as means to "protect" men from women's mysterious powers.

"The puberty ritual celebrates and purifies menstrual blood impurity," Edet writes. "During the ritual, clitoridectomy is sometimes performed with all its accompanying rites. The important elements here, as in birthing rituals, are segregation, purification, and exhibition. The outing day for a confined girl celebrates blood as dangerous and salvific; as contagious and efficacious; as a symbol of life and death. It is dangerous in that red explicitly signifies violence, killing and at its most general level of meaning, a breach in the social order. The symbolism suggests that the young woman is unconsciously rejecting her female role of motherhood, that in fact she is guilty." Further, Edet points out, in certain Nigerian languages, the term for menstruation is synonymous with "being guilty."

A minimum of 100 million women in the world—possibly as many as 150 million—are believed to have passed through one version or another of genital cutting—sometimes little more than bathing or ritual nicking and at other times full removal of the visible clitoral glans or even vaginal stitching, which can inflict severe pain during urination, as well as life-threatening and sometimes fatal infections. For all the African women artists at the Brussels *Body Talk* show, ritual mutilation of women's sexual organs certainly represented a grotesque form of sexual abuse, and yet, the campaigns conducted in the West against female genital mutilation (FGM) also struck most of them as an elitist and demeaning dismissal of African tribal cultures, lumping a half dozen very different practices into a single "barbarian" notion of sexual violence. UNICEF estimates that upwards of 98 percent of women in Somalia, 96 percent in Guinea, 93 percent in Djibouti, 89 percent in Eritrea and Mali, and 91 percent in Egypt—where the procedure is legally banned—have suffered genital cutting. Some sixty thousand women in France, which has a large African immigrant population, have undergone genital cutting.

Today almost all genital cutting has ended in one African nation, Senegal, due in large part to a grassroots education program initiated by a lone American woman, Molly Melching, who had grown up in a small town in Illinois before embarking on intense human rights work in Senegal. The story of her work with native Senegalese women over thirty years to end genital cutting—known simply as "the tradition"—is at once as exhilarating as the razor blade procedure is grotesque, all of it recounted in intense detail by writer Aimee Molloy in her book *However Long the Night.* Facilitators who had been trained by Molly Melching would move village by village to encourage women of child-bearing age to gather in small groups and talk about their personal experiences with "the tradition." Like many physical rites associated with religion, "the tradition" had been simply assumed as a female rite of passage necessary for obtaining a husband in a land where living as a single woman could only be described as ghastly. It was never discussed. The men, who were of course assured that the cutting had taken place, never spoke of it and generally had no idea how, when, or by whom it was performed. Talking, then, was always the first barrier that Melching and her facilitators faced. Very often an hour or more would pass in the first meeting before anyone dared speak. One of those who did at last find the courage to speak was called Kerthio. Kerthio had come with her mother, a stern village matriarch regarded as the enforcer of "the tradition." Kerthio listened as one woman after another began to describe their own agonizing experiences with a village cutter, or the screams they had heard from their infant daughters and in some cases even how those infant daughters had bled to death during the night and day after their tiny clitorises had been cut. At last Kerthio rose to tell her own story, how as a young mother she had lost her first daughter from the bloody procedure, then nearly lost her second daughter and had finally stood up against her own mother and thousands of years of tradition to protect her third daughter from the same mutilation.

For many Western health professionals, genital cutting was simply a primordial, barbarian mutilation of ignorant tribal women. But that was not how Molly Melching approached the issue. She first went to live in villages and work with the women there, learning their language, cooking and cleaning and offering simple classes concerning everything from hygiene to simple business practices, in the process of which she came to understand how and why "the tradition" was such a universal tradition among Senegalese women.

"Why were girls cut?" author Aimee Molloy asks in her book. "It was a silly question, like asking why one breathes. Every woman in the room knew that the tradition was among the most momentous events of a girl's life, preparing her to become a woman, to eventually be deemed acceptable for marriage, and, most important of all, to fully belong and have a respected role within her society. For a girl not to be cut—and to be a *bilakoro*, a name considered among the worst insults in their culture—was unimaginable." A bilakoro was an unclean person, who could never be accepted by "real women," and "the food she cooked would not be eaten, the clothes she washed rewashed by others."

Later, another woman, Aminato, from northern Senegal rose to speak. She had been cut when she was an infant and afterward had been "resealed" —a binding procedure that closes the vagina, barely allowing a woman to urinate, and, once menstruation begins, hampering her monthly bleeding and leaving her more susceptible to infections. At age fifteen Aminato had been presented for marriage to a man chosen by her parents. "On the night before my wedding," she told the group, "my mother explained I would have to be cut open the next morning in order to consummate the marriage. I panicked and tried to refuse all of it . . . I had no choice. The procedure to open me was agonizing. I'd been told that if I wasn't penetrated that night my vagina would again close, but I didn't care. The pain was so severe I couldn't imagine having intimate relations with my new husband." Instead, Aminato ran away and hid for several days. The new husband divorced her.

Just as by the mid-twentieth century the birth control pill enabled women to explore pleasure independent of reproduction, so the ancient practice of clitoral cutting in fact enforced a brutal form of female monogamy by completely divorcing sex from pleasure. Aminato did eventually remarry, but she never found pleasure in sex—only pain—and childbirth was always agonizing and difficult because of the inelasticity of the scar tissue that had formed since she had been cut as an infant. "My body was so damaged, I could hardly be put back together again," she said. As Kerthio listened to these testimonies, she remained silent about how she had protected her third daughter from the "purifying" removal of her clitoral glans.

Fortunately for the women of Senegal, the dominant ethnic population, the Wolof people, do not practice and have not practiced genital cutting, a reality that helped those who did to abandon the practice, which they had until then falsely believed was a requirement of Islam and Christianity. In the other lands where the practice has gone on for thousands of years, long before the arrival of Judaism or Christianity or Islam, little has changed. Somali girls who have not yet been cut are denounced as dirty people and ridiculed in their villages by other children who have been cut. To be cut and purified is still, as it was in Senegal, seen to be a necessary preparation for womanhood when, of course, the women will continue to suffer the monthly denigration of spilling unclean menstrual blood, which will further require them to sequester themselves at home and drop out of school or work. So it is that purification still further codifies and enforces their secondary position and status in the community.

Both the United Nations and the World Health Organization have mounted vigorous public health campaigns to stop female genital cutting. They have, however, rarely acknowledged that very similar practices were undertaken by European and American doctors well into the last century to calm obstreperous and overexcited young girls who were judged to have touched themselves too often or too publicly. Doctors urged mothers to choose undergarments that would not stimulate little girls' sexual terrain and thereby risk activating their uteruses, which could send them into the widely accepted diagnosis of "hysteria." (Sigmund Freud dismissed clitoral orgasm as "infantile" and "immature" when compared to what he called "the mature orgasm" associated with vaginal stimulation.) Those diagnoses and the bizarre notions of female physiology on which they were based have largely disappeared, but cutting of strange or abnormal or simply unfamiliar sexual tissue has not disappeared in American neonatal surgical wards.

Hospitals across America and Europe continue to perform the "sexual assignment" surgery on newborns whose barely formed sex organs are not clearly identifiable as strictly male or female. An estimated one in every two thousand newborn babies, according to the American Medical Association, is born with initially ambiguous genitalia. Through much of the twentieth century, pediatric surgeons were quickly engaged to correct or clarify the ambiguity. At one hospital, Texas Children's in Houston, a special team exists to spring into action when such babies are born. One of the most notorious cases took place in 2014 in South Carolina, where a newborn child first identified as a boy was redesignated as a girl and had his penis cut off. Nearly all fetuses start out physiologically female. Within the first three months roughly half begin to form male genitalia and female forms disappear, while gendered differences in the brain seem to develop in the last months of gestation (see Chapter 16). But in thousands of cases, a child is born with traces of each, including a penis and testicles as well as a tiny vaginal crease. It is sometimes difficult to distinguish between clitoral and penile tissue. In most cases one or the other sets of sexual organs diminishes and disappears, while a few so-called "intersex" children continue to carry both sets of sexual organs. Until the end of the last century surgical correction in advanced surgical wards like that at Texas Children's was common. More recent pediatric research now urges parents and physicians to delay *any* infant genital surgery until much later because individual genital formation can differ widely over time from one individual to another. Whatever the form of the organs themselves, the child's eventual sense of gender, more and more specialists argue, is generally impossible to predict at birth.

On the surface, there may seem to be little relation between primordial clitoral cutting carried out until a century ago in the West as well as in Africa and the microsurgery carried out today by highly trained specialists under ultra-sanitary, anesthetized conditions. One is an obvious mutilation dictated by ancient cultural tradition; the other is a corrective procedure undertaken to render what most medical experts see as physiological abnormality that must be "normalized" so that the infant will not later be subjected to shame, humiliation, and potential hormonal problems. The problem, as the plaintiffs in the South Carolina case argued, is that both authority and control over that child's sexual and gender development was taken away from the child before he even had the ability to speak. Worse, by age eight the child indeed did perceive himself to be male despite his missing penis and testicles. In another case several decades earlier, Cheryl Case was also born with genitalia that puzzled doctors. At first the medical experts decided Cheryl was a boy, and he was given the name Charlie. Later, after the parents became worried about something that looked like a small vagina, another team of surgical experts decided the young child was female. They performed further corrective surgery to remove what looked like a penis but in fact it was a larger than normal clitoris. By removing it, the surgeons had really performed a modern version of the ancient clitoral cutting. In yet another case, David, one of two twin boys, had his penis sliced off during a botched circumcision; unable to construct a new penis, the surgeons went on to model false female genitals and urged the parents to raise David as a girl, named Brenda. But Brenda always refused girl's dresses and games, grew near-suicidal under the pressure, and eventually, with psychological counseling after his parents admitted what had happened, reclaimed David as his name; by his mid-thirties, he had rebuilt his life as a male and got married.

Both American and European pediatric guidelines now strongly oppose surgical intervention in infancy or childhood. Children, they advise, should be encouraged to express the gender in which they feel most comfortable—including diffuse gender responses. The hasty egocentric tendency of Western surgeons to render any child conventionally normal is no more legitimate than is ritual purification cutting in Somalia, they argue; both simply reflect a silent misogyny that reserves sexual pleasure for men and polices women's ability to have sexual relations with men other than their husbands. Be it in Texas or Timbuktu, sexual cutting signals what Michel Foucault called the bio-power of any society's elite to "police" or control the body of any of its citizens—whether they were black slave bodies in nineteenth-century Alabama, white women in the twentieth century who demanded sexual pleasure without risking pregnancy, or voiceless children, girls and boys who, under the mantle of "healthy development," were denied the right to discover and realize their own senses of gender within their own flesh. For the moment contemporary pediatric counselors advise following the model of Scandinavian preschools where children are encouraged to take any role or any costume they like. Surgeons, however, are not known for their diffuse outlooks on normality any more than are Egyptian traditionalists who associate a sensitive clitoris with dangerous sexual appetite. Both surgeons and the matriarchal defenders of "the tradition" aim for culturally constructed normalcy through which bodies and behaviors reflect and uphold predictability. Those who are not normal are, to use the terminology of an earlier time, impure. The language of the pure and the methods of purification may have changed, but the campaigns to enforce purity have not disappeared.

CHAPTER 14
Sexual Capital in Shanghai

Hot tropical drizzle peppered the heavy air as our taxi driver called out to passersby for directions to the faculty cafeteria at Sun Yat-sen University in Guangzhou, China. I had come to meet Yuxin Pei, perhaps the most radical sex and gender specialist I would encounter in this project. Formally a sociologist in the university's anthropology department, Yuxin Pei won global Internet fame with the following posting on her microblog: "Masturbation videos wanted, top cash award of 10,000 yuan."

Ten thousand yuan at the time equaled about sixteen hundred dollars, or five times a worker's average monthly wage.

Yuxin Pei, sometimes referred to as China's "sexy sociologist," is a pretty woman and she enjoys dressing to complement her beauty, but there is a method both in her self-presentation and in her work that aims to rethink the linkage between sex and gender. The masturbation videos she has solicited do not contain images of women actually masturbating; rather they are short reflections by working-class women about their experience with masturbation. While masturbation is not illegal in China and indeed while homosexual acts were decriminalized some twenty years ago, several years ahead of the U.S. Supreme Court's Lawrence versus Texas decision in 2003, circulation of explicit sex videos can still be prosecuted under anti-pornography laws. Yuxin Pei's mission, however, has been to open women up to the notion that masturbation could become a vital tool, indeed a form of "sexual capital," they can use to express their identities as women in conservative China. Chinese women, in Mao Zedong's famous phrase, "hold up half the sky" but that half was in his day mostly staffing the lunchrooms for the Red Army or making itself available for Army propaganda films. Western psychology and sociology, much less "sexology," were banned during the decades of Maoist rule. Love and romance were dismissed as Western bourgeois corruptions. Choice of a life mate was determined by either political or family negotiation, rather as it had been in Medieval Catholic France. Orgasm was the preserve of male privilege. Fashion and self-display, aside from performances by Jiang Qing (Madame Mao) in the Beijing Opera, were a collection of drab blue uniforms.

No more. Although the rabidly market-driven "socialism" of today's China still officially bans "sexy advertising" and push-up bras, glamorous heels and thigh-slit skirts are all over Shanghai's Bund and Beijing's Forbidden City. Sex acts, explicit sex marketing, and sexual art may be carefully shrouded in this second decade of the twenty-first century, but one foreigner asking about sex and gender finds it about as difficult as another asking where to hail a taxi or buy an ice cream cone in August. Kids hawking "pretty lady" or "hot guy" services swarm the tourist zones of major cities. And as China challenges so many other domains in the global marketplace, the 1.3 billion Chinese are set to disrupt and reorganize how the world understands sexuality and its impact on gender. Gay marriage may still be officially unrecognized—just as heterosexual marriage itself carries no certain fiscal benefits until a partnership is registered with the state. Nevertheless, symbolic gay and lesbian marriages though they have no legal standing have become so commonplace on Tiananmen Square that they are hardly noticed.

Yuxin Pei had warned me in a series of e-mail exchanges before I arrived in China that this evening would be her only chance for a meeting. She was leaving that night for an international sociology conference, and it was already a half hour past our appointment time. For my companions and me it was the beginning of a three-week passage through five Chinese cities. Her insights and contacts were vital to the journey, and this would be our only encounter. She had proposed the faculty cafeteria as our meeting point. I had found a table near a large window looking toward the interior grounds of the university.

"Mr. Bro-ing?" a soft, clear, lightly accented voice said from behind. I turned to see two young women towing enormous suitcases toward the table. "Sorry to be late, but did I tell you we are going to Argentina tonight?" The speaker was Yuxin Pei. She had clearly not hesitated to dress herself for the wandering eye. Neither has she hesitated to criticize the subordinate status of women in China's bedrooms or in China's high-rise office suites. Her approach to personal autonomy and gender equality, however, sets her very much apart from that of her Western sisters.

Traveling with her to Argentina was a friend and fellow sociologist from Beijing Normal University, Xiying Wang. They had both become regulars on the international academic circuit, but it is Pei's many scholarly papers linking masturbation to identity development that have drawn the most attention. A year or so earlier she had been invited to speak at the University of Paris III, where she had anticipated a vigorous discussion with French scholars only to discover that most of them sat silent when she uttered the m-word; the French, apparently, were no better at addressing the matter of women's sexual self-satisfaction than were the aging cadre in China's officially communist hierarchy. Male masturbation is a commonplace territory of adolescent humor often enough evident in satiric cartoon papers like *Charlie Hebdo*, but female masturbation remains if not taboo in common public conversation, at least difficult outside the pages of *Penthouse*, *Playboy*, or Hollywood gossip rags. I too felt uncomfortable plunging straight ahead into the topic. Instead we ordered a round of Tsingtao beers and began to talk about mothers and daughters in the New China.

"Mothers now are so proud of their daughters," Yuxin began, addressing the new sexualized sense of style and independence among young women who very often come from rural and working-class settings. "The mothers always think their daughters are living an ideal life," she said. "I have interviewed a lot of mothers and daughters together." The mothers, she assured me, are excited not only about their daughters' financial success but equally about the new sexual freedom their daughters now enjoy.

"What does that tell us about the mothers?" I ask.

"I think it means the living conditions of the mothers and the daughters have changed a lot. Daughters can drive. Daughters have a credit card. Daughters travel around the world. Daughters have handbags. Daughters wear high heels. Most mothers do ask, 'Why do you buy so many clothes and so many shoes?' Twenty years ago, when the mothers were young, these materials were very limited."

Xiying Wang broke in. "In that time you know women dressed like a man, during the Cultural Revolution."

"And most of [the mothers] didn't have a love relationship. They've had very short periods of free love, and then they would enter into marriage," Pei said as the conversation rustled on, each woman picking up the other's sentences. They had grown up in very different parts of China, in different circumstances, but it soon became clear that their research experience was not merely abstract scholarship. They were also speaking about their own mothers' and grandmothers' experiences over the previous half century.

"Sometimes no dating at all," Xiying said. "They just enter into marriage and have children with this man."

"But [now] for the daughters," Yuxin picked up, "They would have a long sexual experience before marriage ... [while] their mothers didn't have [much] sex—or even any before marriage. So for the daughters you can see marriage coming as a result of love, but for the mothers it was not like that at all. It was a kind of political or economic situation."

Yet the mothers are not always pleased, she found, with their daughters' successes.

"You know, even when the daughters have had a good salary or success in business, they often still feel they have failed if they are alone or don't have an ideal husband," Yuxin explained. "They feel very unhappy. When they try to talk about this with their mothers, their mothers always will say, 'Oh you live life in heaven.'"

She cited a thirty-five-year-old editor named Yan who works in a publishing house and had divorced her husband after she discovered he was having an affair with another woman. Following the divorce Yan redoubled her work at the office and soon won a promotion, all the while hoping to find a new mate. She scoured Internet dating sites and signed up with traditional marriage agencies. Still, she told Yuxin, she had failed to "fall in love" with a good man and remarry or even establish a stable cohabitation agreement. As time passed Yan grew more and more depressed. Yan's sixty-year-old mother, a retired schoolteacher, offered little sympathy. She told Yan to focus more attention on career than love affairs. "The mother thinks that if Yan could be more famous, or earn more money, she definitely will have someone admiring her, no matter how old she is," Yuxin said. "She thinks that Yan is at the best age to develop the career: She is young, energetic, without a baby and a husband to take care of, so she must focus on working instead of dating. Yan couldn't convince her mother that 'love' is much more important for a young woman."

Daughters worrying about finding mates and mothers regretting the personal freedom they never had are certainly not restricted to China. Nineteenth-century British novels like *Pride and Prejudice* and *Jane Eyre* revolve continuously about the search for the good husband and the longing for an independent life. But unlike Britain, in modern China the role of moral arbiter has long been and remains the state. Well into the current century the official website of the All-China Women's Federation's continues to publish articles warning of the fate awaiting women who fail to land a proper husband, including, among others, the following: "Eight Simple Moves to Escape the Leftover Women Trap" and "Do Leftover Women Really Deserve Our Sympathy?"

Leftover women in the new China are those who have reached age twenty-seven without being married.

Journalist and sociologist Leta Hong Fincher cited one admonitory essay published in 2011 following International Women's Day: "Pretty girls don't need a lot of education to marry into a rich and powerful family, but girls with an average or ugly appearance will find it difficult. These kinds of girls hope to further their education in order to increase their competitiveness. The tragedy is, they don't realize that as women age, they are worth less and less, so by the time they get their M.A. or Ph.D., they are already old, like yellowed pearls." Even during the Mao years, it would have been unlikely to find those people who held up half the sky described as old yellow pearls. But now under a compulsive market regime when many, many women are millionaires and do run their own companies, Yuxin Pei said the gender pressure is often worse than it was in the old days, particularly for women in their twenties whose families continue to pressure them to study and build a career.

"Yes, if the women are in their thirties or forties, they feel very comfortable being single," she said. "They have already created their own lifestyle to be single. They have their friends, their hobbies. But the younger girls are very anxious not to be single. Even now. My graduate students always complain to me, 'What should I do? I can't find a boy to be married. And I feel so worried.' I tell them, 'Wait a while. When you are older you will feel better. You will know how to deal with life.'"

"I think the problem with the anxious women," Xiying broke in, "is that they don't or didn't know how to have fun. Our education here tells them if you don't get married and have children you will not be happy. They always tell you that in your golden age you will have them."

Neither Yuxin Pei nor Xiying Wang has been promoted to a full professorship in their university. University administrators, they believe, show a blatant preference for hiring men even when they have poorer grades or weaker publication records. They worry that their outspoken articles and interviews may discourage their deans from promoting them, especially as they, like Leta Hong Fincher, explore more deeply into the gender dynamics beneath the campaign for young women not to be "left behind." On the surface the state campaign seems particularly bizarre given that in China there are between twenty and twenty-five million more marriage-age men than there are women. The trouble is with finding so-called "quality men," men whose education and social standing would make a good match for the university-trained women who have consistently outscored the men since elementary school.

~

Everywhere in the developed world, according to the Organisation for Economic Co-operation and Development, girls consistently outscore boys in grades and on domestic and international tests. The decline in Chinese boys' test scores during the last two decades has been worse. One analysis of Chinese university entrance exam scores showed a dramatic plunge in the percentage of young men ranking in the top percentiles: from 66.2 percent male to 39.7 percent male between 1999 and 2008. Poor performance by boys has grown so bad in several cities that school systems have begun to go back to the prerevolutionary practice of offering separate schools and classrooms for the boys to help them catch up. One elite Shanghai high school has experimented with placing sixty boys—a quarter of their first-year students—in separate classes with specially designed curriculum to help them catch up with the girls. A fifteen-year-old boy in the school was plainspoken about his preference for being in an all-boys classroom. "We lack confidence," he said. "The teachers like girls, who answer more questions in class. This program lets us realize we are not worse than girls." Other Chinese educators have suggested sending boys to good schools two years later than girls of the same age, because as both Yuxin Pei and Xiying Wang told me, boys mature later than girls. The result, the scholars say, is that despite the fact that China has roughly 15 percent fewer girls than boys, quality girls now can't find quality boys, and as in many cultures, males are very often disinclined to take up with brighter and more accomplished females.

Which is where the All-China Women's Federation stepped in, warning bright young women that heading into graduate education could trap them in "leftover" cages. The federation has even gone so far as to counsel young women to be "persistent but not willful" in the pursuit of an appropriate male. "When holding out for a man, if you say he must be rich and brilliant, romantic and hardworking . . . this is just being willful." Even if such a perfect man exists, the federation warned, "Why on earth would he want to marry you?"

Mothers, as it happens, don't always see their daughters' options as narrowly as the federation's counsel advises. Later on our visit to China, a young couple who both hold university degrees took us on a sunny Sunday morning to visit the ancient Shanghai Marriage Market, which is sheltered by the spreading plane trees of People's Square. Birds flutter through the limbs above, warbling their own mating messages while a few vendors hawk hot steaming buns from their grills. Row upon row of wooden racks post thousands of scroll-like paper "CVs" offering the talents and virtues of young men and women—as described by their parents. Rarely if ever do the eligibles post their own CVs. This is a market where parents seek to mate their children, described in one site as a cross between a rustic farmers' market and Match.com. Three counselors, who serve as brokers, guide parents through the listings. Family history, education, moral values, physical characteristics, as well as zodiac signs are typically included. Nearly always, our guides explained, the parents of the young men specify that the girl must be younger and shorter than their sons, and nearly always the girl's mother requires that the man be older, taller, and own a car as well as a house or apartment.

Shanghai's marriage market is not in itself a government operation; marriage markets have existed in Chinese towns and cities for centuries, but today in China's go-go real estate economy, the context has changed. One young couple at the market laid out the system simply. "Where does the demand come from? The girl's mother. Our friends, before they got married, were not from Shanghai, so they didn't have a house here. They wanted to get married, but the girl's mother did not agree. Why? The girl's mother said, 'Before you get married, you have to buy a house.' There are a lot of couples like this." When our guides, Chris and Edna, decided to move in together against her mother's wishes, they made an even more outrageous decision. "When we have a baby, whoever is making the least money, which likely will be me," Chris said, "will stay home to take care of the baby and the house."

~

A steaming plate of braised pea shoots and a box of Guangzhou shrimp dumplings arrived midway through dinner at the Sun Yat-sen faculty cafeteria, where I still sat with Yuxin Pei and Xiying Wang. We were at last beginning to inch closer to the matter of masturbation and the sexual satisfaction workshops Yuxin had been leading linking women's identity and their "sexual capital."

"I'll describe a workshop I led last month," she said. "All of the women had tried masturbation before. Some of them were in relationships with men. The women were from different age groups—in their thirties, their forties, and even their seventies. Most of the women who were in relationships told me they didn't achieve orgasm when they had sex with their boyfriends or husbands—even those who were only between twenty-five and thirty-five years old."

We might as well have been discussing culinary technique for wrapping the rice paper around the shrimp or trimming pea shoots. Two men, an American and a Frenchman (my companion), talking about masturbation in normal voices with two women in a Parisian or New York café would have been unimaginable. Here in this Chinese faculty café, English was far from rare; our conversation could have been easily overheard.

"Some women with many sexual experiences did . . . some of them had tried to masturbate," Yuxin continued. "One woman said she told her husband that sometimes she wanted to masturbate, but her husband told her, 'Don't let me know! Don't let me know! I don't want to know.' She can't get any pleasure from her husband. The other women didn't know [how] to masturbate. Some tried to teach their husbands but it didn't work so well. They all want to know how to adjust their relationship, how to make their relationships better by making their sexual life better." Yuxin paused to think. "And yes, some women did say they were very good at teaching the men. Some of the women tried to talk to the other women and teach them how to make their sex life better."

Yuxin stopped for a moment and lifted a shrimp dumpling from its wooden box. She chewed the dumpling slowly. "Some men are teachable," she repeated, "and some are not teachable."

If the male mates are "teachable," Yuxin said, then so much the better, but in her dual appointment in both the department of anthropology and the school of social work, her gender focus is much more concerned with women and how women can come to understand their own bodies and their own sexuality as one form of "human capital." One thirty-year-old woman in her class had dated several young men. "She had had seven boyfriends; after many years she had never achieved orgasm. But once she learned about masturbation, she told me she cried because that was the moment that she could achieve sexual fulfillment without *anybody*. It kind of liberated her." Yuxin paused to watch for our reactions, then eventually added, "Later she became involved with women—ha, ha, ha, ha—rather than boys."

Yuxin Pei had chosen her anecdotes not merely to amuse or shock us or to test our reactions. She wanted us to understand a national culture in the world's most populous nation, which on the one hand pushes girls fiercely in school but then once they've succeeded academically discourages them from building careers or seeking their own independence. Increasingly since she began her doctoral research on women's sexuality at the University of Hong Kong, Yuxin Pei has characterized masturbation as one form of human, or more precisely "erotic" capital, a technique that all women can employ to intensify both their internal and external sense of worth in an ever more market-driven society.

Supported by a grant from the Ford Foundation, Yuxin and her research team posted their "Masturbation Videos Wanted" fliers all around the Sun Yat-sen University campus. Participants were asked to participate in a study of behavior and attitudes toward masturbation. Distinctively, the participants were not asked to fill out questionnaires. Instead each woman was lent a digital video camera and taught how to use it to describe her experiences, her attitudes, and her feelings about masturbation. The women were also encouraged to present creative responses including drawings, stories, and poems.

Nearly half of the women spoke of their own sexual experiences. "Marie," described as a beautiful twenty-six-year-old, was working in a major high-pressure law office in Shanghai. She began by saying she had no time to date.

> I have met some excellent guys . . . It seems part of my work to know excellent guys. But they are very busy as well . . . I like

> to read porn, that's my way to relieve my sexual energy ... I always get satisfied when I read porn ... I always discuss sexual issues with my friends, male or female. They all think that I must be very experienced sexually. No one believes that I am a virgin ...

Monica, who grew up in a small East China city and then earned a graduate degree in England, spoke directly—and representatively—about her experience masturbating herself.

> I'm not sure if we have sex education in schools now. But it's very normal in Europe. They teach you how to know yourself, to know your body, to love it ... I did it [masturbated] one day while I was feeling very lost, you know, in England. I could understand English but never knew what people laughed about ... I did it and I felt great.

Yuxin Pei says that physical pleasure was important to each of the women, but the act of learning how to masturbate and how to masturbate successfully had a profound existential meaning to the majority of the women. Westerners may find it bizarre that adult women would have to learn how to masturbate even if conversations about the clitoris still remain largely taboo in the cafés of New York and Paris. But in China as late as the first years of this century the majority of Chinese women—and the overwhelming majority of Chinese men—had no idea where the clitoris is located on a woman's body. Even further, researchers found that most men didn't want to know anything about female masturbation and the importance of the clitoris to masturbation. Once Yuxin Pei's women learned about clitoral stimulation, they delighted in a new and greater sense of self-realization in part because of the ongoing general taboo on direct, open sexual conversation both in traditional and in modern China.

Do not forget, Yuxin reminded us as we were finishing our dumplings, both psychology and sociology classes and research were banned from universities during the thirty years of Mao's rule. A perfect society, after all, had no need of such inquiry under the Maoist dictate. Another research subject, Juan, a middle-aged divorced woman who had lost her job when her state-owned factory closed, reinvented her career as a labor broker and began earning far more money, which also helped her change her sense of self as a valuable person. Masturbation, Juan said, allowed her to stop thinking of herself as a "withered" person. "Linda" went a step farther in her remarks.

> I learned about masturbation from a very good girlfriend. She told me that we women have five holes in our bodies. If you don't know your body, you don't know how to love yourself. And then, how can you let your partners love you? I learned a lot from her . . . I even taught my boyfriend about masturbation. We both felt good.

Delight in clitoral pleasure was of course not unanimous among Yuxin's participants. A small but significant minority of the women saw masturbation as a bad temptation that they had managed to avoid, an act that would diminish their chances of making a good marriage or that might even drive their husbands away. A few others, however, described their discovery of masturbation—alone or with the help of girlfriends—as a method of maintaining fidelity while their traveling husbands were away for long periods. Still more of the women spoke of their masturbation experiences as a sort of "self-love" that gave them the confidence to train their husbands to become more sexually competent.

Self-love. Self-confidence. Self-respect. These phrases recur persistently in Yuxin Pei's dialogs with the women. They form the basis of her notion of sexual capital—an inner worth uniting mind and body that has enabled them to be more capable and effective both in their private lives and in their social and work experience. Measuring sexual or erotic capital has emerged as an important sociological enterprise around the world, from Finland to Nigeria, from Chicago to Shanghai. Not so surprisingly, defining and measuring an individual's "erotic capital" is fraught with complexity, both psychological and cultural. The concept opens up profound debates among anthropologists, gender activists, family rights proponents (both progressive and conservative), public health promoters, and consumer marketers. In Mauritania and Tahiti, both former French colonies, fatness to the point of obesity has been famously favored as a beauty marker, as it has in many other lands of recurrent famine. Metropolitan France, meanwhile, like most Nordic countries, has long measured both virility in men and beauty in women in terms of slim vigor. To a lesser degree, age and youth have competed for priority in attractiveness, the Finns celebrating "sauna freshness" and many Mediterraneans valuing fuller, "riper" development complemented by makeup, tattoos, and skin piercings. Yet as much as the measures may vary according to age and local culture, erotic promise and performance turn out to be more and more strongly acknowledged assets in almost every domain of life, be it succeeding at trade, accumulating wealth, or winning political power.

Most contemporary social researchers who examine "cultural capital" return to the brilliant work of Pierre Bourdieu, who organized and codified the importance of cultural capital in getting ahead—making the right jokes, dropping the right names, displaying socially appropriate literary and artistic references, remarking on seemingly unrelated though significant current events, even wearing the "just-so" sort of worn-out but trendy shoes and jackets. Until very recently, erotic capital remained absent from that catalogue of contextual assets. Then came British sociologist Catherine Hakim's work on general attractiveness and women's social standing in today's consumer environment. In her book *Honey Money*, Hakim counseled smart women to take advantage of all the fashion options and cosmetic tricks available from the modern pharmacopeia to get ahead in the battle for men, status, and money. To many Western feminists *Honey Money* seemed like a terrible retreat into what they saw as the prettiness trap of an earlier era. Hakim declined to retreat. Men and women alike have relied for millennia on myriad obvious and subconscious fields of engagement to win their objectives and outmaneuver their competitors. Those fields—linguistic cleverness, hierarchical name dropping, disarming dress, musculature—may change across time and culture, but they do not disappear. More particularly, Hakim argued, it is a fatal flaw to rely on rational argument alone to win the day: Erotic capital is present in nearly every human transaction whether we wish to admit it or not.

Contemporary China, Yuxin Pei pointed out as we were finishing our dinner in Guangzhou, is passing through the heat of a multidimensional social recovery that pervades the dialogues and confessions made in the videos recorded by the female research subjects. For many older women who simultaneously suffered and were enthralled by the decade of the Cultural Revolution, New Shanghai and New China have succumbed to brazen ambition and a consequent state of moral degradation. During most of Mao Zedong's tenure the notion of erotic capital was inconceivable. Even if erotic attraction and reward very plainly existed in the population, the strict taboo on discussing anything about sexual life or erotic impulses had simply blocked the possibility of expressing such thoughts. In other published work Yuxin Pei has traced year by year how such so-called "Western psychological concepts" gradually gained currency from 1980 to 2005, largely through medical forums where even masters like Freud, Carl Jung, Alfred Adler, or B. F. Skinner initially were unknown. But just as such "capitalist-roader" concepts had been purged from that China, so today's culture of corporate skyscraper marketing has effectively purged the outlook and discourse of Mao's China.

"In China, everything goes so fast," Yuxin Pei emphasized. "Now the government always wants to push us to make a very successful life. And it's the same for women too. Every city wants to be the biggest in China or in the world, to be the most ambitious, and the city's ambitious dream is internalized into everyone's heart." She stopped after glancing at her wristwatch and pulled an iPhone from her purse. "Sorry, we must get to the airport now," she said as she called for a taxi. She and Xiying had to rush to catch the night flight to Buenos Aires, where they had been invited to speak at a conference on women, sex, and property relationships—a new topic in China and a new topic that China was bringing to the rest of the world. These two very liberated women aim to bring China and Chinese experiences to the larger world just as they have been pivotal figures in exposing their friends and colleagues to new ways of thinking about gender, sex, and eroticism in general. Sex, as we discovered in the coming weeks of our Chinese travel, is on sale, both metaphorically and literally, in every large city we visited. As elsewhere, opening the door to erotic and gender exploration can prove threatening to top-down authoritarian regimes: It provokes individuals to question and reimagine who they are, who they might become, and their willingness to accept the roles to which they have been assigned by tradition—even a tradition with four thousand years of history. The prospect of upturning China's sex and gender roles excites Yuxin Pei. While she dialed for their taxi, Xiying picked up the theme. "If you go to Shanghai now and talk to the original Shanghainese people, they are very proud of being Shanghainese. If you talk about Hong Kong, they will tell you, 'Hong Kong will go out of fashion very soon.'"

Yuxin snapped her phone shut. She stood up to go but also to make her point stronger. "Shanghai people, if you speak of London or New York, they will say, 'Oh, we have this in Shanghai. In Shanghai, everything is more beautiful than there.' The ex-mayor has written that [now we must] push people to be New Shanghai People."

"What does it mean to be New Shanghai People?" I asked.

"It means you must dream of the new city. You must have a house, and you must have a high salary."

"What about a richer sexual life and a larger sense of your gender?" I asked.

She paused with a grim smile. "You don't have a life. You just have a future."

PART V

Gender and Being

CHAPTER 15

Gender and the Techno Mind

Maria Klawe was the first and to date only woman to lead Princeton University's College of Engineering and Applied Science before moving on to become the first female president of Harvey Mudd College in Claremont, California. When we met, she had recently marked her seventh year as president of Harvey Mudd, the science and tech wing of the Claremont Colleges, an hour east of Los Angeles. Her office was bright, bristling with the double light of Southern California's high desert. Every wall that didn't have windows was covered by Klawe's paintings, mostly quasi-expressionist landscapes. Painting, which she talked about at some length, is but one of her passions. Cracking the intensely male world of digital engineering for a new generation of women is another. Our conversation, which started with her addiction to painting, moved on quickly to what it was like to run Princeton's engineering school.

"Was it as smug and intransigent as its reputation?" I asked. She lowered her head and smiled and offered only two words: "No kidding." Princeton and its eating-club attitudes were not, however, what she had invited me to talk about. The matter at hand was why the titans of Silicon Valley could not find the women they claimed they desperately wanted to hire to enlarge their engineering and code-writing teams. Twitter, Google, Apple, and Microsoft (on whose board she sat) were, she assured me, genuinely dedicated to bringing more women onto their teams and to breaking the gender caste that typified the boys'-club reputation of Silicon Valley.

However noxious the gender barriers in the industry, she said, they begin to be erected much earlier—in college or even junior high school. "When I was a student studying mathematics both at the undergraduate and the graduate level," she said, "I would have faculty look at me and say, 'I don't see why you're doing this, why aren't you doing art or something?' even though I was not just the best student at the time. I was the best in like a decade. It wasn't that they thought I wasn't good at it; it just didn't make sense to them."

Report after report on gender imbalance in the high-tech universe—most notably research conducted by Stanford University's Clayman Institute for Gender Research—has reiterated the same point. The seats in high school computer science classes are overwhelmingly held by boys. The same is true for advanced mathematics and advanced physics classes, which are frequently seen as prerequisites for university computer science admissions and majors. One female code writer even told me how in the British system, the girls in junior high were regularly discouraged from taking any science besides biology and psychology. Despite all the discouraging, patronizing counsel, Klawe advanced undaunted.

When I asked her if she was sure that boys' brains aren't simply more adept at games, gadgets, and machines, she thought for a moment and spoke about her childhood. "I grew up being convinced and my father was convinced too that I was a boy. I always wanted to do all the things boys do. And he . . . he thought I was his son. The first time I was pregnant, he looked at me and said, 'That is not physically possible.'" A sturdy woman, beginning to gray, but decidedly feminine, Klawe was clearly adept at steering the direction of most any interview. She waited for me to catch up.

"I think that made a huge difference in my ability to go into math and science. I just thought all the things that boys and men did were intensely interesting. And the things that girls got to do were not interesting. I think I was nine by the time I went to bed without thinking I would not wake up the next morning female." Having played with my visible confusion, she hastened to add, "I don't mind having sex with men. I've been married for thirty-three and a half years and I adore my husband. He's a very quiet, shy individual. I'm like a fly buzzing around and he holds the string." I realized then that her initial presentation and incidental conversation about her life as an amateur artist was more than polite small talk. Nor perhaps was it altogether strange that her undergraduate professors had tried to direct her toward "art" or other "womanly" studies—never mind that successfully exhibited female painters and sculptors and musicians are just about as rare as female code writers. "Initially I thought of it as 'women should just be more like men.' They should be more aggressive. They should be more goal oriented. Which is what I was.

"I guess it was when I was becoming a manager at IBM—I was turning thirty-two—all of a sudden I realized there might be women who liked fancy clothes who could be good at science too. Before, it was like there ought to be more women like me. But then I started thinking, no, science should be more open to everyone whether they're poets or artists or football players. My life goal has been to make the culture of science and engineering more ... nurturing, more accepting, more supportive of everyone, independent of gender or race."

Feisty self-confidence and determination appear to run in her family. Her sister, Jennifer Chayes, cofounded Microsoft Research New England in Cambridge, Massachusetts, and then four years later Microsoft Research New York City. Look her up on the Internet and nearly a hundred published scholarly papers pop up immediately on MathSciNet—many of them coauthored with one of her two husbands. Early on she too defied conventional gender wisdom about the sort of work women should do, plunging into higher math and theoretical physics in high school, eventually earning a doctorate in mathematical physics and pursuing post-doctoral work in theoretical math at Harvard and Cornell, which eventually led to her creation of the theory and modeling unit within Microsoft.

"Jennifer and I are both extremely outspoken. We fight for things," Maria Klawe said of herself and her sister. "We do just fine in the tech culture, but the whole point is you shouldn't have to be like Jennifer and Maria to succeed." The second of four sisters, she admitted to always having been the difficult sister though she always performed well academically. Each of the four was encouraged to excel at one talent or another. "I got math, science, and art. My oldest sister got languages. My next younger sister got dance plus she has a Ph.D. in anthropology and religion. Now she's doing these online courses in math and computer science. That door had been closed to her because she was the quiet, peaceful one. Now math! She's loving it! So this whole bit about natural inborn abilities? *Phhh!* What I say all the time is that people learn things at different rates."

Klawe's family story may seem exceptional, and undoubtedly it is. But major ongoing research at Stanford's Clayman Institute suggests that her younger sister's quiet—some would say more feminine—demeanor is strongly linked to the gender barriers within the high-tech universe. A "buddy culture" marked by incessant "guy sports" talk and superficially aggressive "put-downs" typical of men's college dorm humor casts many quiet or reticent women as outsiders to the club regardless of their training or expertise. To get at the dynamics underlying gender exclusion in "the Valley," Clayman undertook a detailed survey of work and personal perceptions among 1,795 men and women in seven key Silicon Valley high-tech companies. A little over half of those surveyed held mid-level positions, 20 percent held high-level jobs and a quarter were entry level. The first not very surprising finding was that men are almost three times more likely than women to hold high-level positions, even though the men and women held equivalent levels of advanced degrees in business technology. Sharper distinctions showed up for minority women, or, as one entry-level Hispanic woman commented, "I'm the only Hispanic person in my group . . . There are very few Hispanics in my technical field. Sometimes I look around and I'm 'both.' I'm the only Hispanic and the only woman." Another woman noted, "I'm used to it [being the only woman in my group]. I've been used to it since engineering school in India where I was one among fifty men. So I never questioned it and it never bothered me, partly because I had to accept it."

Learning how to "get along" inside an overwhelmingly male work club turned out to be a persistent comment made by the female respondents to the survey, but the stereotype of the "hacker" as a compulsive, noncollaborative engineer holed up and glued to screen and keyboard until ten or eleven o'clock each night was equally off-putting. "Research clearly shows that the classic hacker stereotype curbs the desire of both women and underrepresented minorities to enter and remain in the technology profession. In fact, practitioners have identified this stereotype as one of high-tech's greatest challenges to recruiting women and underrepresented minorities," the report concluded. But when Clayman's researchers pushed deeper into the stereotype, they found that the obsessive geek image so commonly perceived outside Silicon Valley was itself out of date. Mid-level employees instead characterized successful technologists as people "who are careful and critical, and yet who take initiative by thinking outside the box. Chief among attributes for success is analytical thinking, followed closely by innovative, risk-taking, and questioning behaviors." Collaborative style ranked well above insular geekdom for successful technical innovation—values that sociologists have long associated with women's work styles more than with men's. Both men and women saw themselves as first being analytical, followed by being ready to take risks, and lastly being assertively personal, confounding typical gender assumptions that women are nonanalytical, risk averse, and unassertive. Yet men's greater readiness to believe the stereotypes about themselves and about women creates an atmosphere in which the women feel compelled to demonstrate their worthiness more forcefully. "Women are absolutely undervalued in the technical world. When both men and women have equal skill set/education, women are consistently assigned to program/project responsibilities while men are assigned the 'pure engineering' responsibilities," one mid-level woman in technology wrote. "You have to be able to blow your own horn," said another. "You have to be convinced that you're smarter than everybody else and everybody should listen to you. This is a certain ego trait that I don't think is rewarded in women. It is certainly not seen as feminine . . . whereas those same personality traits in men are somewhat admired."

Another key difference the Clayman researchers found revolved around the conflict between work and family. The women surveyed consistently reported feeling that their success would be measured by their readiness to work extra hours, nights, and weekends, while relatively fewer men expressed the same anxiety. Across the board women reported part-time work, flex time, or maternity leaves as either unavailable or sharp career negatives, and in general working at home online is deeply discouraged. Whether the women's anxiety was real or projected as a result of their minority status, or whether the men's confidence came as a collateral advantage of their training and education, was unclear—except when the question of family duty arose. While 60 percent of all the respondents described themselves as "family oriented" and while more than 80 percent described themselves as being married or in a "partnership," both the men and the women spoke of "the family penalty" faced by technology workers who have children to mind. Despite a steady increase in sharing domestic duties among middle-class couples, other census data still demonstrate that working women continue to face the "second-shift" obligations of cooking and childcare far more often than men do. None of the women found it wise, however, to bring up family obligations when negotiating jobs or promotions.

Deep at the core of the Clayman study was the notion of a "masculine culture"—a term that relatively few males either acknowledge or seem to understand. One typical response from a high-level male technology employee said simply, "It's not about gender, it's what have you done?"

Another Silicon Valley male responded with great self-confidence, "In the technical world, it's ninety-five percent about what you know and what you've done. Then there's personality and odds and ends in there. In the technical world, I haven't seen political positioning and posturing." Their views couldn't be farther from how the women working in high tech saw their experience. "I had general expectations that I'd be evaluated on my merits alone and not necessarily on my gender. That was the case earlier in my career," a senior-level woman responded, but then as she rose past middle management she discovered how important it was to "be in the right place at the right time. Other factors definitely come into play the more senior you become . . . It becomes a club." Statistically, 66.4 percent of the women saw the work groups inside their company as competitive with each other while only 47.1 percent of the men did—or in short, women working in mid-level technology jobs experienced their work life very differently from the way the men did. At the same time all employees tended to judge female managers as "less technically competent" than equivalent male managers. Of course it may well have been that in each case the female supervisor was less competent, but the women managers themselves told a different story. Said one, "I was constantly getting interrupted, even from people who I didn't consider to be jerks . . . When I would suggest something, people would talk over me. Then a guy would suggest the same thing and, of course, people didn't talk over him." Another high-level woman said, "I've had a couple of experiences where I've worked with guys and it was very hard for them to take me seriously until I proved myself. It might be a little bit harder for women than for men. If a guy walks into the room, it's easier (especially if it's a room full of guys) for him to believe that he knows what he's talking about. If you're a woman, you have to try just a little bit harder until you prove yourself."

Beliefs and attitudes are one thing, but there is also data. Most major American companies are required to report race and gender statistics annually to the U.S. Department of Labor. The Silicon Valley corporations had been notable laggards in their early years; then after the turn of the current century they agreed to turn over their figures, but only if the Department of Labor would regard the figures as "trade secrets" and withhold that information from the public. A reporter for the *San Jose Mercury News* sued the department and forced it to release their gender and ethnic employment data—up to the year 2005. The numbers were not shocking to the handful of women who work in the high-tech trenches. Three quarters of the tech positions were held by men. Several years later Josh Harkinson, a reporter for *Mother Jones* magazine, managed to get fresher figures from Google and nine other Silicon Valley giants. The proportions, he found, had grown worse. By 2010 men held 83 percent of the technical jobs and nearly 80 percent of the executive positions.

In May 2014 a group of women technologists in the Valley issued a signed open letter to the industry detailing their experiences in the companies. Their letter was a blistering indictment of what it is like for women to work in the leading high-tech corporations:

> We've been harassed on mailing lists and called "whore" and "cunt" without any action being taken against aggressors.
>
> We get asked about our relationships at interviews, and we each have tales of being groped at public events. We've been put in the uncomfortable situation of having men attempt to turn business meetings into dates.
>
> We've witnessed the few female co-workers and male allies we've had get fired or bullied into leaving at companies that had so few of them to begin with.
>
> We're constantly asked "if you write any code" when speaking about technical topics and giving technical presentations, despite just having given a talk on writing code. We've been harassed at these same conferences in person and online about our gender, looks, and technical expertise.
>
> We regularly receive creepy, rapey e-mails where men describe what a perfect wife we would be and exactly how we should expect to be subjugated. Sometimes there are angry e-mails that threaten us to leave the industry, because "it doesn't need any more cunts ruining it."
>
> We have watched companies say that diversity is of the highest importance and they have invited us to advise them. After we donate much of our time they change nothing, do nothing, and now wear speaking to us as a badge of honor. Stating, "We tried!"
>
> We've grown cynical of companies creating corporate programs and paying lip service to focusing on women's issues in the tech industry without understanding the underlying reality. We've experienced a staggering earnings gap in our field. We've been told repeatedly that our accomplishments were due to our gender and our role as the "token woman."

The letter sent shock waves through several Silicon Valley executive suites—including an acknowledgement from a senior Google vice president that "being totally clear about the extent of the problem is a really important part of the solution." Analysts at the Anita Borg Institute for Women and Technology (originally housed at Xerox) in Palo Alto, as well as another scholar at the Clayman Institute, praised the Google statement publicly but expressed doubt about how real change in the gender balance would come.

Ann Mei Chang, a frequently cited star of the tech world before she went into public service, had risen to the top rungs of Google's hierarchy, running the company's mobile app division. She told me she never experienced any overt bias against herself as a woman technologist, but at the same time she learned early how to behave "like the guys." Some men, she said, were uncomfortable or intimidated by women who didn't conform to their notion of the nurturing caregiver female; that produced problems, but finally she thought that most seemed to accept her because they simply quit seeing her as a woman. They saw her as an Asian techno-colleague; her gender disappeared. "There was a little discomfort [around me]," she said over tea one afternoon near her home in San Francisco, "because I was younger. I never found any overt antagonism, but I could sense it sometimes." A little later, she added in passing, "Maybe I had an easier time of it in the tech atmosphere because I'm a lesbian. I'd bring girlfriends to the companies' parties. They reacted to me as one of the guys because I wasn't a typically gendered woman. There wasn't that tension there. That made it easier for me. They looked at me as gender neutral. They were different with the women who wore dresses to work, who were deferential or who flirted. They didn't treat them seriously."

Most of the barriers to women, Chang believes, are based on indirect cultural issues. "The way people work is constructed in a very male way. Work late at night. Sit at the computer by yourself . . . writing code. That's not inaccurate for software engineers [even if] there are lots of studies that show pair programming [working in pairs] is more effective. The way the work environment is constructed tends to favor the way men like to work." Men, she told me, "seem happier than women sitting before the computer all day. So what I see is that a lot of women who make it into the workplace, in time they just opt out. It's not that there's no discrimination, but over time they tend to adapt to careers that give them more interaction and more social contribution. Business development or product development or I-design (infotech design). These recent fields enable them to interact with users, be more interactive and collaborative in general. It's just the way women tend to prefer to work." The Clayman Institute's research indicated the same difference between how men and women relate to technical design. Chang addressed the issue personally by going first into company management and then becoming a State Department advisor for third world technical development; eventually she joined and spent several years at Mercy Corps as the agency's chief innovation officer, focusing on how high tech can help develop socially valuable businesses and agencies in some of the world's poorest countries.

Clayman's research suggests that at the base, males tend to be tinkerers while females are pragmatic people interested in solving bigger problems. But their findings along with Chang's personal perception of divergent gender approaches to software engineering do not address a deeper question. Why should boys or men be more drawn to solitary tinkering and girls or women be more engaged by cooperative, pragmatic problem solving? Is this divergence evidence of a hard-wired distinction between the genders? Or is it the consequence of the roles imposed on men and women across the millennia? Maria Klawe had no answer to that question when she took the reins of Harvey Mudd College. But about one thing she was very confident: If digital engineering and computer science were creatively presented to women, the women would be just as attracted as males had been. Never an incrementalist, she initiated a radical reformulation of how the college teaches computer science (CS). On her arrival in 2006, barely 10 percent of CS students were women; seven years later enrollment in CS classes was evenly divided between males and females, and the high-tech giants were snapping up the female graduates as quickly as they turned the tassels on their mortar boards.

"It's all about making it interesting, making it relevant, making it fun," she told me. "A very common experience as you go to your first computer science class is that there are maybe two or three males who just talk all the time, who answer every question, who are talking about all the detailed things they are excited about. It's not that they're trying to intimidate everyone around them. Often they are people [guys] who knew way more about computer programming details than the teachers they had in high school ... and finally they're in college and here's a real computer scientist they can talk to and they just go Phoof! And it's terrifying for the other people in the class. I call this the macho factor."

Teachers never want to blunt a student's enthusiasm, but at Harvey

Mudd, and more recently at similar introductory classes at University of California, Berkeley and at Stanford, teachers pull the dominant talkers aside and have what Klawe describes as "a quiet conversation" about their classroom behavior. Frequently they are unaware of how they intimidate other students. Sometimes teachers push them into more advanced classes. At Harvey Mudd there are five computer science "streams" for students—gold (the school color) for students with no previous computer education, black for those with some experience, and three other streams for those who come with advanced CS skills. Yet even then, many of the most advanced students, who are usually male, continue to push aside kids who are more timid. Then, Klawe said, she's encouraged the instructors to be clearer with those people in private talks and say, "You know, Joe, I love having you in the class. It's just so wonderful to have someone who's so enthusiastic and so well prepared. I'm sure you don't realize this, but when you talk so intensely in class, it's really intimidating for the other students who assume they have to know as much as you do. So if we could just continue to have these conversations one on one, it would be really great," and usually the problem goes away.

Equally important, Klawe set about making the CS classes "relevant and fun." Turning math or physics into "fun" sets off alarms for many serious, intense scientists and educators. And I, having never found anything fun about math—I'll never forget getting a score of 64 on my algebra final exam—was unable to hide the doubt in my eyes and the stiffening of my neck, but Klawe did not back off. "Fun" as she explained it, is about the content to which a mathematical procedure is addressed. "The fun part is all about the problem sets."

As an example she chose the notion of "recursion in an N-factorial," which, I vaguely remember from my miserable algebra class, is the projection of a series of numbers or integers that repeat themselves in smaller and smaller quantities down to the smallest unit, one. In math language a factorial is expressed with an exclamation point. The classic example is $5! = 5 \times 4 \times 3 \times 2 \times 1 = 120$. Taken as a pure mathematical problem, mastering recursions seems to be about as much fun as eating a mud pie filled with toxic worms. I didn't say so, but Klawe understood my doubt and explained that it's just a way of "looping" that is used every day in computer programs in biology, robotics, and architecture. Epidemiologists studying how diseases spread use recursion modeling, as do chemists and physicists looking at how one element bonds progressively with another in a chain reaction. Architects use recursion factorials in designing spires and reducing the weight of buildings as they grow taller, and they are essential elements in designing self-reproducing image algorithms in digital art. The basics of code writing and design could grow in any of these directions. As it happened, Klawe had taken me on a short tour during which we passed a classroom that displayed a set of numeric curves, one of them illustrating the mating habits of frogs, another of lions.

"Are you telling me that might *not* have been a biology class?" I asked her.

"Yes, that might well have been something else. That might have been a math class, but who knows, it could have been a psych class. That's what I mean by making it fun." The basics of computer modeling are all but infinite. Some months later I recalled that conversation during a visit to Toulouse in southwestern France where the California sculptor Jorge Pardo had redesigned color and lighting displays in a former convent to illuminate the magnificent ancient capitals that were mounted on several dozen bland columns. He and his team had worked out the entire operation with computerized models in his Mexico City studio. Pardo himself hadn't written the software codes for the project, but members of his team did have that competence. It wasn't just the coding references and their underlying mathematical knowledge that I recalled as Pardo explained how he had built the installation. It was also his reliance on his *team*.

"We do a lot more teamwork now," Maria Klawe explained, and that approach has changed how students are coming to understand computer science courses. "A lot of people enjoy learning more if they do the work together, even though computer science is often seen as very solitary work." Result? More than 40 percent of the students in Harvey Mudd CS classes are women. A large number come from Scripps, the women's college across the street. Word about how much "fun" the course is had been spreading through all five schools in the Claremont Colleges group; by autumn 2013 more than 60 percent of the CS students came from outside Harvey Mudd. To make the class more accessible to non-techies, it's taught in Python, a coding language generally seen as more forgiving than Java, the industry standard. "So, if students are trying to explore a concept, they might write the code in Python first and then they would translate the pieces that need to run fast into Java. So you could actually get a summer job." Those who get hooked move on to higher-level CS classes, leading them into still better summer jobs. "They can see all the job offers the seniors are getting, with starting salaries between eighty-five and one hundred ten thousand dollars."

"It's crazy," she added, slightly embarrassed. "My son, who does software development for a hedge fund, gets paid three hundred thousand K a year. It's twice his father's salary. Crazy."

Harvey Mudd's approach to opening computer science beyond traditional techie kids has been the model followed by Berkeley, Stanford, and other elite universities. Still, the gender balance and gender attitudes inside the industry have changed little—as the Labor Department statistics, the Clayman Institute's study, and the collective letter written by the women technologists in 2014 illustrate.

IBM and Microsoft have the highest proportion of women employees, while several other tech leaders have seen a decline over the past decade. "But it's still awful especially if you look at the start-up world. I was just talking to a guy from [the venture capital firm] Kleiner Perkins," she said. "In the program they have for putting interns in start-up companies, the first year they had twenty interns. Two were female. The next year they had thirty and two were female. The first year they made offers to eight female students and they got two. The next year they made offers to twenty and they got two. The start-up world is probably like 5 percent female."

Klawe doesn't believe that male buddy culture explains everything about the high-tech gender imbalance. She also agreed with Ann Mei Chang that whether it's innate biology—which she doubts—or ingrained cultural teaching and training, young women in America and most of Europe simply are more risk averse than young men. As well, she pointed out, one of every ten start-ups fails. She also believes, with Chang, that young women are more drawn to the world of code writing and design when it's presented in concrete and potentially pragmatic task-driven contexts rather than as an end in itself.

But why should that be, I pressed her. Did she really think that there are innate gender differences between men's and women's brains that exist from birth—an assumption that many neuroscientists flatly rejected a generation ago but that has once again begun to gain favor? "I don't think we'll ever know," she answered after a reflective pause, "because our culture is so gendered. Girls are rewarded for different things than boys. Boys can be messy and loud, and fall out of trees, and people just say 'boys are boys.' Girls are supposed to be neat and tidy and helpful and good with younger people, respectful of their elders. We expect different behavior from boys and girls. Why should we be surprised if they behave differently on average?"

For her own part Klawe was just then embarking on a profoundly new, for her, learning project: ballroom dancing. "Nobody's been able to teach me how to dance," she admitted. "Ever. Many people have tried. One of my students who's a senior has asked me every year. We have this dancing under the stars thing, and he's one of the leading male dancers. So, I'm learning! You know," she said, lowering her voice in perhaps faux astonishment, "it's so much easier than I thought—and the reason is . . . I could never follow a lead. But I found out you don't have to follow a lead . . . if you're following a routine."

CHAPTER 16

Bodies and Brains

"Contrary to convention," I said to Wolf, "I've never understood the assertion that girls are worse at math than boys." Wolf, who retired after having launched a successful epidemiological software company, waited for more and sipped at the homemade aperitif we had concocted out in the country. "Girls," I continued, "always won the math bees in my school."

Math bees?

Math bees were like spelling bees in grade school except you had to do multiplication and long division problems without pencil and paper. Wolf's backstory was rather unlike mine: rambling Upper West Side apartment, child of two doctors, sent to private school, undergraduate and master's degrees at UC Berkeley, longtime sexual health consultant to the CDC in Atlanta. My village two-room school had no indoor bathrooms or plumbing, and it was heated by coal hauled inside by the students, boys and girls, from a pile in the playground next to the well. When I moved on to high school, seven miles down the road, there were two math whizzes in my class, Mary, and Sherrill, a boy. Both were timid people and both paid far more attention to their homework than I did. Sherrill I lost track of. Mary became an information technology specialist and financial analyst in a time when people with two X chromosomes were nearly unknown in those spheres. There were three math teachers in our high school; two were women. The most advanced class they taught was trigonometry, offered every second year. I did well at geometry, but I didn't dare try trig. Calculus wasn't taught. It wasn't until I entered university that I saw a demographic shift.

"Demographic?" Wolf queried.

Two thirds of the students in beginning algebra were boys. Of those who bit off calculus, 90 percent were male. Most were headed toward engineering majors. A few were pre-med students. Until then I had no inkling that engineering was almost exclusively a male terrain. I did have an uncle who had been a construction engineer in Cincinnati, but somehow I also knew, likely from one of my spinster aunts, that women had played key roles in designing British military signaling and code systems and building California freeways, and a few at least had played key roles in creating aerospace guidance systems. When as a freshman I'd eat lunch on the grounds beside the newly constructed campus engineering building, however, the gender demographics were obvious. Judged by the hallways inside, the building might have been a fraternity house. A few girls lunched on the sloping lawn, but most of them were sitting with their would-be engineer boyfriends.

"Berkeley was easier for us," Wolf said.

In the 1960s the trouble with math and science wasn't gender, at least not overtly. It was war, the Vietnam War. "We thought of physics and chemistry as Pentagon tracks," Wolf reminded me, "preparation for building new kinds of bombs and rockets. Even if it wasn't true. Except for a few of us interested in medicine, not much of anybody then had heard of epidemiology. Polio was over and AIDS hadn't started."

Wolf—I never learned exactly when or how that name fell on such a small, tender brunette—was one of the first women I knew who excelled at medicine and hard science as well as at math. Nothing about her was "wolfish" besides the fact that she had persisted and succeeded in an overwhelmingly male profession and, like my high school classmate Mary, she had sailed gracefully through higher math. Possibly her blend of style and mental acuity intimidated her male colleagues. I'd had no inkling that men were almost universally regarded as innately superior to women in both math and science, nor did I have any inkling of how profound and nasty the academic battles would become in the coming decades with the partisans of pink brains versus blue brains—the assertion that the female and male brains are born with essential functional differences.

At the pop-media level several generally respected TV physicians have waded, and continue to wade, into the neuro-universe of brains and gender. Dr. Jennifer Ashton, first at CBS News and then ABC, has regularly assured her viewers that there are "vast" functional differences between women's and men's brains—from the greater mass and weight of gray matter in male brains to the slightly greater amount of white matter in female brains, as well as citing autopsy-based evidence that female brains have more trans-lateral "neuro-wiring" than male brains in the corpus callosum tying together the right and left hemispheres. These measurable volumes and linkages, Ashton maintains, help explain how and why men excel at "processing information" while women excel at connecting or linking the "processing centers" within the brain. Quick translation: women are "linkers"; men are "thinkers." Back on the street and in the kitchen, Ashton has suggested, we find a justification for broader assertions that women are "innately" more adept at multifunctioning and maintaining interpersonal connections while men triumph at singularly focused, concentrated thinking. By extension, according to this pop-reduction, women were seen as better at nurturing, defined as picking up the crying child, feeding it a snack while stirring the soup, minding the roast in the oven, and talking to grandma on the telephone.

From superficial observation, I asked Wolf, mightn't these distinctions make some sense? Wolf smiled but said nothing.

I raised the assertions of female superiority at multitasking with another longtime friend, John W. Krakauer, a British neurologist at the Johns Hopkins School of Medicine. Krakauer's work the past thirty years has concerned stroke recovery and what happens in the human brain when people are engaged in what gets called "multitasking." Because he is also a teacher, Krakauer was patient with me in his response. "It all depends, you see, on what you mean by multitasking. It might very well be true that many women are more often engaged than men in what your friends regard as multitasking, at least as they experience it in their homes or their offices. But they probably don't think about what happens when a pilot lands an airplane manually—and pilots do that more often than you might imagine. Speed. Flaps. Wheel and wind brake controls. Tower communications. Attitude of the fuselage. Lateral alignment on the runway. All at the same time or in very precise sequences." He began to rattle off several more sorts of work that rely on multitasking teams, not least cardiovascular surgeons, usually male, who receive continuously updated information from nurses and assistants and electronic monitors, all of it used to guide the knife and regulate the other instruments that keep the patient alive.

The next time I saw Wolf, she led me to one of the few published experiments that have attempted to measure men's and women's performances at multitasking. A team of English and Scottish psychologists led by Gijsbert Stoet of the University of Glasgow organized two experiments in 2012–13 designed to measure several sorts of multitasking. In the first experiment 120 men and 120 women of various ages were asked to respond on a keyboard to a series of shapes and colors appearing in sequence. In the second experiment 47 male and 47 female undergraduates were presented with a series of arithmetical problems and then they were given special "search" problems: They first were asked to locate restaurant symbols on a map of an urban area they didn't know and then they were asked to find a key that had been placed in a large visual field. In each experiment, all the images were presented on a computer screen, be they a city map or a field or a series of squares and diamonds or a number of rings in concentric circles. The participants were generally given fewer than four seconds in the math and matching exercises and somewhat more time in the searching tests. Most importantly, the participants were sometimes asked to answer very similar questions sequentially, but at other times different sorts of exercises were intermixed. In one of the two experiments they also had to answer a set of phone calls in which they were asked unrelated questions, for example naming the capital city of France or Poland. The object in all the exercises was to evaluate any differences in accuracy or response times between men and women, as well as the "cost effect" of having to shift back and forth between different sorts of images or computational questions.

Conclusion: All the study subjects, men and women, performed more quickly when they responded to similar operations sequentially and without the interrupting phone calls. When the operations were "interleaved" back and forth, errors and response times both rose sharply. On the arithmetical tests, men scored very marginally higher than women. On the city map test, men performed about one percent ahead of women. On finding a key in a field, the women did slightly better than the men. More broadly, the researchers concluded that the women had a small but measurable advantage over the men when different visual and mental tasks were mixed back and forth. Sequential task management is associated with conventional business management or social planning approaches in which tasks are placed in hierarchical order of importance and performed over time. For that sort of multitasking the women also scored better than the men.

After plowing through all the caveats and marginal statistical distinctions, I turned back to Wolf for guidance. She offered none, but instead asked what my conclusion was.

"Hard to see much of any gender advantage—at least among these middle-class college-age students," I said. She peaked her eyebrows, smiled, and turned back to her laptop, where in a minute or two yet another still more provocative, multiyear piece of research emerged that addressed a much deeper and more complex issue: Even when differences in brain function can be measured between men and women, how do we know whether those differences are innate or whether they result from what psychologists and neurologists call "brain training?" The notion of brain training is far from new. Language educators and brain scientists have long known that acquiring a new language is on average much easier after a person has already become proficient in two languages. And it's not just about the diligence of the student. Our brains become more supple at integrating and organizing new vocabularies and grammar structures after we have stocked two languages in our heads and become operational in both. (Bilingual or trilingual people also seem less susceptible to early senility. For parallel if slightly different reasons, athletes who have become proficient in basketball often do very well in soccer, volleyball, touch football, and other sports that rely on rapid hand-eye coordination and response. Improved muscular strength is enhanced by parallel mental agility.)

The second study that Wolf drew up on the screen, originally published in 2004 in *Nature*, took these analogues farther, examining how learning to juggle alters our gray matter. Twenty volunteers who had no experience juggling first underwent fMRI brain scans to establish the form and size of their gray matter in the middle visual cortex of their brains. Then after one week and then a month of training and practice with standard three-ball juggling, they underwent new brain scans parallel to the first pretraining scan. Their gray matter in the middle cerebral cortex, which is where our capacity for visual-muscular coordination is seated, had expanded. A control group of twenty people who had not learned to juggle underwent the same scans—with no growth in gray matter.

In itself the growth in gray matter tells us nothing definitive. What is significant is what happened in the jugglers' brains two months after they quit juggling. Their gray matter shrank back to its original dimensions. Four years later the same research group repeated the experiment with twenty more volunteers. Again, they found that gray matter grew and changed form slightly during training—but only as long as they kept up their daily juggling routines. Continuous exposure to and exercise of new experience was required to maintain the same gains in gray matter. Our brains expand. Our brains contract. They become more "plastic," both in perception and in function—and they can become less "plastic" as our experiences in the world expand and contract. *Use it or lose it,* as the popular adage would have it.

Still, what in the world does a modest athletic exercise tell anyone about gender—or sex—and the brain?

"First and most importantly," Wolf explained, "any single snapshot of anybody's brain at one moment only tells us what that brain looked like at that moment. It doesn't tell us anything about the form of that brain when the person was born or when the person died. Nearly all the images of people's brains—men's brains or women's brains—have been made either in single fMRI images or in autopsies after the person's death."

"Not to mention, I suppose, comparing the weight of male brains and female brains?" I asked. She didn't bother to respond.

Beneath, behind, and circling all around these issues of sex, gender, and body—remember, our brains are simply a part of our bodies—hovers a half century of battles over what we mean by gender and what we mean by sex. Sex, recall, refers essentially to the division between people born with two X chromosomes—females—and people born with one X and one Y chromosome—males. Other very rare chromosomal possibilities exist, but they seldom surface in the bigger public debates. When Christian, Muslim, and other fundamentalists speak and demonstrate against "gender radicals" as "betraying" nature, they generally are protesting any variation from the social roles traditionally associated with having an XX pair or an XY pair of chromosomes. As they experience the world, any variation between chromosomal reality and gender behavior is simply unnatural. On the other hand, so-called gender activists regularly assert that all or nearly all sexually related behavior aside from procreation is a socially constructed "performance" enforced by conventionally organized societies dominated by men at work, on the street, and within the household. Increasingly, and especially during the past two decades, neurological researchers have begun to reveal a much more fluid relation between sex and gender that starts at nearly the moment of fertilization and continues until the concluding breath of life.

For most people in the developed world, "sexing" of a newborn begins in a hospital delivery room when the doctor or midwife helps extract the baby, taps it lightly on the back to help it suck in its first breath, and looks between its legs to declare the wrinkled pink mass a "boy" or a "girl." In most cases—apparently between 95 and 97 percent of cases—that newborn matures into the male or the female body that the first look would suggest. However, for between 1.5 and 3 percent of newborns those exterior "sex" markers are not so clear. There may be a vaginal crease *and* a tiny penis or there may be undetectable testes that might or might not appear later. Until recently, sex identification or sex assignment was left to the supervising physician. Well into the last century, as we saw in Chapter 13, many doctors confronted with what appeared to be underdeveloped male genitalia and some vaginal evidence would apply the knife and declare the child female. Though far more rare, a slip of the knife made during male circumcision would result in the same thing with grim psychological consequences fifteen years later.

Increasingly, medical ethicists discourage doctors and parents from undertaking any early, irreversible surgical procedure—even when quick DNA or chromosomal analysis confirms that the child is an XX or an XY person but the child doesn't show the usual external genitalia. Not the least reason is that other sex and gender indicators—some physical and some within the brain—develop many years later as the child grows toward puberty and maturity. No single researcher has probed more deeply—or controversially—into the zone of biology and gender than Brown University professor emerita Anne Fausto-Sterling. In a series of public lectures and interviews, Fausto-Sterling carefully dissected the arguments about the apparent differences between left-brain functioning, typically associated with emotive and empathic response (and therefore with femininity), and right-brain activity, typically associated with cognitive acuity (and therefore male reasoning).

"When people say 'it's nurture' or 'it's nature' in making us male or female, I take the middle ground and say that it's a combination of both," she told a *New York Times* interviewer. "That's not a popular position to take in today's academic environment, but it is the one that makes the most sense." That interview took place in 2001, but in the decade and a half that followed, the nature-nurture battlements seemed only to have grown more rigid between the opposing camps, neither of which generally possesses much formal training in either biology or neurology. Fausto-Sterling, meanwhile, has continued to pursue work she began during the 1980s when gender theorists like Judith Butler and Judith Lorber began publishing philosophical and sociological analyses that saw most gender roles as societally constructed. As classically defined marriage roles began to disappear in double-income families and as women began to bypass men in math, science, and engineering schools, and indeed as transgender identities became more and more common in the mass media, Fausto-Sterling found herself ever more intrigued by the interactions between molecules and society. How can we be so certain in the face of such rapid social change that biology and social experiences are not at some level interactive? Are we sure that the language of science used to describe biology is not itself skewed to produce the answers biologists want?

She famously (in her field) and shockingly (to some) suggested that the two basic hormones associated with sexuality, estrogen and testosterone, ought not be called "sex" hormones but "growth" hormones. "The molecules we call sex hormones," she said, "affect our liver, our muscles, our bones, virtually every tissue in the body. In addition to their roles in our reproductive system, they affect growth and development throughout life. So to think of them as growth hormones, which they are, is to stop worrying that men have a lot of testosterone and women, estrogen." While it is generally true that testosterone is more heavily concentrated in males and estrogen more so in females, anyone who walks down the street can easily spot women with touches of facial hair (associated with testosterone) or men with nearly no facial and chest hair. Breasts, Adam's apples, bone weight and strength, hip and breast development—the so-called secondary sexual attributes—all vary enormously among males and females even if they are popularly taken as clear sex markers.

Fausto-Sterling, however, was more deeply interested in the relationship of the body to the brain and how these simple sexual categories are affected by individual experience.

For many years she focused her research on children born with uncertain sexuality—the 1.5 to 3 percent of infants then commonly called "intersexual" who might or might not later go on to declare themselves transsexuals. Specifically, she helped lead a campaign to stop surgical sex assignment to those children at birth. "People deserve to have a choice about something as important as that. Infants can't make choices," she said, "and the doctors often guess wrong. They might say, 'We think this infant should be a female because the sexual organ it has is small.' Then, they go and remove the penis and the testes. Years later, the kid says, 'I'm a boy, and that's what I want to be, and I don't want to take estrogen, and by the way, give me back my penis.'" As the global movement toward transsexual declaration grew more public (well before square-shouldered Bruce Jenner became slinky Caitlyn Jenner, never mind ancient Rome's plainly transsexual Great Mother deity described by Plutarch) and as surgical intervention began to decline, the once "obvious" liaisons between sex and gender also have become less and less clear. Fausto-Sterling spent many years researching a variety of physical, hormonal, and neurologic coordinates associated with transsexuality and intersex biology, largely as an approach to understanding the most extreme variations in human form and expression. Then gradually she moved well beyond questions of transsexuality toward what she calls a "dynamic systems" approach to understanding how sex, hormones, and experience interact within the plasticity of our brains across our lifetimes.

Dynamic systems approaches are far from new. They have marked how everyone from aerospace engineers to developmental child psychologists look at growth and change in relation to surrounding circumstances. At the biological level, most psychologists long ago abandoned seeing childhood development and maturation as a series of fixed stages from infantile need through puberty and adolescent independence. No one seriously questions any longer how the death of a parent, divorce, poor diet, or lack of rest can seriously alter or degrade a child's physical, mental, and emotional growth: All those forces exist in larger, dynamic interaction in which the child exists and matures. However, Fausto-Sterling did make waves when she began to look at the formation of sexuality and gender presentation in a similarly dynamic manner—especially when she published a slightly tongue-in-cheek essay entitled "The Five Sexes." In choosing the number "five," she intended only to suggest that the Platonic notion of dimorphism—or two obvious sexes—neither describes human reality nor enables human beings to express the nuances of their sexual and social being.

Applying the biological term "phenotype," or obvious characteristics, to gender, she asked herself how concrete personal experience might affect everything from so-called right-left brain variations to the ways people speak, walk, dress, or express sexual appetite—in short, how "the individual things that are going on day-to-day and moment-to-moment in infant and child development lead to global outcomes." Unlike the purely sociological "gender theorists," Fausto-Sterling and her collaborators specifically sought to build on the basic understanding of brain plasticity—or brain training—to trace how differences in sexuality and gender display manifest themselves in any single individual. Her approach initially threatened all camps, be they the transgender and homosexual "essentialists" like Lady Gaga, who insist they are born with a fixed genetic destiny, or traditional religionists who maintain that any variation from Biblical doctrine amounts to a sinful (if not Satanic) challenge to God and Nature. From the point of view of biodynamics, each side seems stunningly fundamentalist.

All of which can return us to the earlier exercise in learning to juggle: What happens in our brains, especially in the corpus callosum (which might be compared to an Internet switching center), as our eyes, hands, balance, sense of touch, and sensitivity to light activate the axons to communicate more quickly and more fully between the right and left hemispheres as we develop the capacity to juggle. Nothing that goes on inside our brains is isolated from the activity outside and around our heads. Whether you're striding down Fifth Avenue or the Champs-Élysées on a spring morning or marching through an Alaskan forest in February with an ice ax on your shoulder, the manner of your walk and your attentiveness to your surroundings is not merely a matter of current awareness. Each activity is a performance, developmental neurologists have shown: each is a learned way of being. Just as certain communities of traditional Albanian women were once known for their broad shoulders and competence at maneuvering heavy equipment, and as tribes of northern South American warrior women terrified the conquistadores, history, culture, and circumstances contributed to developing their aspect and behavior. No serious human biologist today would consider them as genetically apart from other humans, and had it been possible at the time, neurobiologists like Fausto-Sterling could surely have tracked distinctive differences in how the brains of the conquistadores and the warrior women foes had grown and developed. The effect of war on the brain, of course, is hardly surprising, as illustrated by the thousands of soldiers who have suffered "shell shock," as it was known during World Wars I and II, and more recently, post-traumatic stress disorder (PTSD). Quieter but still more startling evidence of brain change has come out of research at Yale and the University of Denver in 2013 directed by Pilyoung Kim. A group of new dads underwent brain scans during the first month after their infants were born and again during the fourth month. Changes in new mothers' brains had already been established, but it turned out the fathers' neural activity was also altered by caring for their children: "Fathers exhibited increase in gray matter (GM) volume in several neural regions involved in parental motivation, including the hypothalamus, amygdala, striatum, and lateral prefrontal cortex. On the other hand, fathers exhibited decreases in GM volume in the orbitofrontal cortex, posterior cingulate cortex, and insula. The findings provide evidence for neural plasticity in fathers' brains. We also discuss the distinct patterns of associations among neural changes, postpartum mood symptoms, and parenting behaviors among fathers," they reported in the journal *Social Neuroscience*.

Although this inquiry into the nature and destiny of sex and gender is hardly the domain for a descent into the extremely rich and convoluted territories of neuroscience, what scientists have clearly proven is that brain plasticity, or brain education, extends far beyond the basic motor skills that a two-year-old child develops while learning to walk—which seems to be permanent—and what an adult can pick up learning to juggle—which seems to be temporary. Different parts of the brain are engaged in each activity and not all develop at the same time or at the same pace. Aside from the well-discussed left and right hemispheres and their supposed relation to cognitive capacity (left) and empathetic sensitivity (right), neuroscientists interested in sex and gender (among other behaviors) have concentrated on a nest of four other key areas of the brain: the thalamus, the amygdala, the hypothalamus, and, smallest of all, the pituitary gland. Eating, drinking, smelling, breathing, heart rhythm, and sexual function are all either linked to or governed by the interactions among these four key areas. Autopsies famously performed in the 1990s on gay men who died with AIDS appeared, for a while, to suggest significant differences between homosexual and heterosexual males in the size and weight of certain parts of the hypothalamus. Other efforts at radio imagery, however, cast doubt on those claims. Nonetheless brain scientists, mostly studying rat and monkey brains, have reached a fairly common consensus that sexual attraction, arousal, and orgasm are largely governed in these cerebral zones. That in itself wasn't much of a surprise. Monks, meditators, and philosophers of several traditions have told us for millennia that sexual appetite and sensitivity, not to mention sexual performance, are far more matters of the brain than of our genitalia. Rather newer, on the other hand, is the finding that arousal, including masturbation, in some monkeys is stimulated and governed by a different part of the hypothalamus than is ejaculation. Similarly, aggressive behavior can be moderated or exacerbated by electrical stimulation or surgical elimination of parts of the amygdala—an almond-shaped piece of the limbic brain that governs fear, anger, and pleasure responses.

The complexities of all these interrelated actions and perception bits of our brains appear to grow more baroque every few months as brain explorers develop new tools to peer inside our heads and, still more importantly perhaps, become freer and freer to watch our brains perform as we are subjected and exposed to the sorts of suggestive sounds, images, fragrances, and storytelling that would have been regarded as scandalous and unimaginable when Indiana University's Kinsey Institute researchers were studying American sex life in the 1940s and '50s. Take, for example, the now relatively commonplace acknowledgment that anal stimulation of men or women can provoke either intense fear and anxiety or intense erotic excitement, both responses visible on fMRI scans in the brain depending on setting and circumstance. Not only was neurological monitoring unavailable a half century ago; it was also then unimaginable for university researchers. Though the Kinsey team, under Dr. Alfred Kinsey, gingerly addressed all four varieties of oral-genital activity, again, neural monitoring of exposure to these pleasures remains rare to nonexistent. Likewise, undertaking fMRI monitoring of men clothed and performing as women, and vice versa, remains at the edge of the research frontier.

Why, many readers might ask, should neuroscientists waste ever scarcer research dollars on such studies? What beyond the scientist's own prurient curiosity is to be satisfied by monitoring how the brain responds to these sorts of arousing images? The simple response is that conventional male-female penile-vaginal intercourse may in the West remain the majority sort of erotic contact, but ongoing Kinsey-modeled research at the beginning of the twenty-first century suggests that it is only barely the predominant form of erotic contact people imagine having. I well recall one of the few times I engaged in a conversation about sexual activity with my father, who was never prudish, just after I had published an exposé report in *Penthouse* (!) magazine about the ravages of corporate strip-mining in Appalachia. *Penthouse* in the 1970s was the preeminent male publication dedicated to cunnilingus, and that issue was replete with what could have been regarded as a visual, step-by-step user's guide. "Who looks at this magazine?" he asked in moderate shock. "I can't believe there are many people who actually engage in ... in that sort of sex." This from a worldly man who had passed his twenties in Paris and Berlin. A quarter century later his reaction would strike almost any American TV viewer as nearly monastic. The same would go for shock reactions to same-sex households, transsexual parents, and cross-dressers of nearly every sort. The terrain of the research on bodies, brains, and gender has sharply shifted from the 1990s when Anne Fausto-Sterling and her colleagues concentrated most of their energy on the mismatch between genitalia, desire, and the gender roles among atypical children. Since then pop-science articles on brain plasticity and sexuality have become nearly as common as the latest hybrid tomato variety. Alas, much of what appears in newspapers and magazines exaggerates early and non-replicated research. What neuroscientists do know is that repeated exposure to attractive images—food, sex, champagne bottles, roulette wheels—stimulates production of the neurotransmitter dopamine, one of the brain's most mischaracterized chemicals, which produces different effects on different receptors in the brain. Repeated exposure to pleasurable acts and images, it appears, amplifies dopamine production, which during orgasm in turn releases a flood of other neurotransmitters including oxytocin, nitric oxide, estrogen, and testosterone. Acts and images that at first may provoke mixed reactions in that way can become, with repetition, more and more attractive. At its simplest metaphorical level, that is how we learn to like artichokes, sour cherries, or bitter Italian Averna. Or nipples, penises, and clitorises. Doubtless, an appetite for the delights portrayed in *Penthouse*'s photographs must have set off neural reactions in my father's inexperienced brain not unlike what happens to a child who taste's her first sour cherry. Though not all children come to adore sour cherry pies, most do. Oral sex, as actor Michael Douglas insisted on telling us, is likely to take place in suburban homes now more than baking a cherry pie. The ability to study how our multiple brain centers respond in real time to different kinds of images and stimulation has challenged and reordered older purely physiological arguments that had sought to distinguish "male" and "female" responses along static left brain–right brain dichotomies.

At the same time our understanding of the left and right hemispheres has become messier than ever. Aside from the primary left-right cabling lines in the corpus callosum, it turns out that another communication linkage, the anterior commissure, is consistently larger in women's brains than in men's despite the fact that male brains (like their bodies) are, overall, larger than female brains. One of the anterior commissure's primary functions is to communicate sound, smell, and sight information, which presumably would provide women an advantage in musical performance, culinary invention, and visual arts. Anyone who's ever gone to a symphony concert, dined at three-star restaurants, or visited the Louvre Museum would be hard-pressed to find even a quarter of those institutions dominated by women. Similarly there is mounting evidence that women enjoy greater translateral access across the corpus callosum between left and right hemispheres than do men: Men's mental activity, remember, tends to be concentrated, sometimes isolated, on the so-called cognitive side while women, on average, access both right and left hemispheres more readily. For some researchers and their activist followers, that cerebral fluidity helps explain women's supposed richer access to intuition and creative insight, which one might suppose would enhance their advantage over men in both the sciences and the arts. Alas, few societies anywhere in the world seem yet to have profited from that advantage, suggesting that socially created gender regimes consistently trump innate "sex" differences. Perhaps women's greater success at university will one day change that.

Analis Kaiser, at the University of Freiburg, has argued that while those gender prejudices and barriers certainly exist, a part of the problem rests with the cloudiness that surrounds how we use sex and gender terminology and therefore how both biology and social science explore those differences. Kaiser looked at the way gendered selection of words can change how language itself can alter the meaning of scientific findings about men and women. In one case subjects' responses to certain words light up fMRI scans in a different place and in a different dimension in a male brain than in a female brain. Is this a consequence of biological sex or of how the male and female brains have been "sexed" by social experience? In short, has gender experience altered neurological and therefore biological function? Kaiser's answer is plainly that sex and gender are very often inseparable as each individual ages, develops fears, discovers appetites, adopts habits, and then reinforces all of them through repetition. Differences between adult men's and women's brains, she points out, do clearly exist, citing again the famous example of women apparently having less ability to visualize an object in rotation. Similarly, the pleasure centers that respond to eating chocolate appear radically different in male and female brains. While both differences might appear to demonstrate fixed biological distinctions, there are well-documented differences in the availability and marketing of early childhood treats and toys for boys and girls, including warnings and rewards for each, that are plainly gendered. Who gets the blocks and trucks in the toy store? Who gets the dolls and the ribbons?

Still more perturbing is how scientists formulate language categories in their research and how, over time, the terminology of categories shifts. Reanalyzing sixteen years of neurological research, Kaiser tracked how a gradual shift in terminology slowly changed the outcomes of the fMRI scans aimed at examining brain lateralization (or cross-hemisphere responses) to words and language. She found that from 1995 through 2002 seventeen separate teams explicitly set out to measure the differences in male and female bilaterality as against one project focused on measuring the similarities in male and female responses across the brain's hemispheres. The number of studies measuring the difference in men's and women's neural responses continued to grow year by year through 2010 for a total of sixty-seven over the whole period. But beginning in the early years of the last decade other researchers began trying to measure male-female similarities in lateral and bilateral responses, starting with only one such study in 1999, five in 2003–2004, and then a big leap in 2009 to thirty, for an overall total of sixty-one by 2011 in which researchers specifically sought to identify the neurological similarities between men's and women's responses.

How researchers frame their notions of similarity or difference very clearly shapes the outcomes they discover. How great or how small the difference that they discover becomes, at the end of the day, less significant than the accumulation of research demonstrating that difference exists. When the underlying paradigm shifts and when researchers begin to look for similarities, they find them—even if at varying degrees. Tying up her analysis of the research and its relevance to popular assumptions about male and female neurological differences, Kaiser quotes a dialogue in the Zurich weekly magazine *Die Weltwoche* with a renowned neuropsychologist, Mathias Plüss, who dismisses out of hand notions that women are unable to read maps or that men don't listen:

> PLÜSS: [T]hese are all secondary, tertiary or even quaternary effects. They are biologically irrelevant. There is no biological background whatsoever that makes women slower in mentally rotating an object.
>
> *INTERVIEWER:* Then what?
>
> PLÜSS: It has to do with other interests or a lack of practice.
>
> *INTERVIEWER:* And the congenital emotional differences you acknowledged before, you attach no importance to those?
>
> PLÜSS: Yes, they are relevant mostly when selecting a partner . . .
>
> *INTERVIEWER:* Are these different strategies still relevant today?
>
> PLÜSS: Absolutely. All data indicates this. Women choose partners mostly for their status, that's why men are on average five years older than their wives and have a higher income . . .

Aside from Plüss's seeming apology for men's and women's discriminatory pay difference, his and Kaiser's fundamental critique stands: how scientists formulate sex, gender, and brain research all too often predetermines the outcomes. Few people have made the argument more clearly than Diane Halpern at the Claremont Colleges group, the very same institution that has transformed women's participation in computer science education. Like Fausto-Sterling, Halpern has upset both the biological determinists and the gender fundamentalists, but with data.

"Consider the finding," Halpern wrote in one provocative essay, "that, in more gender-equal societies, females perform as well as males in mathematics, much better than males in reading and much worse than males in visuo-spatial tasks. No simple theory, such as the hypothesis that sex differences reflect societal norms or that gender-equal societies will reduce all sex differences, can explain this pattern of results." Halpern, a former president of the American Psychological Association, has for more than twenty years lectured and written books attacking what she calls "junk science" of the sort cited by Dr. Jennifer Ashton to demonstrate gender-based competence at various tasks. But she is equally frustrated by counter-arguments that seek to wash out any biologically based differences. Certain mental and cognitive disorders are more frequent in boys than in girls, and the effect of hormones both in utero and in childhood development and even in old age alters how our bodies and brains work. The gritty details of sexual function and desire are merely the most obvious examples. As we experience those physiological and environmental changes, our brains change how we organize our perceptions and our physiological responses. "The question is not whether female and male brains are similar or different, because they are both. The questions we need to answer are: How can we understand the ways in which we are similar and different? And how can we use that knowledge to help everyone achieve their fullest potential?"

CHAPTER 17

Gender and Resilience

Two women face each other at a small table at the back of a café in Berkeley, California. A hot autumn sun pulses through the glass. One of the women, sturdy in a chambray shirt and large glasses, shakes her head with a false smile: "Then I just lost it."

Her friend, a slightly older sixtysomething in running shoes, sits across from her, her lean left knee tucked below her chin, nodding in understanding.

"Mary Beth was stuck. She had nobody to call except me," the first woman goes on.

Mary Beth, I learned through discreet eavesdropping, was a lawyer. Her kids had needed to be picked up from primary school early the day before, which would have forced her to cancel an important client negotiation that was going badly. Her husband, an apparently high-powered something or other in a techie start-up, had called earlier in the morning to say he'd have to stay an extra day in Denver to close a deal with a new client. Mary Beth had had no one to call for help with the kids except her mother, the stocky woman in big glasses who had "lost it."

"It was the second time this week that happened. I love my grandkids. I love my daughter, but . . ." I wondered if she was going to scream or cry. Her friend in the running shoes listened attentively, but she spoke so softly I couldn't hear her. It was the end of a week I'd spent in Berkeley, taking my daily espresso infusion each morning at the café. Almost everyone there in the morning was over sixty. They were fairly equally divided between men and women. It was also playoffs week for the National League pennant, and the San Francisco Giants were one game away from the title. Aside from one or two conversations in a language I didn't understand, nearly all the men's tables were dominated either by baseball talk or the upcoming nonsensical governor's race in which the lifelong Democrat, Jerry Brown, was sure to win his fourth term.

"Pretty standard," Andy Scharlach chuckled when I described the morning café scene. Scharlach directs the Center for the Advanced Study of Aging Services at UC Berkeley's School of Social Welfare. Men, no matter what their age, he said, usually talk sports or politics and women talk family and relationships. It is one of the abiding clichés about gender and how the earliest habits of childhood lead most of us into very different strategies for facing life's latter years. Men tend to blather about safe topics circling over and around their tender anxieties, while women are ever more pragmatic and direct about the foibles and frustrations brought on by the passage of time.

I was at first startled and disbelieving when older women friends began to share with me their exasperation with their post-retirement male mates and friends. Beata—Polish for Beatrice—was one of the first women to do so.

"What puzzles me is the fact that I am surrounded by bright people—more than when I was younger. So how come so many guys of my generation—I'm fifty-seven—guys that were interesting, really interesting, promising, exciting, cool guys when I was younger, become rigid, dull, not as quick-thinking, not as excitable, when they pass sixty? No, not all of them, but a lot of them—their . . . their vitality is gone. Intellectual curiosity is also gone. Conversations are all about proving they're right instead of exploring a thought, and thinking forward." The first time Beata recounted that experience was by phone; a few months later we spent the better part of an evening sitting outdoors at a café near Cincinnati. Autumn light descended quickly. Tarnished oak leaves had begun to pave the ground. The sadness and distress in Beata's voice echoed the season. "When I was younger," she went on, "I never felt that guys treated me differently than they treated other guys . . . I always thought I was one of them. I talk. They talk. We agree. We disagree."

Between the first time Beata and I had spoken about her dilemma and that autumn evening, I'd had at least a half dozen parallel conversations with other women whom I'd known for twenty years or more. Increasingly they spoke about a sort of *reinfantilization* of their male partners and friends. The men no longer had shops or businesses to run or secretaries to handle their mail. They no longer had assistants to unravel their computer software glitches. More and more, the wives said, the men had taken to yelling into their telephones to vent their frustrations. These men had, apparently, lost any sense of meaning or purpose in their existence. Worse for the wives, the loss of a regular workplace meant that the men no longer had any sense of social network through which to speak about their shrinking lives. They were drawing inward, unable—or unwilling—to look beyond their own experience or even hear counsel from others.

Beata recounted a recent meeting with four male colleagues she had known for many years. They wanted to organize a non-profit social service organization. "We were talking about getting grants and certain legal requirements concerning non-profits. I'm the only person at the table who had actually incorporated a non-profit, who had run it for a long time and gotten grants. Their [proposed] non-profit is in the same area of industry as mine. So you'd think it would be natural that I would be the one they would turn to and ask, 'Do you know anything about this?' or 'How to do that?' That did not happen. I wait quietly, but clearly they are not figuring it out. Finally, I barge in and tell them how to get started. They listen. There is a moment of silence. Then the conversation moves on to a different topic, without acknowledging that I had just answered their question. So they basically brushed me off."

That men, especially businessmen, ignore women's counsel is hardly new. But Beata had collaborated on many projects with the same group of men for more than a decade. What had changed was the age of the participants. Little by little she reduced her contact with them. Had Beata's example and observations been exceptional, I might have heard it as a matter of her personal style and behavior. She is not a timid woman. But after listening to repeated parallel experiences from other "early senior" women—and having been forced to acknowledge some similar behaviors in myself—I decided to look for deeper analyses of how gender roles and reactions evolve with age. The most startling and widely reported body of research surfaced far away—in Japan—where social psychologists have developed a specific diagnosis they label "retired husband syndrome." The diagnosis applies not directly to men but to the woman who upon her husband's retirement finds herself smothered by the man's perpetual presence, judgments, grumpiness, and dependence in the house where previously she had exercised personal freedom and autonomy. Some estimates have placed the incidence of retired husband syndrome at 60 percent of Japan's middle-class Baby Boom families. Not surprisingly, divorces among seniors have spiked, doubling from what they had been two decades previously.

Japanese society, widely perceived in the West as conservative and rigid in role relations, is far from exceptional. Parallel studies of aging and gender have found broadly similar trends in Austria, Finland, and the United Kingdom. A study of 1,315 U.S. military veterans published in 2014 by the journal *Psychology and Aging* tracked the men's self-reported daily moods over several years. Like the Japanese, grumpiness, aggravation, and frustration was minimal for the men in their fifties, but it intensified after they reached age sixty-five and spiked at around age seventy, though their material conditions and living circumstances had not changed significantly—aside from witnessing the steadily increasing deaths of good friends. Other studies have shown age sixty-five as a turning point in male grumpiness. U.S. census data show divorce initiated by men over sixty-five doubling between 1980 and 2008—from 5 to 10 percent—while divorce initiated by women in the same age group tripled over the same period, from 4 to 12 percent.

Not surprisingly, marriage or couples' counseling for retired people has enjoyed a parallel boom in the last decade, and by some measures incidence of retired husband syndrome may be worse in the United States, where women now in their sixties profited from second-wave feminism in the 1970s and '80s, creating dynamic careers for themselves once their children had grown up and left. Taking care of paunchy, "infantilized" gray-haired husbands was not at all what they had looked forward to, or, to use the almost clichéd phrase of a retired friend from South Miami, "I married you for better or worse but not for lunch." When her high-profile nuclear physicist husband retired at seventy, she injected herself into the retirement negotiations to be sure that he would keep his office for life—and guarantee both of them time apart. Learning how to pass an entire day with a mate who's been absent most of the day for most of the couple's life has proved to be a territory rife with expectation and disappointment—expectation from women in traditional marriages that her male mate will share household work and disappointment when he not only doesn't but he also expects her to take over the daily support his previous female assistants had provided him at his office.

If gender-based misunderstandings over work and leisure are a frequent source of conflict in the retirement years, they reflect divisions between men's and women's social formation and education, argues Louis Primavera, dean of Touro College's Graduate School of Health Sciences in New York. "Women," he said in one widely circulated interview, "are generally more socially integrated, having more and stronger emotional ties to friends and family. Men, in contrast, have fewer close relationships, and many depend on their wives to keep them socially involved. A certain amount of social dependency is reasonable. But for some wives dependency can become extreme. In fact, we found that many men expect to be the primary focus of their wives' attention when newly retired. This of course is not at all realistic nor is it healthy for either spouse. And many wives might become angry and resentful if they have to surrender more of their personal time than they'd like to." On the surface the distinction between male and female sociality may seem only to repeat old and outdated behavioral clichés. Gerontologists who have looked closely at markers of successful aging do argue that there are major gender differences and that those gender cleavages persist across the modern, developed world. But, just as late-life physical health depends on earlier exercise and agility, they see late-life psychological issues as rooted in early life experiences when little girls and little boys discover the barriers and opportunities that they face.

Susan Folkman, who spent the last decade of her professional life as a distinguished professor of medicine at the University of California, San Francisco, has been deeply engaged in studying how men and women address age and its inevitable relation to caregiving and care-receiving—or care and coping. Her first work addressed the premature aging that often marked AIDS patients in San Francisco during the 1980s when thirty-five- and forty-year-old men found themselves forced to take care of their dying friends and mates. From there her work expanded to the broader profiles of the kinds of people who learn and succeed in caregiving—especially as they age. "From a very early age," she told me, "boys are indoctrinated with the athletic metaphor: You don't give up. You keep going after that success. You fight for it. You don't take a second. You just fight harder. I don't think women are brought up with that metaphor. I'm not sure what women are brought up with, but it's not the athletic metaphor." During her graduate training in Berkeley in the pre-AIDS era, she had interviewed young men and women about how they perceived stress either as a challenge or a threat. Nearly everyone, she said, understood threat as presenting physical danger. But men nearly always interpreted a "challenge" in athletic terms—something you had to win or master or control. For the women, "challenges" also had to be mastered but, more importantly, they had to be understood. "I think all that's very embedded very early in males and females," she said. Early understanding of barriers and difficulties—as opposed to vanquishing them—continued to mark men's and women's differential behavior and outlook throughout their lives.

Across San Francisco Bay in Berkeley, Andrew Scharlach frames those distinctions in what he calls *resilience*. His research team has looked specifically at how men and women display resilience as they age, and, like Folkman and other gerontologists, he thinks the templates for developing resilience are set very early—often even before boys and girls learn to read. "You become resilient by dealing with small-scale stressors that you're able to learn from," he told me. "Women have many more opportunities to do that in their lives than men do."

"More opportunities?" I asked.

"More exposure to the stresses that come from being excluded from the privileges that come automatically to little boys. And that continues throughout women's lives as they carry different burdens and expectations from men. Women still carry more child-rearing responsibilities. They carry more of the emotional load in families. The gender biases that exist either beat you down, or you develop a sense of yourself and others as being okay." Very early on girls learn the kind of games that are reserved for them, the sort of toys they usually receive and how they are different from boys' toys, even the sorts of shoes they wear and how they differ from the shoes boys wear, which encourage rough-and-tumble activity. Equally, he pointed out, children even younger than four observe the sorts of roles that are mostly given to either men or women.

And that's not all: "A second source of female resilience has to do with what many sociologists and social workers have noticed in gender relations across the lifespan: Women develop richer social networks than men that are not as work bound, and not as sports bound, or activity bound." Susan Folkman laughed when I mentioned Scharlach's comments about gender and social networking. She and her husband had always shared domestic duties and chores even when he ran a large corporation. Now that they are both in their eighties, they each have regular lunches and social groups with their friends. Most of hers are with women; most of his are with his dwindling number of male friends.

"I have my woman friends," she said, "and we talk about things that [would cause] my husband to get up and leave the table . . . like the nature of our relationships with our children and children-in-law. The men prefer things that are easy to speak about where everything is beautiful and perfect." She paused and looked directly at me. "But everything is not beautiful and perfect. Being able to complain about a child or a child-in-law, or a grandchild, is socially unacceptable. You can't do that in public. But with your close women friends, you can just lay it out. Women in the geriatric dining room also talk about the families they grew up in. Many of the women talk about that—the men much less so." After that long riff, she smiled and added, "I don't know what men talk about."

Our conversation was drawing to a close when Folkman turned her well-coiffed head and again looked at me more intensely. She asked if I was aware of the difference in spousal mortality rates following the death of a partner. Men, she reminded me, are much more likely to die in the first six months following the death of a wife than are women following the death of a husband. While there are slight differences concerning race and ethnicity in what's called the "widowhood effect," the greater death toll among men appears to be a worldwide phenomenon. "Why do men have much higher mortality rates in widowhood than women?" she asked rhetorically. "Because we prepare for our partner's death ahead of time. On an often quite unconscious level we imagine ourselves as a widow. Women are simply much more likely to do that than men are."

Janice Schwartz, another gerontologist at University of California, San Francisco, has also focused on gender gaps in health, longevity, and caregiving. She is even more convinced of the negative consequences of conventional men's inability to form close friendships and strong social networks following retirement. "My husband and his friends do not talk," she told me. "I know more about what's going on with his friends and their partners than he does. They just hang out and do good-ole-boy speak. They talk around things. They don't ask. They don't know. I don't get it, but I had to learn how to 'good-ole-boy speak.' How men say things without really saying it. And I say, 'why don't you just say it?' Direct?"

Schwartz's research extended well beyond the upper-middle-class territory of doctors, businessmen, and technologists. She spent several years interviewing and following aging residents of a residential retirement trailer park in Sonoma County, north of San Francisco, where she found the same differences she had observed between her and her husband's friends. She even puzzled a bit about whether male unwillingness to talk about failures and frailty might be genetic across animal species. "Sick male animals hide because it's threatening to show illness.

Men are such babies when they get sick. Maybe that's a predictor of how they will cope later if they were babyish when they were younger ... When [my husband's friends] get together they talk stocks. When his friends' wives and I and the others get together, we talk about how we're doing, how our families are—new grandchildren, new illnesses, new diagnoses. Parents' problems. I'm the only active physician. There's a lawyer, a landscape architect, one housewife and Planned Parenthood volunteer. What we have in common is we know what's going on in each other's trips and their families, which things need help, which things don't, or a common question is, 'Okay, but how are YOU doing?'

"When one person's husband was in the hospital, of course we all knew, e-mailed, texted each other ... Our book club goes like this: We talk about the books, then we talk about each other. The guys go to dinner and none of that comes up. I'll ask my husband if they talked about X's problems. 'We didn't talk about that.' What do you mean it didn't come up! I'm hearing it from his wife."

Then, as Susan Folkman noted, there is the matter of mortality and how—or even whether—men address death. We all know we are going to die, but death remains a reality most Americans tend to avoid until the loss of an important family member—usually a grandparent. Here again the gender differences in acknowledging mortality are major. "The first time men begin to talk about mortality is when they confront a major illness," Schwartz said. "Women think about mortality all the time. They're worried about their kids dying. They're worried about who's going to take care of them [their kids] if they themselves die. Women face it in their thirties, when they ask, 'Do I have another child or not?' They think about their reproductive lives being over. The men think about it when their working lives are over. Women have thirty more years of adapting."

Even erectile dysfunction—the so-called "andropause" that has pushed the boom in magazine advertising for Viagra and Cialis—remains verboten at the guys' clubs. "Men don't talk about it, and men don't write about it," Janice Schwartz continued, drawing on her own geriatric psychological research. "They don't go to consciousness groups. Nobody's going to be surveying them, because if a woman did it, they wouldn't agree to it. And the men aren't going to think about doing it. So it doesn't happen. Men ask about taking testosterone when they notice their muscle mass going down."

~

No matter the causes, the gaps in male and female lifespans are well established and cut across cultures around the world. In America women's life expectancy is roughly eighty-one years against seventy-six for men. The gaps are similar in most of Europe, although it is beginning to narrow slightly in wealthier American zones and in the Nordic nations while the reverse is true in Russia. Greater female longevity might seem like good news for women. But often it's not in modern societies where extended families and cheap caregiving have all but disappeared.

"Yes, women do age more successfully than men," Janice Schwartz agreed. "But why? Women put up with disability better. Women face the problems of aging—notably menopause—at a younger age than men . . ." Just as she was beginning to recount a number of psychological and physiological advantages women enjoy, another younger colleague, Kristine Yaffe, a neurologist, joined our conversation and added a few darker notes. "But aging women are also more likely to be socially isolated than men. As they get older and the male dies off, and there they are left alone, right? If you look at the percentage of adults that are completely homebound about 1 percent of adults over sixty are completely homebound, 4.5 percent are almost homebound, and between 6 and 10 percent need help. If you look at the people who are homebound, they're more likely to be women, minorities, and people with primary illness. The men have already died."

Given lifelong wage disparities between men and women and the consequent effects on pensions and Social Security, widows' incomes also drop sharply on average following the death of a husband. Overwhelmingly, home caregivers are women, usually wives but also daughters and sisters—and increased male longevity very often spells a longer period of caregiving required by those worn-out men in poor health. As one friend's mother recently told her son, while she missed her late husband, his final years had offered no real companionship—only relentless burden. Against the dark specter of gender and aging, there are of course a few bright spots. Once the medical and psychological risks of the grieving phase are past, women with a secure income find themselves free to travel and have experiences they had never been able to have during their married lives. More and more often they set up "housekeeping" with other widowed friends to cut costs and build new social lives. Or, like my own octogenarian mother-in-law in France, who lives on a limited income, they visit children, grandchildren, or even great-grandchildren at no more cost than staying at home.

One of the most creative American alternatives to the limitations and isolation of old age is the proliferating Village Movement, which itself emerged from aging-in-place campaigns aimed at helping older people avoid nursing homes and senior assisted-living compounds. Aging in place touches everything from single-floor architectural redesign to installing digitally monitored pill dispensers. But at a broader societal level the builders of the Village Movement, which started in Beacon Hill, Boston, sought to create grassroots membership communities of people living at home who would help each other overcome the barriers and constraints of age.

Pat Sussman and Shirley Hamerfeld were neighbors who had known each other for decades. They would meet regularly at a Berkeley, California, street corner where commuters pick up extra riders to avoid paying tolls on the Bay Bridge into San Francisco. One January day in 2007 while they were waiting for a ride, they began chatting about a newspaper article Sussman had read about the Beacon Hill Village. Sussman and Hamerfeld were in their late sixties at the time and, while they were both healthy and professionally active, the limitations of age had begun to be undeniable, especially concerning illnesses that each of their husbands had developed. The seed for what came to be known as the Ashby Village with three hundred members was planted in both women's minds that early morning.

"We said let's send out some e-mails to all the people we know in the neighborhood," Sussman recounted when I met her in the small house where she and her semi-invalid husband, Peter, live in south Berkeley. "The silence was deafening," she laughed. "Nothing. No one said anything. So we decided to send a second set of e-mails. Nothing." At the time, Hamerfeld was preparing to move her very elderly mother into her own house. She had been looking for advice and help from the Alameda County senior services agency but to no avail. Again and again she had called the telephone numbers listed on the agency's website only to find herself shuffled from one telephone extension to the next and placed repeatedly on hold. She had been disconnected multiple times and finally had been advised to call back another day. She was working full-time in a junior high school. Her time was limited, and her mother's arrival was imminent.

"She was frantic," Sussman recalled. That was when she and Hamerfeld changed their strategy. Instead of sending out general e-mails, they focused on other women. "We decided to call about five or six women in the neighborhood. We each called our own friends. The conversations would start with what do we want as we age. We put it in the context of what did we see with our parents aging." One woman's response captured the sense of nearly all the rest. "She said, 'I want to be able to stand at my front window and look at the people coming down the street and watch the children playing.' This is what everyone was saying: I want to be in my neighborhood. I want to stay in my house."

Next they became more serious. They contacted the Beacon Hill Village, whose leaders had just self-published a thick book describing how they had organized themselves, how they had won foundation support, how they had organized voluntary services such as drivers to take members to the doctor or to go shopping, household handymen, companionship networks for recently widowed members, and even assistance with completing the bureaucratic forms required by Medicare or other local, state, and federal agencies ostensibly created to help the elderly. If Beacon Hill was the founder of the Village Movement, North Berkeley's Ashby Village soon found itself barraged by aging Baby Boomers across the country who wanted to follow in the same path.

Since the Beacon Hill Village started out in 2002—and grew to include other Boston neighborhoods—the Village Movement has spawned elder villages in every sector of the country—from New England to the Northwest to Texas and South Florida. As the movement grew, it also steadily drew the attention of gerontology specialists who were concerned by the rapidly expanding elderly Baby Boom population being confronted by a steady decline in public services. Andy Scharlach at UC Berkeley has dedicated most of his scholarly concentration on the Village Movement. The movement, he says, is profoundly American in that each village is autonomous and completely voluntary (which makes it seem bizarre to many European gerontologists, who see services to the aging as an obligation of the state). "These are organizations that grow more or less organically from people sitting around, asking the question what do we want for ourselves as we get older. Why don't you and I and Sally and Marge try to create something."

That is where gender comes back in. Almost without exception, the villages have been initiated by women. About two thirds of the members of the Village Movement are women, according to Scharlach. Partially that is simple demographics. Women in America outnumber men six to four by age sixty-five and eight to four by age eighty, and by almost all measures women in old age are healthier and more active than men.

Demographic distribution alone is not the end of the story, or, as Scharlach suggested, "This is the kind of social networking that is more in the wheelhouse of women than of men."

Pat Sussman offered a slightly different interpretation.

"I don't believe men think in the same terms as women do," she said. "I don't think they're as grounded in the realities of life. Really."

Sussman's husband, Peter, a lifelong journalist who has difficulty walking, had been listening to our conversation from his upstairs office. He decided not to remain silent. "I'm the other gender," he declared, speaking from the stairs across the room. "Let me just say the person who formed the Ashby Village group on modern poetry is me. It includes two men and three women. The photography exhibit was organized by men. I set up an e-mail, Yahoo group . . . I saw that as a way to help keep everyone in contact."

Pat had just undergone reconstructive foot surgery. She lay stretched out on the living room couch. She couldn't turn to see her husband, but she was pleased that he had joined the conversation. Peter's voice was strong and clear. "My personal sense," he continued, "was that as far as Pat was concerned she really wanted it to be her thing, and the women wanted it to be more of a woman's thing. I think it was a big and important deal that women were the cofounders. My sense was that they wanted to be the founding mothers. I sensed they wanted to be all women. I would have been more involved. I loved the idea and I was aiding it in any way I could, but I pulled back."

Pat listened patiently but finally broke in. "I don't think that's true, love. I think you and a lot of the men involved in a lot of other things were not willing to give the great amount of time that it took to get it started. Meetings and all these phone calls. You were enormously helpful in writing and telling the world how fabulous it was."

Peter cut back in. "Part of it was just the way it happened. They were talking on the street corner and I wasn't there. Pat and Shirley and sometimes Jane would just meet on the street corner and just talk, and I wasn't there."

Pat smiled.

"We did try to get men involved in our original work, and they didn't come. They were very wary. That was years ago, love."

Peter was not buying it.

"I think it's a vast overstatement," he answered. "A more relevant fact is that men of my era who went through the women's lib movement recognized we had been overbearing, and we were sensitive to that when women felt they wanted to do something. So the men held back. That's my generation." Peter turned to hobble back upstairs to his office.

Pat turned her head toward him. "You were very supportive of what we were doing," she said, calmly.

Parallel stories, according to Andy Scharlach, have marked most of the groups in the Village Movement. But even if the "action agents" or initiators were almost always women, roughly half of the volunteer managers or administrators turn out to be men, and men are often the drivers for the women who need lifts. Scharlach does not find the role division surprising. "So much of men's identity, their roles and their sense of purpose, is based on action, on activity, on doing something. Most of the evidence suggests that personalities don't change dramatically through our adult lives, and that includes gender roles." Or, in short, people—men—removed from the sort of action roles that Baby Boomers have had throughout their lives, are more likely to suffer social-psychological deficits after retirement than are women. Little surprise then that women, who all the researchers agree are more adept at building personal networks, have turned out to be the Village creators while the men find positions similar to what they did in their working lives. "What I'm suggesting," Sharlach elaborated, "is not to take the men and women out of the context of their lives, whether there are differences in pasts of men and women in the Villages, or in the kinds of services people use and participate in according to their gender."

Without question the Village Movement represents a creative window into addressing old age for both the men and women who participate in it—even if its emergence seems directly due to the highly gendered and historic "networking" roles women have developed to survive in a world largely governed and controlled by men. Still, the slice of society that is currently benefiting from these aging-in-place villages remains tiny and shows little probability of changing. Nearly all the villages Scharlach has studied are middle- to upper-middle-class and overwhelmingly they are white. In the Ashby Village, one retired African American health professional had joined and remained for several years but then left out of a sense of isolation. Very few to no Hispanic women participate in the villages, nor do Asians, possibly because the kinds of help and solidarity the villages offer are still being offered by extended families in their ethnic communities. A new North Oakland Village has attempted to recruit black members, but with annual family membership dues steadily approaching one thousand dollars, the price tag has proved too steep.

~

Finally I come back to my friend Beata, who was the first to speak to me about the intense differences she observed in how men and women address aging, how even women who are desperately poor seem to flower in their sixties just as the men she knew were drawing inward, angry and difficult. She asked me if I knew about the Red Hat Society, a social organization of women aged fifty and older. "It was made up of women who'd decided that after a certain age they're free to do and wear what they want. So they wear purple dresses and red hats." They organize groups and have lunch together—*without men*—and talk about whatever they feel like, be it children, grandchildren, naughty affairs, movies, or pumpkin pie recipes. "It's like, 'We don't have to accommodate our husbands or their perception or what they want us to wear and how they want us to behave.' We can put on our purple dresses and don red hats and go parade around without caring a damn who sees us. It's 'Look at us! We have power.'"

The Red Hat women who slightly preceded the Baby Boomers didn't look to psychologists or gerontologists to justify themselves, but in their own way they presaged the explosion of psychological literature that has arrived with the Baby Boomers' entry into retirement. Newspapers, magazines, and even network television programs report almost weekly on the proliferation of "grumpy old men" and the presumed causes for their descent into personal darkness: declining testosterone and its effect on male alertness and memory; greater neurological decay and an increase in the brain's white matter; and cognitive decline linked to reduced cortical blood flow in the base of men's brains. Men on average display greater confusion and a sense of inadequacy in meeting today's daily requirement for digital competence. There is also evidence of intensifying resentment over older women's seemingly greater mental and physical resilience as well as women's slow but steady encroachment across all ages in universities, governance, and business. Gerontologists argue among themselves over whether the spiral of male negativity begins in middle age or at sixty-five or at seventy—but that it exists and that it intensifies with many if not most men over time is not in question.

There is always a tendency in the realm of gender talk to draw a sharp line between biological and societal explanations. Sex differences are innate, it is argued. Gender differences are the result of how society has been organized—mostly by men. Yet just as biologists have noted about penguins, whose males are the nurturers and females the explorers, conventional wisdom is frequently misleading. Fiercely heterosexual males do design clothes. Hyperfeminine women do excel at brain surgery. And increasingly, the first rank of gender scholars argue that sex (or biology) and gender (social roles) are deeply intertwined. How we live and how we've been raised to imagine our lives has profound effects on our individual hormonal production, and those hormonal expressions evolve with age—still more evidence, as Yale University's Richard Bribiescas has demonstrated (see Epilogue), of the inseparability of nature and nurture. Or as University of California, Berkeley's Andy Scharlach expresses it, "aging is something we learn how to do and learning is always a developmental process."

In one of our earliest conversations, Beata asked rhetorically, "What happens to a woman when she starts going into menopause? She's not planning to have children at fifty years old. So that doesn't bother them. What you suddenly realize is from now on I'm going to be aging rapidly. What's coming? Wrinkles. Dry skin. And it's coming fast. So I want to live NOW! I don't want to wait until some other time to get a life. You perk up. You start compensating for time. You start growing inside yourself. It's not that you want to look younger; you want to LIVE younger. You want to live as much as you can. The women over sixty that I see become more active. If you have money, you travel. [Maybe] your kids have young kids. So you stop working and you become a grandmother. You go and help raise those kids and pay attention to them."

And what about the men, then, I asked. "The men?" She paused. "They seem to be lost."

EPILOGUE

The Fate of Gender

We were all of us, those born with the tags and apparatus of a male, once female, or nearly so. In those first hours, days, and weeks of fetal life, our bodies could not be distinguished from the fetal bodies of our sisters. No matter that at the molecular level the distribution of our X or Y chromosomes had already been established from the instant of fertilization, the bodies that were forming inside our mothers' wombs all appeared the same, or, as Richard Bribiescas has frequently pointed out, in the beginning we were all generic embryos. "Everyone comes from a common genetic and developmental framework that is tweaked by sex hormones," he said in a famous interview published in September 2014 in *Men's Health*. Though we each carry sets of male or female sex chromosomes, those Xs and Ys do not meet their destiny until our growing shrimp-like bodies begin to be bathed in a wash of powerful sex hormones. Had our mothers' supply of testosterone been weaker than it was, had the stock of estrogen in her amniotic fluid been greater, then in all probability that thin seam that joins the right side of a boy's scrotum to the left (the raphe line) would have developed as a girl's vaginal crease; and had there been insufficient concentrations of two other male hormones, MIS and DHT, the tiny bud that grew into a penis would have rounded up into the hypersensitive female clitoris. And by the end of our manly lives, as many gerontologists have also noted, the distinctive physical qualities that distinguish the male from the female also gradually subside, bone structure notwithstanding, into unitary decay.

So goes the biology of sex, or nature, as opposed to the notion of gender, commonly taken to be a product of society, or nurture. But as Bribiescas has also argued with elegance in his memoir-essay, *Men: Evolutionary and Life History*, the popular tendency to separate nature from nurture is so fundamentally flawed as to be not only meaningless but worse, misleading. As we have seen in earlier chapters, hormonal expression in those warm wombs where we all once swam is deeply affected by the trials and tribulations our mothers faced during our gestation as well as by how many boy fetuses or girl fetuses had previously resided in those wombs. Moreover, even once our sexual tagging has been set, still more hormonal and physiological activity influences the neurological wiring, or "sexing," that helps shape our fetal brains, which in turn helps form our sensitivities, our sensibilities, and our emotional expression once we pop out of our mothers' bellies. More briefly, while it may be useful descriptively to separate "sex" from "gender," in evolutionary terms, our gender expression is inseparable from our biology, and both reside at particular moments in our social and biological evolutionary story. If we cannot be fully separated from our primate ancestors and how they worked out their gender roles, neither can we expect that our descendants will live and perform quite the way we do today.

Consider, for example, muscles. Physical anthropologists long ago learned how very different our hominid ancestors' muscles were from our own today. Their longer arms required the same sort of extended, sinuous muscles that apes and chimpanzees still use to swing themselves through forest canopies. Once we descended to the ground, then our upper arms became rounder and stronger, required for lifting tools, gathering harvests, and thrusting weapons at our enemies. While predicting future evolutionary change is rarely advisable, the obvious reorganizing of work seems likely, in the view of many anthropologists, to continue altering our musculature. Unless you're a firefighter, for whom lifting heavy weights is critical, there is little utility at the digital keyboard for maintaining those thick pectorals and biceps that almost all humans needed a mere century ago when most of our ancestors dug and scratched at the ground to produce food for survival. Likewise, body hair appears to be slowly but steadily disappearing both as a source of warmth and as a marker of virility (as it was perceived by the early Greeks and their predecessors). Darwinian natural selection, whether realized through the elimination of the less fit or through the proliferation of body forms regarded as esthetically superior, remains at the root of these changes, marked not least by the reduction of body weight given over to bone and muscles at the expense of larger and larger brains.

The one certain evolutionary change in both our physical form and our esthetic-behavioral profile is our "racial" appearance. The distinctive physical markers of racial difference that anthropologists tracked during the nineteenth century—skin color, skull shape, height, and girth—are washing away with unprecedented speed thanks to cars, trains, planes, boats, motorcycles, and sturdier shoes that have made mass migration a universal daily reality. With migration and racial mixing come evolving ideas of human beauty. Where women of the 1950s sought to lighten their skin tone, now darkeners are the cosmetic leaders. Where sturdy, thick men—think John Wayne, Robert Mitchum, Rock Hudson—were the film icons of the 1940s and '50s, lean figures lead the pack today: Johnny Depp, Brad Pitt, Leonardo DiCaprio. While blond has hardly disappeared among beautiful stars, sultry olive skin and curly locks are rapidly catching up in the West. Fashion, of course, is fickle, but the blending of the races and the emerging body types that accompany the mixing is plain fact, much to the dismay of white supremacists. Tall, square-shouldered white males, the minority that has ruled the world for the last several centuries, will almost certainly disappear in fairly short order before the fertile flood of the far more numerous darker-skinned bipeds. Natural selection will triumph—and there is every reason to believe that the gendered behaviors that have marked the white world dominance will also wash away along with them.

When the former Olympic athlete Bruce Jenner stole the global media spotlight as a surgically remade woman named Caitlyn just a year after Conchita Wurst won the 2014 Eurovision contest, anxious traditionalists began worrying seriously about the much-ballyhooed gender revolution. Just as whiteness seemed doomed, they worried, "Is gender dead?" Was *Vive la différence!* a mere nostalgic illusion? Such worries, as Richard Bribiescas and nearly all other evolutionary biologists respond, are plainly absurd. The animal attraction of male for female remains as fierce as it ever was. At the same time molecular neurologists produce more and more evidence that male brains *do* function differently than female brains. *La différence* is in no danger of disappearing. But if gender difference is far from dead, the democratization of gender roles and their influence on society is provoking rapid radicalization. The aging white boys' club may rant and rave about their slowly diminishing authority, but the facts are too strong to ignore:

- women's income either equals or exceeds their male mates' income in more than two thirds of U.S. households;
- women held 89 percent of U.S. bank accounts in 2010 and controlled more than half of the national wealth;
- women make more than 83 percent of all U.S. consumer purchases;
- women constitute more than two-thirds of high school valedictorians; and
- women earning university degrees exceed men by 20 percent in the United States, and a solid majority of law and graduate degrees go to women while slightly more than half of all science and engineering degrees go to women. (The same is true across Europe and the gap is even greater in Russia.)

For nearly thirty years the greatest growth in job creation has come from small start-up firms. Increasingly, those firms are being run by women; the same is even more true for Latina women, the strongest growing demographic in the United States. Meanwhile, men's place in the economy is falling. Two thirds of the jobs lost in the 2007–08 recession were held by men in heavy industries, many of which departed for Asia and South America. At its worst, male unemployment during that recession hit 11 percent while female unemployment capped at 8.3 percent.

Women's wages, even in the liberal Nordic nations, still run a quarter to a third less than men's, though the gap is slowly narrowing and the greatest job growth expected across the next generation is in soft industries, where women already dominate the workforce. In few to none of these new growth sectors do heavy bones and mighty muscles count for much.

Economic measures are not the end of the story. A global hunger has emerged since the dawn of the current millennium not merely for women to hold positions of authority, but for human values and sensibilities usually associated with women: attention to personal relationships, a reduction in aggressive responses to difference and conflict, greater readiness to discover negotiated resolutions to problems, and, perhaps most surprising to the Henry Higgins variety of males, a greater sense of pragmatism in meeting daily challenges. There is surely no guarantee that women's ascension up the ladders of power and authority will guarantee any of these outcomes. The records of Margaret Thatcher and Golda Meir are hardly promising, but both of those larger-than-life figures were by definition gate crashers who ruled in social and political contexts that were overwhelmingly male—and male in a very traditional cast. If there is anything globally significant in all the attention paid to the transsexual movement, it is very likely not the surgical splash that has captured so much media attention, but the validation of sensibilities that these sexual voyagers have described—sensibilities that, among those transitioning from male to female, refer to a deep discomfort with conventional male thinking and perception complemented with a greater attachment to so-called female sensibilities.

Does that suggest that what we are now witnessing in the gender arena is the first wave of massive transsexualization of humanity? Hardly. What it does suggest is that the shame once associated with men who embrace "feminine" styles and sentiments is by fits and starts gradually fading away. Rarely in the gender schema are good men now praised for their simple brutality and muscular force, desperate jihadists notwithstanding. Those great arbiters of conventional male discourse, the *New York Times*, *Le Monde*, and the *Guardian*, not only report more than ever before on the intimate dimensions of modern life, but their share of steadily declining newspaper readers continues to rise, according to regular reports by the Pew Research Center. The gender balance in book purchases even more strongly favors women, who make up roughly two thirds of American book buyers.

As women's market share continues to rise, so have editors' news choices evolved—ever more toward addressing the pragmatic details of daily life: weather predictions, personal health and fitness, disease prevention, education, which lead the list of women's media interests. Even further, the steady and dramatic shift away from conventional news sources to online social media reflects women's much greater presence on the Internet at large and particularly on social media sites. And while online personal blogs capture far more female readers than men, Pew researchers consistently find that women are far more attentive to reported risks of public violence than are men and are about equally responsive to political campaign news. What lags consistently in print media is the readiness of still mostly male editors to seek out comment and analysis by women on foreign affairs and global issues (aside from concerns about global warming).

What then do these steady and uni-directional gender shifts in public discourse suggest? Backlash by major power centers like the Russian Orthodox Church and Salafist Islamists cannot be ignored. The savage slaughter of mostly young people in a Paris theatre as well as in several cafés and restaurants in November 2015 was conceived and organized by the most radical Islamist militants under the direction of the would-be Islamist Caliphate. In claiming credit for the attacks, the leaders of the Islamist State, or ISIS, specifically praised "the soldiers of the Caliphate [who] set out targeting the capital of prostitution and vice, the lead carrier of the cross in Europe—Paris. This group of believers were youth who divorced the worldly life and advanced towards their enemy hoping to be killed for Allah's sake, doing so in support of His religion, His Prophet (blessing and peace be upon him), and His allies." Certainly the ISIS attacks in Paris concerned the so-called Caliphate's greater strategic interests, but the particular focus on a heavy metal concert and outdoor terraces where men and women sat together talking and drinking reflected Western notions of feminism and gender independence. An earlier "manifesto" from "Women of the Islamic State" very clearly damned Occidental notions of women's equality with men, decreeing that girls as young as nine could be taken in marriage by young men and that their duties, aside from jihad, should be restricted to knitting, cooking, and cleaning. The century of French women's public independence and display, represented by the targeted clubs of the 11th Arrondissement in Paris, was nothing less than an insult to male authority. That tens of thousands of Twitter comments celebrated the slaughters suggests not merely a "backlash" but a statement of outright warfare against the gender liberalization exemplified by women's conduct in cities like Paris, New York, and San Francisco. The regular rape of women they regard as infidels constitutes even plainer evidence of the rage radical Islamists hold toward independent women.

Were those attitudes limited to desert enclaves, they might be easily dismissed. But they are not. Evangelical preachers across the American South regularly denounce feminism and the gender transitions of the last half century. Owen Strachan, a leader of the self-described Christian "complementarians," draws an ever larger following when he argues that the Bible, like the Quran, specifies that men and women have been made for separate roles in the home, at work, or in prayer halls. As for stay-at-home dads, he and many Christian evangelicals denounce them as "man-fails." At the same time the incidence of rape, defined as involuntary forced sex, appears to be growing on ordinary college campuses. And indeed plain gang-rape has reportedly also risen in college fraternity houses, many of them at elite universities. Arguments that resurgent rape is a direct result of the shifting gender panorama or the ubiquity of birth control are suspicious at best. Even so, there can be little doubt that a global backlash against the revolution in gender roles is well underway, be it in Syria or San Diego.

Backlash, however, is just that: a reaction based on resentment to a forceful change in public values and conventions. Without any question the world's population appears to be more and more exasperated with the models of male power and morality that reached its apogee during the Victorian era and the first half of the twentieth century.

Global warming, famine, public health, and mass migration at the hands of murderous male tribalists, issues that as late as the 1980s were mostly relegated to the back pages of major media (and even there often were portrayed in the language of racial inferiority), now increasingly lead the news. While these catastrophes are rarely if ever characterized as overt gender concerns, the fact that women pay more attention to them and that they now lead the news is ample evidence of a profound gender shift in public perceptions.

As I write these concluding notes, I find it hard not to reflect on a recent visit to one of Europe's most enchanting sites, the Musée des civilisations de l'Europe et de la Méditerranée (Museum of the Civilizations of Europe and the Mediterranean), or MuCEM, perched just at the opening to the port of Marseille. The curators at the MuCEM have from the beginning strived to avoid the pumped-up French sense of cultural superiority, opting instead to open its prism onto the broad array of stories, arts, and civilizations that make the entire Mediterranean basin a vast mysterious and provocative piece of geography. Just now there are two major exhibitions at the MuCEM. One focuses on the shared sacred sites of today's three great monotheisms: Judaism, Christianity, and Islam, religions "of the book" for which there is one and only one singular, invisible, all-powerful male force that from time to time demands that his followers engage in massive purifying bloodletting of all those who do not follow his strict commands. It seems to be the inevitable heritage of monotheistic religions.

But around the corner in this light-shimmering museum is another exhibition. This one draws us back to a time that preceded the notion of a unitary deity, when all the gods were continuously changing their shapes, their names, and very often their genders according to the wants and needs of ordinary folk. The Egyptians, the Greeks, the Romans were all wanderers and as they wandered and conquered (or were conquered) they took their gods with them and met new gods along the way. Osiris, the Egyptian, became Dionysus, and Isis became Aphrodite, though the characteristics of each changed as they were adopted and renamed by new peoples. Zeus, the most almighty of Greek gods, gave birth through his thigh to the beguiling Dionysus. Tiresias, son of a Greek shepherd, was transferred by the goddess Hera into a woman and became one of her servant priestesses. Fierce as the warriors and their warrior gods may have been, they existed as a collection of spirits, a pantheon of deities to which mere mortals could look to for succor and defense. Rather than insisting on the fixity of contemporary monotheism, the icons of these myriad gods and goddesses gathered at the MuCEM speak to us as well today as they did to their ancient followers. Across the Mediterranean they spoke to the complexities and uncertainties we find within ourselves when we dare to look at and accept our own fluidities and uncertainties. What we now call the gender revolution may indeed represent not merely a rejection of the rigid roles imposed on us by those stern monotheist deities, but instead an ever expanding array of the multiple deities and identities that reside within and around all of us.

Acknowledgments

A great number of friends, colleagues, and counselors have provided wise advice and inspiration for the completion of this book, most notably Nancy Miller, editorial director at Bloomsbury and her associate Anton Mueller. Others include Sandy Close, Dan Hubig, Linda Hunt, Deborah Johnson, my literary agent Jennifer Lyons, Erica Marcus for translation help in China, Dorothy McGhee, Lynn Meyer, Wendy Miller, Sharon Silva, Natasha Williams, Brenda Wilson as well as Paul Kleyman of New American Media, which with the Gerontological Society of America provided a generous grant to support reporting on gender and geriatrics. And as always, for patience during the dark periods, my companion, Christophe Sevault.

Bibliography

Altman, Dennis. *Global Sex*. Chicago: University of Chicago Press, 2001.

Ariès, Philippe, and Georges Duby, eds. *A History of Private Life from Pagan Rome to Byzantium*. Cambridge, MA: Harvard University Press, 1987.

Badinter, Élisabeth. *La Ressemblance des sexes: de l'amour en plus au conflit*. Paris: Livres de Poche, 2012.

Bagemihl, Bruce. *Biological Exuberance: Animal Homosexuality and Natural Diversity*. New York: St. Martin's Press, 1999.

Baker, Jean H., *Margaret Sanger: A Life of Passion*. New York: Hill & Wang, 2011.

Beam, Cris. *Transparent: Love, Family, and Living the T with Transgender Teenagers*. New York: Harcourt, 2007.

Bech, Henning. *When Men Meet: Homosexuality and Modernity*. Chicago: University of Chicago Press, 1997.

Benkov, Laura. *Reinventing the Family: The Emerging Story of Lesbian and Gay Parents*. New York: Crown, 1994.

Berry, Wendell. *Sex, Economy, Freedom & Community*. New York: Pantheon, 1992.

Boswell, John. *Same-Sex Unions in Premodern Europe*. New York: Villard, 1994.

Bremner, J. Douglas. *Does Stress Damage the Brain: Understanding Trauma-Related Disorders from a Mind-Body Perspective*. New York: W. W. Norton, 2002.

Bribiescas, Richard G., *Men: Evolutionary and Life History*. Cambridge: Harvard University Press, 2006.

Butler, Judith. *Bodies That Matter: On the Discursive Limits of "Sex."* London: Routledge, 1993.

Califia, Pat. *Public Sex: The Culture of Radical Sex*. San Francisco: Cleis, 1994.

Carrier, Joseph. *De Los Otros: Intimacy and Homosexuality Among Mexican Men*. New York: Columbia University Press, 1995.

Center for Disease Control and Prevention, *Assisted Reproductive Technology Success Rates*, 2007, Atlanta: Department of Health and Human Services, 2009.

Chang, Leslie T., *Factory Girls: Voices from the Heart of Modern China*. New York: Doubleday, 2008.

Cherlin, Andrew J., *The Marriage-Go-Round: The State of Marriage and the Family in America Today*. New York: Vintage Books, 2010.

Coontz, Stephanie. *Marriage, A History: From Obedience to Intimacy, or How Love Conquered Marriage*. New York: Viking, 2005.

———, *The Way We Never Were: America's Families and the Nostalgia Trap*. New York: Basic Books, 2000.

Connell, Raewyn. *Gender in a World Perspective*. Cambridge, UK: Polity Press, 2009.

De Beauvoir, Simone. *The Second Sex*. New York: Vintage Books, 1989.

———, *Coming of Age*. New York: Putnam, 1972.

Dollimore, Jonathan. *Sexual Dissidence: Augustine to Wilde, Freud to Foucault*. Gloucestershire: Clarendon Press, 1991.

Edelman, Lee. *No Future: Queer Theory and the Death Drive*. Durham, NC: Duke University Press, 2004.

Friedan, Betty, *The Feminine Mystique*. New York: W. W. Norton, 1963.

Foucault, Michel. *The History of Sexuality*. Vol. 2, *The Use of Pleasure*. New York: Vintage, 1990.

Gerzema, John and Michael D'Antonio. *The Athena Doctrine: How Women (and the Men Who Think Like Them) Will Rule the Future*. San Francisco: Jossey-Bass, 2013.

Glassner, Barry. *The Culture of Fear*. New York: Basic Books, 1999.

Halberstam, J. Jack. *Gaga Feminism: Sex, Gender and the End of Normal*. Boston: Beacon, 2012.

Halpern, David M. et al, *Before Sexuality: The Construction of Erotic Experience in the Ancient Greek World*. Princeton: Princeton University Press, 1990.

Hardy, Robin, with David Groff. *The Crisis of Desire: AIDS and the Fate of Gay Brotherhood*. Boston: Houghton Mifflin, 1999.

Herdt, Gilbert, ed. *Third Sex, Third Gender: Beyond Sexual Dimorphism in Culture and History*. New York: Zone Books, 1994.

Hochschild, Arlie Russell. *The Outsourced Self: Intimate Life in Market Times*. New York: Metropolitan Books, 2012.

Isay, David. *Mom: A Celebration of Mothers from StoryCorps*. New York: Penguin, 2012.

Kass, Leon R. *Life, Liberty and the Defense of Dignity: The Challenge for Bioethics*. New York: Encounter Books, 2002.

Kimmel, Michael S., *Manhood in America*. Oxford: Oxford University Press, 2006.

Kunin, Madeleine M., *The New Feminist Agenda: Defining the Next Revolution for Women, Work and Family*. White River Junction, VT: Chelsea Green, 2012.

Molloy, Aimee. *However Long the Night: Molly Melching's Journey to Help Millions of African Women and Girls Triumph*. New York: HarperOne, 2013.

Lorber, Judith. *Gender Inequality*. Oxford: Oxford, 2012.

——, *Paradoxes of Gender*. New Haven: Yale University Press, 1994.

Mercer, Kobena. *Welcome to the Jungle: New Positions in Black Cultural Studies*. Routledge, 1994

Mercer, Kobena. *Welcome to the Jungle: New Positions in Black Cultural Studies*. London: Routledge, 1994.

Miller, Toby. *Sportsex*. Philadelphia: Temple University Press, 2001.

Moss, George L. *The Image of Man: The Creation of Modern Masculinity*. Oxford: Oxford University Press, 1996.

Mulgan, Geoff, ed. *Life After Politics: New Thinking for the Twenty-First Century*. New York: HarperCollins, 1997.

Nimmons, David. *The Soul Beneath the Skin: The Unseen Hearts and Habits of Gay Men*. New York: St. Martin's Press, 2002.

Nowotny, Helga and Giuseppe Testa. *Naked Genes: Reinventing the Human in the Molecular Age*. Cambridge, MA: The MIT Press, 2010.

Nussbaum, Martha C. *The Fragility of Goodness*. Cambridge: Cambridge University Press, 1986.

Okin, Susan Moller. *Justice, Gender, and the Family*. New York: Basic Books, 1989.

Parker, Richard G. *Bodies, Pleasures and Passions: Sexual Culture in Contemporary Brazil*. Boston: Beacon, 2001.

Pinker, Susan. *The Sexual Paradox: Extreme Men, Gifted Women and the Real Gender Gap*. Toronto: Vintage Canada, 2008.

Putnam, Robert. *Bowling Alone: The Collapse and Revival of American Community*. New York: Simon & Schuster, 2000.

Ryan, Christopher and Cacilda Jethá. *Sex At Dawn: How We Mate, Why We Stray, and What It Means for Modern Relationships*. HarperCollins, 2010.

Sandberg, Sheryl. *Lean In: Women, Work, and the Will to Lead*, New York: Random House, 2013.

Solomon, Andrew. *Far From the Tree: Parents, Children and the Search for Identity*. New York: Scribner, 2012.

Stacey, Judith. *Unhitched: Love, Marriage, and Family Values from West Hollywood to Western China*. New York: New York University Press, 2011.

Vidal, Gore. *Sexually Speaking: Collected Sex Writings*. Jersey City: Cleis, 1999.

Warnock, Mary. *Making Babies: Is There a Right to Have Children?* Oxford: Oxford University Press, 2002.

Warren, Elizabeth and Amelia Warren Tyagi. *The Two-Income Trap: Why Middle-Class Parents Are Going Broke*. New York: Basic Books, 2003.

Williams, John C. & Rachel Dempsey. *What Works for Women at Work*. New York: New York University Press, 2014.

Wolf, Alison. *The XX Factor: How Working Women Are Creating a New Society*. London: Profile Books, 2013.

Yuchun Xiao, and Fang Lee Cooke. *Work-life Balance in China?* Melbourne: Asia Pacific Journal of Human Resources, 2011.

Index

A Note on the Author

Frank Browning grew up on an apple orchard and tobacco farm in Kentucky. He now lives in Paris. A former NPR science reporter, his books include *The American Way of Crime* (with John Gerassi), *The Culture of Desire*, *A Queer Geography*, *Apples: The Story of the Fruit of Temptation*, and *The Monk and the Skeptic*. He writes on art and culture for the *Huffington Post* and has contributed to the *Washington Post Magazine*, *Mother Jones*, *Playboy*, *Salon*, the *Progressive*, and other publications.